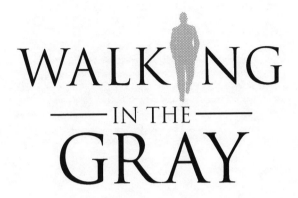

WALKING
—— IN THE ——
GRAY

HOW TO SUCCEED WHEN THE RULES
ARE NOT BLACK AND WHITE

RICKEY L. JASPER

WALKING IN THE GRAY
HOW TO SUCCEED WHEN THE RULES ARE NOT BLACK AND WHITE

iUniverse books may be ordered through booksellers or by contacting:

iUniverse
1663 Liberty Drive
Bloomington, IN 47403
www.iuniverse.com
1-800-Authors (1-800-288-4677)

ISBN: 978-1-5320-9113-1 (sc)
ISBN: 978-1-5320-8932-9 (hc)
ISBN: 978-1-5320-9114-8 (e)

Library of Congress Control Number: 2019921237

Print information available on the last page.

iUniverse rev. date: 12/31/2019

*To my wonderful wife, best friend, and partner, **Sheila Denese Jasper,** who for over 33 years has stood by my side, in front of me, behind me, under me, and/or over me - wherever necessary to keep me going or to hold me up. When others left, she stayed. When they said I could not, she said I could. When my burdens got heavy, she helped me to bear them. When I slowed under the load, she gave me a push or a pull. When I wanted to surrender, she shared a word of encouragement. When she ran out of words, she prayed until something happened.*

*To my two young men, **Rickey Lane Jasper II and Desmond Tyler Jasper** who taught me through their birth and life that life is about giving; that there is more to life than just the accumulation of things; that life is about a legacy - not the things you get or the stuff you gain. Life is about what you leave behind.*

*To my **Lord and Savior, Jesus Christ**, who has ordered my steps, taught me how to go in and out among people, expanded my territory and made all these things possible.*

CONTENTS

Introduction ix

PART 1–WHERE DO I GO FROM HERE?

Chapter 1–Have a Destination 1
Chapter 2–Know Where You Are 29
Chapter 3–Commit to a Course of Action 89

PART 2–WHO AM I? SELF-AWARENESS

Chapter 4–Know What You Bring to the Table. 103
Chapter 5–Identify Your Motivation. 135
Chapter 6–Own the Outcomes. 149
Chapter 7–Increase Your Value 181

PART 3–WHAT TO DO WHEN YOU DON'T KNOW WHAT TO DO

Chapter 8–Identify and Modify Your Success Strategy 199
Chapter 9–Take a Step and Get Moving. 207
Chapter 10–Stop Tripping: It Is a Journey, Not a Trip 221
Chapter 11–Encourage Yourself and Know Your Why 235
Chapter 12–Believe in Yourself. 245

PART 4–HOW WILL THEY KNOW?

Chapter 13–Be the Best You That You Can Be 259
Chapter 14–Expand Your Territory (Network) 273
Chapter 15–Help Somebody by Sharing Your Story. 283

INTRODUCTION

OVER TWENTY-FIVE YEARS AGO, I STARTED WRITING A book entitled *Walking in the Gray* to share my thoughts on how to succeed in life. After many starts and stops and the passage of many years and experiences, it is time to share the book with you. While this text has been a long time coming, I felt, given the number of books and documents on the subject, I owed it to you to have ascertained the validity of my ideas through practice and proof. To that end, in addition to my experimenting with and using the ideas, I have shared and seen others use them successfully. I am confident that you too will benefit from the many thoughts and ideas as well as the encouraging and motivating words found within these pages.

I have been in the workforce since I was nine and a half years old, and I have gone from the cotton fields in Parkdale, Arkansas, to the executive suite in the federal government. I have learned how to succeed in areas where success was unlikely, unexpected, and not previously proven possible for someone with my background or pedigree. As a matter of fact, my success occurred in environments, organizations, offices, and agencies where neither my origin, nationality, associations, nor education created the opportunity.

I did not grow up knowing or understanding how organizations functioned; nor was I taught, mentored, or tutored on how to succeed when one employed me. However, I owe a debt of gratitude and appreciation to my mother, Louisie Mae Grayson, who despite her poor and humble upbringing, never stopped dreaming and taught my siblings and me to dream. She taught us the value of a dollar, the ability to economize, and the value and necessity of good ole common sense. She taught us that we had to be better than our competition, "to work four times as hard to get half as much," to be the best we could be, and to value and build relationships.

Walking in the Gray as a topic came to me as I boarded a plane to leave the country for temporary duty. Having graduated valedictorian in a class of twenty-two students from Parkdale, I had a successful run through undergraduate school in three years and graduate school in a little over a year. I had married the girl of my dreams (Sheila Denese Jasper) from college, and now I had secured a good position with the federal government. I felt I had experienced a level of success that was worth sharing with others. So I started to write, but then I began to question whether what I had learned in life and observed in academia was transferable to the work environment. I asked,

- Would the principles I applied at school operate the same on the job?
- Would my people observations and interactions operate the same in the workplace as they did in academia?
- Would my academic knowledge and understanding of organizations hold true?
- Would my view of the organization as an organism prove to be more than a theory?
- Would my ability to drive outcomes through motivations and understanding of the landscape prove applicable?

I questioned my ideas, my observations, and myself, and I waited, studied more, and tested my thoughts. For the past quarter century and more, I have successfully "walked in the gray." I have also enjoyed both the journey and the success of others who utilized the ideas I freely shared with them to change their walk and outcomes.

I chose the topic "walking in the gray" because it lets you know that we are going to discuss something that is unclear. It tells you that

- we are going to discuss becoming successful when the rules of engagement are not written or, if they are, are unclear;
- we are going to discuss a topic that is secret, unknown, or not publicized; and
- I am not going to talk about the obvious things that are clear, known truths, if they do exist.

What am I going to discuss? The answer is things that are not so obvious, not so clear, or not so known. We are going on a journey together to areas less traveled or perhaps frequently trekked to but undisclosed. I also chose this topic because as the topic suggests, we will discuss things that are not necessarily unknown, unseen, and unrecognized. They are just unclear. These are not real secrets, as they are not hidden to all, and they can be learned, seen, and observed.

It is worth noting that this places me at a bit of an advantage to those who desire to debate with me about this topic, as this work is a report on my observations and empirical experiences while walking in the gray.

Walking in the gray neutralizes our visions. What you see and observe may not be the same as what I do. What separates or determines the accuracy of what we see or saw is the outcome. Gray places each of us on the same level playing field. It limits each of our views and does not consider our backgrounds, education, ethnicity, beliefs, and so on. You cannot see any more clearly than I can. What separates us is what we learn from each step we take. If I cannot see the pitfall in front of me and I fall, I can learn something from that experience and use it going forward or on my way back.

For the past decade, I have told people that I am a code breaker, much like Neo in the movie *The Matrix*. I can see and understand the ones and zeroes. I say this because I have studied and, more importantly, observed the ideas, thoughts, concepts, and principles in this book in action enough to know that they work.

It should be noted that this book is not an academic research work on my findings intended to be analyzed and statistically validated. However, I encourage the academicians to validate my findings, as I have empirically observed their successful results in government, industry, ecclesia, and life in general.

It was summer, and all the children (our relatives and friends) we played with were working. They would leave before dawn in the morning, and if it did not rain, they would return just before dark. Despite their youth, they did not have a lot of energy left to play. And even if they did, it was too late, and they would have to work the next day, if it did not rain. When it poured, the clouds were gray, and things appeared gloomy, but our playmates were home. I am not sure if we cared about the weather or only noticed it because we had to stay inside, out of the rain. I am not sure we noticed the cloudy gray sky. Despite the rain, clouds, and gray sky, we succeeded in having fun.

The gray did not prevent our success in this case. It created the opportunity for us to succeed. If it did not rain, there were no clouds, and the sky were not gray, our opportunity to be together would not have happened. Once we were together, we either looked beyond, ignored, or did not see our challenges. We took advantage of what the challenges provided us, that is, time together, and we had fun.

My twin and I were a little over nine and a half years old when the boredom of being home alone together (an oxymoron) got the best of us. We pleaded with and convinced our mother to get "the boss" to let us begin work early. (Back then we could work in the fields at age ten.) In hindsight, we must have been just short of crazy because we were pleading with our mom to join our brother, cousins, and friends on the front line of the cotton fields, chopping cotton. The weather was hot, and the work was hard. The boss was at times unfriendly, and the food was never the best, but we were with our relatives, friends, and people.

We would grab a hoe from the back of the truck that we rode to work on and go to work just at the break of day. The mornings were cool. The cotton and the grass we were sent to remove were wet. As the morning rolled on, everything dried up, and it got very hot. The cotton rows appeared to be a country mile, never ending. And the grass got taller and increasingly harder to cut.

Somehow amid all of this, we managed to have fun, to make the best of a bad situation. We talked a lot, played games, sang songs, made fun of each other, competed on getting the work done, and united around our dislike for the straw boss. Despite the heat, the difficult work, and the other challenges, we still managed to have fun. It should be noted here that the amount of fun we were having determined success as a kid of nine or ten years of age.

We did not let the gray skies, the heat of the day, or the difficulty of the task define our experience. We somehow managed to look beyond the task, environment, weather, and person we collectively did not like and focus on the fun. Although we were walking in the heat of the day, working beyond our physical strength, and being pushed to do more when less seemed only possible, we pressed on. We found a place amid our challenges where purpose and destiny drove the present. We walked and worked in a space where the work got done and we had fun, even when this seemed impossible.

Maybe it was the relationships. We worked with our cousins, friends, and acceptable acquaintances. Perhaps it was the realization that the day would end, as it had every day before. Maybe we had grown tough to the task or found a place to work where good met evil, easy met difficult, and light met dark. Possibly we discovered how to succeed in a space called gray where the unknown and known collide, struggle and success coexist, plan and purpose participate, and black and white mingle and create gray.

Gray is that color that either exists between black and white or consists of black and white. While it has often been perceived as a dull and uninteresting color, it works with most colors. To validate this truth, you only need to spend a few minutes matching it with other colors in your wardrobe, for example, blue, black, white, pink, mauve, yellow, green, and brown. The fact that gray blends well with other colors has prompted its use with blending in, not standing out. When we hear the term "going gray," we understand that the person is not going all the way dark—not entirely. We know that they are hiding or hidden, but not completely. When we hear of someone "walking in the gray," we understand that they are not breaking the rules but just bending them.

While I can understand how these thoughts of gray can be grasped, I would like to offer an expanded look at the gray and suggest that if we are true and honest with ourselves, we would agree that we spend most of our lives in the gray. We seldom know the black or white of anything. We rarely know the beginning and ending of anything. We infrequently know the how, what, when, or where of things. In 1 Corinthians, Paul writes,

> For we know in part, and we prophesy in part. But when that which is perfect is come, then that which is in part shall be done away. When I was a child, I spake as a child, I understood as a child, I thought as a child: but when I became a man, I put away childish things. For now we see through a glass, darkly; but then face to face: now I know in part; but then shall I know even as also I am known. (1 Corinthians 13:9–12 KJV)

While Paul notes the limited understanding of children, he also calls out the limited vision of adults. "We see in part." There will come a day when light will overtake darkness, when we will know even as we are known, but until then, we will continue to walk in the gray. I have learned that life is about walking in the gray.

When I first thought about writing on this subject, I was going to document the impact that color has on your dreams and look at skin colors, both black and white. I was a black man growing up in what I then perceived as a white man's world. As I matured and progressed, I came to understand that walking in the gray was the lack of clarity on the rules of engagement, lucidity that could make one's professional journey more manageable. I finally came to know and understand as Paul did and expressed to the Corinthians that life is a walk in the gray.

In this book, I offer you some thoughts on how to succeed in life, the workplace, school, marriage, and church, knowing that gray is your new white for clarity, your new black for definition, your newfound friend to walk with. Let us begin our journey together.

WALKING IN THE GRAY

Walking in the gray is about walking in an area where it is neither black or white, things are unclear or unknown, there are no or unclear written rules, or you must figure it out as you go along. I decided years ago to write this book, but I thought it would be best if I experienced success first. I believed my testimony of success would be more acceptable or accepted if I had experienced what I was telling people or writing about. In short, I needed to experience what I was going to write about before I jotted it down.

So my life has been an interesting journey because I have been able to see the fulfillment of the things I share with you in these pages. I have tested the concepts and ideas with people for the past thirty years as a professional, and I have grown increasingly convinced than ever that they work. I have also become assured that understanding where you are walking, what you are doing, and what is going on around you will determine whether you succeed or fail. Everybody wants to be a success, but very few people understand what it means to be successful or what is required to be successful. Everyone wants a quick overnight fix for success—like putting food in the microwave—immediately. But I have learned over time that quick-gained success is often short-lived.

The journey to success is just that, a journey. It is not a trip. (If people understood and accepted this fact, they would stop tripping.) As a result, if you want to be successful, you must put in the time. That said, I believe you can shorten your journey to your destination if you understand the trip—where you are going and how to get there. I graduated from undergrad in three years. I was able to accomplish this because I understood my destination and what was required to get there, not because I was so much smarter than other students who graduated in four years. Once I understood the cost of my destination and realized I had the requisite resources, all that was required was a decision and a commitment to use the resources to pay the cost. In this case, time, hard work, and commitment were it. It took around 150 class hours to graduate with an undergraduate degree. If I did this in four years, I would have to commit to approximately eighteen hours per semester.

However, if I took twenty-one hours and attended summer school and took nine hours there, I could graduate in around three years. These facts were known and doable; however, what I did not know was the difficulty of carrying such a heavy load and the impact it could have on my health and GPA. So once I decided and committed to completing the requisite task in a shorter amount of time, the outcome was academic.

There is nothing new or novel about identifying a way to shorten the time it takes to do something. People do this all the time. When you know and understand what is required, then it is up to you to decide how much time, energy, or effort you want to dedicate to completing the task. Some people take an hour to do a thing while others take thirty minutes to do the exact same thing.

What is the difference? If the task is the same, the difference must be the individual's talent, effort, or time dedicated to the outcome. It is shorter because of their focus. What you will discover in this book is an understanding of what is required to be successful and how walking in the gray, where the rules are not written, can be determined and defined by you—and you can shorten your path to success. You just need to understand what is required and determine if you are ready to commit.

The intent of this book is to provide you with the tools that you can use in life, the workplace, church, school, the household, and so forth to make you a success. The tools I will provide you, if applied, will allow you to get from A to Z—A being your present state and Z being your desired state—in a reasonable, if not a more accelerated, amount of time.

Because you are reading this book, I am assuming that you are willing to commit the desired time and effort to doing these things. What you may find in this is that a number of these concepts are very basic and elementary. However, too often, what we manage to do is forget the basic things that need to be done to accomplish our desired end/outcome. The big things do not cause failure in business and relationships. More times than not, it is the little things. When we get away from doing the little things, the big things suffer. Businesses and relationships oftentimes fail because of minor issues, not big ones.

Often the small things in life cause us to fail. We forget the basics. With this being the case, I believe a lot of what you may hear and gather from what you read will take you back to the basic details that will have somewhat of a new spin. The goal of this book is not to give you an alphabetical or sequential way to get from A to Z but provide you with concepts, thoughts, and ideas that, if applied properly, will create the possibility of your success. Let's get started.

We will spend most of our waking lives in a gray area, a zone where we lack information, guidance, details, insights, or understanding. When we are born, we learned from our society, family, and friends whom we are and what our local norms, protocols, and acceptable behaviors are. Once we managed to get a handle on our little world—one where we learned to get food, water, and attention by simply crying—things changed.

But we were taught as we got a little older that crying was not the answer. In fact, we were taught that crying for what you need was unacceptable. We were often left in our cribs, crying for what seemed like hours for attention, something that never came until our behavior changed. Many nights we cried ourselves to sleep until we finally realized that crying did not work.

We spent the next several years trying to please our parents and appease our friends. We were not sure what our parents wanted. They were constantly correcting us and trying to get us to be like them, but it did not seem they knew what they really wanted.

Regardless, for a period of years, we made it our lives' calling to please our parents. As soon as we had a handle on that, something happened to our bodies—physically, hormonally, and psychologically—that changed our outlook on life. And nothing was clear anymore. It seemed that gray became grayer. What we thought we knew and wanted was reversed. We no longer wanted to please our parents or be like them. We just wanted them to understand us.

There was only one problem: we did not understand us. Peer pressure was on us, and we wanted to please our peers, but they were us and had no clue what pleased them. One day we were best of friends; the next day we were worst enemies, only to return and become the best of friends. Once we realized that this was not the end of the world, life changed. We no longer had our parents to decide what was best for us or our friends to pressure us. We only had ourselves, and we were simply trying to figure it out.

If we decided to attend an institution of higher learning, we were in the gray again. We not only had to learn new norms and behaviors, we had to make new friends and determine how best to engage them. Once we got a pretty good handle on this, we graduated and had to start over in the workforce.

Before I tackle this period of grayness, I want to introduce one more era, our adult lives and parenthood. This is the time in our lives when we became the parents. If it were not already gray enough, it really got out of hand. How many times have you said or heard someone say, "Parenting did not come with instructions"? Being a parent myself and married to the best wife and mother in the world, I think I can speak for a lot of parents when I say, "We made it up as we went along."

Parenting is a very dark shade of gray. There are so many factors to consider, that is, so many moving parts and so much unknown. When we were done with the punishments, permissions, support, spending, guidance, and graciousness, we were still left saying, "Only time will tell if we got it right." And even if we did, we still did not know what we did right and why it worked.

While you will spend most of your life in the gray, in the dark, it is my contention that you do not have to do so without understanding and making progress, moving to the light. The light that you see is not the end of the tunnel; it is your way out of the gray right now. We spend far too much time focusing on the current destination and not on the journey. Life is to be lived. Jesus said, "I have come that they may have life and that they have it more abundantly" (John 10:10b KJV).

How can your life be abundant when you spend most of it with your eyes half seeing and viewing your current destination as your journey? Open your eyes and see the course that you are traveling. Enjoy your time in the gray. Yes, I know that we are only strangers and sojourners down here, pilgrims who see through a glass darkly. As Paul told the Corinthians,

> For we know in part, and we prophesy in part.
> But when that which is perfect is come, then that
> which is in part shall be done away. When I was
> a child, I spake as a child, I understood as a child,
> I thought as a child: but when I became a man, I
> put away childish things. For now, we see through
> a glass, darkly; but then face to face: now I know
> in part; but then shall I know even as also I am
> known. (1 Corinthians 13:9–12 KJV)

That said, even Paul recognized some clarity and growth with maturity. Even knowing in part, we are faith walkers, and as such, we do what Paul declared to the Corinthians, "We walk by faith and not by sight" (2 Corinthians 5:7 KJV). Faith takes us out of darkness and into the light of hope. It permits us to walk, now seeing the light at the end of the tunnel here with us illuminating our path. Faith connects the then with the now, the not yet with the right now, and tomorrow with today. It makes sense out of what we are going through because it allows us to see where we are going to.

In this book, we are not going to walk out of the gray in every aspect of our lives, but we will identify some tools, steps, and things that you can do and apply in your life that will help you whenever you are in the gray. This book is not designed to be a religious manuscript nor an academic piece. It is designed to be plain talk from one who has walked and currently walks by faith in a world that is not faith based.

In the following chapters and pages, I want to show you how to come out of the grayness of your organizational life into the light. I want to share with you how easy it is to work your way out of the unknown, understand the unwritten rules, formalize the informal channels, manage the grapevine, accomplish your goals, and fulfill your mission and vision. Thank you for joining me as we shed some light on your gray areas.

PART
1

WHERE DO I GO
FROM HERE?

HAVE A DESTINATION

WALKING IN THE GRAY IS ABOUT WORKING WITH THE unknown, taking actions without all the details, and walking between the black and the white. It is about moving forward with purpose without knowing the right next step, when the next step is critical. It is about walking—moving forward—even when you do not have what you think you need to do so. It is about not allowing what you do not know to keep you from doing what you know you should do or what needs to be done. It is about deciding and making a choice with inadequate information. It is about getting out of your own way and not allowing yourself to settle because you lack the details to move. It is about having a destination without the detail, the where without the how. It is about identifying a way forward and moving in that direction even when you do not know if the way you are going is forward.

Far too many people take the lack of details as a cause for pause, a reason to surrender, stop, or give up. In this book I want to highlight the fact that we all live and move in a gray space. I want to encourage and excite you to accept this area as your new normal and incite you to understand and move in this space as if it were black and white. (Besides, gray is just the combination of black and white.)

In this life, if we are honest with ourselves, we live daily in a gray space. How much do we really know about anything for sure? Do we know what the future holds? Do we know what is going to take place tomorrow, today, the next hour, or the next minute? There are so many knowns and unknowns that we do not control or are even unaware of. Even if we were informed, we would be misinformed to think we know enough to control the outcome of our next decision. We are all walking in a gray space.

We are all required to make decisions that are not fully informed and to rely on a level of truth and a set of facts that are incomplete at best. It could be true, and the facts could be accurate; however, it could be false and not factual. We close our eyes each night not knowing if we will open them again tomorrow ... if tomorrow comes for us. We open our eyes each day hopeful but not knowing what our expectations will yield. Our daily reality is walking in the gray.

Meteorologists have studied the weather for years, and they have yet to consistently and accurately predict the weather—to get it right all the time and make their weather predictions black and white. They have advanced tools, empirical evidence and details, historical data, and comprehensive analysis, and yet they cannot say without a shadow of doubt what the weather will be. They can only forecast (predict or estimate) the weather.

While we can rely on the meteorologists' forecast to make decisions on what we should wear tomorrow or what the weather is going to be, our reliance on their forecast is another example of walking in the gray. Even with the best tools, access to a vast amount of information (historical and empirical), understanding of the weather, and the wisdom to predict what would, could, or should happen next, their best forecast is an educated guess, a matter of fact ... not fact. How many times have you planned your day based on the weather report or decided what to wear or take an umbrella, only to be disappointed because they got it wrong again?

One could argue that your decisions were good, given they were based on the facts or at least the information you were given at the time that was accumulated, analyzed, and announced, data posed as facts or at least a factual forecast. (Perhaps this is an oxymoron.) Is it the meteorologist's fault?

I live in an area where there was a time the meteorologists seemed to have predicted the weather so inaccurately that many of us started using the opposite of their forecast to inform our decisions. People questioned, "What is the one occupation you can be wrong half the time and still be employed?" Answer: a meteorologist.

In fairness to the meteorologist, they too walk in the gray. Yes, meteorologists use proven scientific methods and the latest technology to forecast or determine the weather and have the latest equipment to measure past and present atmospheric conditions, but they do not control the weather. There are too many unknowns. The best they can do is make an informed and educated guess, a forecast.

Since the dawn of time, humans have been trying to forecast the weather. Jesus acknowledges the study of the weather in scripture. He stated, "When it is evening, ye say, it will be fair weather: for the sky is red. And in the morning, it will be foul weather today: for the sky is red and lowering. O ye hypocrites, ye can discern the face of the sky; but can ye not discern the signs of the times?" (Matthew 16:2b–3 KJV).

It would seem in Jesus's day they (people in general) accurately predicted the weather. Jesus said they were weather-wise, able to "discern the face of the sky." Maybe they got it right most of the time; perhaps global warming was not an issue. Possibly they did not rely as much on the weather or its report to make their lives' decisions, or they were more accepting or tolerant of the mistakes.

Today, however, we rely on the meteorologists' weather forecasts to make many of our decisions: what to wear; what to take with us during the day; whether to go shopping, golfing, or to see a movie; and when to take a trip. Meteorologists know this and have made major advancements and improvements to be more accurate. They use computer-based models that take many atmospheric factors (current weather and sky conditions, weather patterns, etc.) into account, and yes, they are only right some (maybe most) of the time. That said, billions of dollars later, the weather forecast is still an educated guess. Why? They are walking in the gray, working with unknowns and uncontrollable outcomes.

Business is no different. While business is in business to do business, to positively affect the bottom line, they struggle, strive, or succeed based on how they cope with or walk in the gray. Business and industry have been able to determine market trends, cycles, investment strategies, and customer needs and then deliver products and services just in time to impact the bottom line. They have increased revenues, cut cost, reduced waste, managed taxes and interest on debt, and optimized the allocation of resources. At the end of the day, the cycle, the period, and profitability are only measures of success. While they serve to inform all concerned on what worked, they are really a testament of the company's ability to walk in the gray. There are too many unknowns (variables) to ascertain what will work repeatedly in a dynamic and changing environment.

Poor profitability only indicates that something is not working. There are too many other contributing variables we must consider in order to recreate repeated success. Success or failure, positive or negative numbers, only indicate or reveal that something is or is not working. If management gets it right one time because of their strategy, mission, vision, and goals, it does not mean that they will get it right the next time, even if all leading indicators are consistent. They are walking in the gray.

Like meteorologists and businesses, individuals are also walking in the gray. In this book, I want to share how individuals in all walks of life can take certain actions or steps to ensure that their walk in the gray is on the side of success. I am going to offer suggestions, recommendations, ideas, thoughts, and tried-and-proven practices that, if implemented and followed, will position you to walk and succeed in the gray.

Let me be clear: there are no guarantees, no silver bullets, no absolutes, no one-size-fits-all, no shortcuts, and no quick fixes to your success. Success is a long game. To experience it, you must recognize and accept the fact that you must put in the necessary time and effort. However, knowing how to better allocate your time and effort will prove helpful. After all, there are things that you can do that will improve your situation, create better opportunities for you, or position you to make success a real possibility even when you are in a gray space.

It is a forgone conclusion that we are all walking in the gray and have been doing so since we entered this life. It could also be argued that people were created to live life in a gray space. 1 Corinthians 13:12 (KJV) declares, "For now we see through a glass, darkly; but then face to face: now I know in part; but then shall I know even as also I am known."

It is worth noting that I began the thought of writing this book because I felt I was a "black man in a white man's world" and I needed to learn how to walk in the gray in order to survive. The gray is an area or place where you are not accepted by your own and not received by others for the same reason. You are trying to better yourself, to be the best you that you can be.

At this time, my gray area was limited to the color of my skin. One might think this surprising given the day I was living in and the time in which I was considering writing this book. It was not the 1960s or earlier. It was the late 1980s, a time when you might think we would be living the dream of Martin Luther King Jr., one in which we would "be judged not by the color of our skin but by the content of our character."

In many ways, this is still a dream. Once I entered the workforce, my gray area expanded beyond skin color to the gray space of organizational behavior. This is the space where organizations operate somewhere outside, around, above, beneath, or near their documented guidance, directions, rules, regulations, policies, and procedures. It is the space in organizations where unwritten and often inconsistent, subjective, and inequitable decisions are made about their personnel, procedures, and policies.

I learned that in order to succeed, I could not allow myself to play the victim or get upset about gray areas like hall files, unwritten rules, "good ole boy" networks, and glass/bamboo ceilings. While I had no intention of buying into or accepting these ideas, I learned to acknowledge and accept their reality.

In order to make change, you must first fully understand the thing you want to alter. To that end, to modify the organization, I made it a point to learn everything I could about the organization. In the process, I learned that some things were not going to change, that in order to succeed or thrive with their existence you would do well and best to learn everything you could about the organization and it gray areas—what they are, how they operate, and how best to operate with them. I learned how to walk in the gray, to see the organization for what it was.

While it was important to me to see the organization for what I wanted it to be, more times than not, this created more frustration for me because my perception and reality of the organization did not match up. To balance this, while attempting to make changes, I made it more critical to understand the organization as it existed. This meant I had to learn the unwritten rules and how to walk in the gray and make the best of a bad situation at times. As if this were not enough, I learned that the gray space expanded beyond the organization. That is, it was our way of life.

I realized that we were placed here, and we exist in a space where we do not fully know or understand all. We are in the gray. While we serve an omniscient God, we are limited in our knowledge and understanding of all the pieces that go together to make life work. We are in the gray. A hymn I learned at a young age speaks to this walk, "We Will Understand It Better By and By" by Charles A. Tindley[1]. The refrain says,

> By and by, when the morning comes,
> when the saints of God are gathered home,
> we'll tell the story how we've overcome,
> for we'll understand it better by and by.

---

[1] Author: Charles Albert Tindley (1905)
Tune: BY AND BY
Published in 65 hymnals
Printable scores: PDF, MusicXML
https://hymnary.org/text/we_are_tossed_and_driven_on_the_restless

The songwriter was on to something significant. In this life, we experience difficulties and good times—being tossed and driven, having success and sunshine, or seeing clouds and rain. What does it all mean? Are difficulties more important than successes? Is sunshine better than rain? The songwriter does not attempt to answer these questions but encourages the hearers by letting them know that they will understand all of this in time. In time, the hearers will understand whatever experience they had.

It is worth noting that the whole of Christianity is based on walking in the gray—walking by faith and not by sight. It does not let what you see in the natural determine your fate, outcome, or future. In fact, faith is described as "the substance of things hoped for and the evidence of things not seen" (Hebrews 11:1 KJV). It is seeing what does not yet exist but knowing it does. It is proof of tomorrow today, things to come, and things not yet seen. It is evidence that change is coming and this is not the end of the story. Faith is our walk that is not evidenced or proven by what we see, what we know intellectually, or what the tangible facts are. Our Christianity is defined by our ability to walk by faith, not by sight, to walk in the gray. It is confidence in an unseen God and a not-yet existent outcome. It is the belief in the then ... now.

It must be noted too that the scripture also speaks of us each having a measure of faith (Romans 12:3b) and encourages us to operate within it. This tells us that we do not all have the same amount or level of faith. This should come as no surprise to anyone, as we are all different. What it says to us, however, is that while we are all walking in the gray, some of us will survive while others will thrive and still a few will barely stay alive.

That said, whether we survive, thrive, or barely stay alive is not dependent on your measure as much as it is on our use of the measure we are given. Each of us is given a measure of faith equivalent to our need. Some need more than others to do the same thing. Think about it: whether a person weighs 100, 150, or 200 pounds, each has 206 bones and about 700 named skeletal muscles. However, each will perform differently depending on the amount of time and effort put into building their muscles. The individual weighing 100 pounds may be able to lift more weight than the person weighing 200 pounds. How much one can lift is dependent on one's strength, not the measure of one's weight. The amount of time one spends growing muscles determines one's strength. The same is true of our faith. Our faith, like a grain of mustard seed, grows (Matthew 13:31).

As you know, not all of us grow at the same pace, and we rarely mature at the pace and way we want to. We can facilitate our growth and aid in its health. As you may have surmised, the same is true of us walking in the gray. We will all walk and succeed differently; however, we can facilitate our growth. We can aid in the outcome of our walk by growing, understanding to walk successfully, and doing things that have a direct impact on the success of our walk. A walk in the gray will remain consistently dark or dreary unless we identify ways to improve our walk, that is, shed more light on the path, learn the lay of the land so well that you can walk it with your eyes closed, and create a path for yourself.

If we are going to be successful in a space where things are not black and white, we must learn how to walk in these unknown, unclear, undetermined places and spaces. This will not be an easy feat and is likely to elude many. But it is doable. It has been done. To be successful in a gray space, we must take certain measures to ensure that our footing is firm and we can stand and move forward one step at a time. While we cannot guarantee the outcome, we can better position ourselves to affect the outcome, to set ourselves up to succeed.

HAVE A DESTINATION BUT BE FLEXIBLE

The first step is knowing the answer to the question, "Where do we go from here?" What is our ultimate destination today? I state today because we must not become rigid or inflexible. We must not set our destination in stone. Change is constant, and flexibility is a must. If we agree that when walking in the gray, we are walking in a space that is unknown, unwritten, and dynamic, we should agree that to thrive in this space, we must be open to change and be flexible and more dynamic.

If you refuse to change when change is necessary, you will fail. History is replete with stories of failure resulting from individuals, teams, groups, churches, companies, organizations, governments, and countries unwilling to change. Without any specific details, if you look back, you will see things gone that you thought would last forever. Something new and, in some cases, improved have replaced them. For example, whatever happened to the record player and cassette deck? They were replaced by the CD player, which was replaced by digital solutions (e.g., iPods and smart phones). What happened to the rotary phone with the party lines? Cell phones eventually replaced them. What happened to Blockbuster? Redbox, Netflix, and online movie purchases eventually replaced them. Where did all the mom-and-pop stores go? The bigger stores, for instance, Walmart, replaced many. Why have the Walmarts and Giants become super? Everything changes. If one thing is certain and evident in our society and life, it is change. Harold Wilson said it best, "He who rejects change is the architect of decay. The only human institution which rejects progress is the cemetery."

Look at where we are today: we are living in a technological age. You would have been hard-pressed to convince generations before us that today would be what it is. There were no pervasive indicators. Yes, there were visionaries, seers, mavericks, and those who saw things different from the norm, but they were not normal, not the majority, or not popular.

It was quite the contrary. Time and change have been good to them and us, but when stepping on the scene, they were not popular or readily accepted. It took time, proof, and one convert at a time for change to gather momentum and get a foothold. This should strike each of us as odd, given that change is the constant.

Change is the one thing that we have been able to depend on, the one consistent occurrence in our world/society, the one thing that has kept us moving forward.

Change has been the constant to ensure both our success and survival. If you look at where we are today and consider where we were yesterday, the affect of change is evident. It has not been so long ago when service was our calling. Society seems to thrive on being a service industry. As time passes, the ages seem to pass more quickly. Did the Stone Age, Bronze Age, Iron Age, Middle Ages, and Renaissance all last longer than the Agricultural and/or Information Age? Did the Age of Enlightenment last longer than the Technological Age?

Honestly, the answer to these questions matter little, if at all, but their existence highlights and supports the fact that the world is changing at a rapid pace. Maybe we have the Information Age to credit this with. If we do not change with the times, we will be left behind and die.

When the Wright Brothers labored with the idea of putting an object in the air, they were clearly outside of the norm. However, thanks to them, we now have airplanes. Do you think they even thought of the idea of an unmanned aircraft, a satellite in space, or a drone? When Nicholas-Joseph Cugnot invented the automobile, he was outside the norm. Do you think he thought of mass production, electric cars, or self-propelled vehicles? I assume neither of these inventors thought ahead of what they were doing, as they were already ahead of their time.

Herein lies genius. While these inventors' changes were not done to accomplish what came after, they each set the stage for the next change. One could say, "If *a* had not happened, then *b* would not have been possible." I tend to believe that when change happens, whether it is resisted or received, wretched, or welcomed, it sets the stage for the next change (something better). Change creates the opportunity for improvements, and we should always be looking for opportunities to improve or change. In the words of St. Jerome, "Good, better, best. Never let it rest. 'Til the good is better and the better is best." The benefit of change is that it creates the opportunity for more change.

A study of child development will reveal the truth to the reality and importance of change. Even when a child is in the mother's womb, change is taking place. A child does not go from crawling to running track. A child grows, which is another way of saying changes. A child goes from childhood to youth, adulthood, and then old age.

In school, a child starts with preschool, kindergarten, first through twelfth grades, and then on to college. In college, they generally go from freshman to sophomore, junior, senior, graduate, and postgraduate studies. Change is a process, one that opens the door to the next change event. Change is evolutionary and contributes to and creates the next change event.

This is important to know and understand when we establish our destination. We must know and understand that we set or determine our destination with today's limited knowledge and information. We should be careful not to fix where we are going in stone, as each change event will have an impact on our journey and destination. Flexibility is a must because we only know what we know. However, if we are willing to learn, we can welcome change, make the requisite adjustment on and to our journey, and ensure that change does not prevent but facilitate our travel to an even better destination.

Imagine getting into a car to go to an address in another city. You have maybe three points of information: where you are, where you are going, and what your current plans to get from here to there are. What you do not know is what is between here and there. You start your trip, and you encounter construction, a roadblock, an accident, a police trap, potholes, weather, and traffic. Each or all of these will have an impact on your journey. If you expect change, you can plan for it. If you are surprised by it, it could cause you to cancel your trip or not enjoy it at all.

When we go down south, every now and then, we take I-95 to Richmond. One thing has been consistent with this route. There will be traffic and lots of it. With this information, we make plans so we are not so negatively affected. To that end, we try to leave when the traffic dies down a little, earlier in the morning or later in the evening. Even with the best-laid plans, the amount of traffic continues to frustrate us a bit.

Because of this, for longer trips down south, past Richmond, if reasonably possible, we will route our trip to avoid I-95. We assess the weather, and what we encounter still surprises us. We map out our travel, use the GPS, and secure traffic information, but we still encounter things that we did not plan for or expect.

So to continue our journey, we make the adjustments and proceed. I normally have a time in mind that we will arrive our destination. While I cannot brag about 100 percent success in meeting our timeline, we have been blessed to always make the destination. That said, we often arrive using a different route and after more stops than planned. And on one occasion, it was in a different vehicle than we started out with.

However, we have been blessed to always make it. We arrive either exhausted or rested. A few times we are rushed. We are either on time or late. And sometimes we are ahead of schedule. But we have been blessed to always make it. We have never turned around and quit or return home before making our destination.

Our success rate did not come without adjustments. We made unplanned stops, unscheduled hotel naps, unanticipated rest stops, and roadside fifteen-minute recuperation sessions. We turned up the music to max and the temperature to cold (even in the winter). And we rolled down the window to stay alert and not fall asleep.

Most of these actions we did not plan for; we did them on the fly. We made game-time decisions. When we started out, we thought we were rested and ready. We thought we had a good plan, and we did. However, there were unknowns. So in order to make our destination, we made the requisite adjustments. Much of our success can be attributed to our flexibility. We were not rigid. We did not insist that we had to go one way and one way only or arrive at a predetermined time. Yes, we had a schedule in mind, but we knew starting out that it would change. We set our destination, but everything else from start to finish was subject to adjustment or change.

If you are going to be successful, you must have a destination. Your destination could be fluid or firm, but it must be determined or defined. Lewis Carrol was right. "If you don't know where you're going, any road will get you there." An example of this is provided in the conversation between Alice and the Cat in *Alice in Wonderland*.[2]

> "Would you tell me, please, which way I ought to go from here?"
>
> "That depends a good deal on where you want to get to," said the Cat.
>
> "I don't much care where—" said Alice.
>
> "Then it doesn't matter which way you go," said the Cat.
>
> "—so long as I get SOMEWHERE," Alice added as an explanation.
>
> "Oh, you're sure to do that," said the Cat, "if you only walk long enough."

Without a destination, it is not impossible to arrive. You just will not know if you have. Without a destination, you will wander and wonder, *Have I arrived?* And you may continue past where you want or need to go. Without a destination, your journey could become a series of trips, falls, blunders, and stumbles. Without a destination, it is certain you will make it somewhere, but where? You may arrive and not know. Or worse, you may never arrive and could have.

How can you lead people to a place when you don't know where you are going? If you do not have a destination, you do

---

[2] Khurana, Simran. "Lewis Carroll Quotes: Alice in Wonderland." ThoughtCo, Oct. 20, 2019,
thoughtco.com/lewis-carroll-quotes-alice-in-wonderland-2832746.

not know where you are going. If you do not know where you are going, you do not have sight. You are blind. "Leave them; they are blind guides. If the blind lead the blind, both will fall into a pit" (Matthew 15:14 KJV).

Herein lies the risk of not having a destination. You don't know where you are going. If you don't know where you are going, you are not likely to arrive or know that you have, and you could lead others astray. If, however, you are fortunate enough to arrive, you will not even know that you have done so.

Therefore, the first step to improve your possibility of success while walking in the gray is to determine your destination, which does not have to be right, firm, fixed, or forever, but it must be chosen. The destination may be short term, midterm, or long term, but it must be one. This is the beauty of a destination. You don't have to see it; you just identify it.

When a destination is not selected, it is too easy to get frustrated and want to turn around because you feel lost, like you are wasting your time, spinning your wheel, going in circles or nowhere, or not making any progress. However, when a destination is identified or selected, you can begin to make plans, set goals, determine objectives, and take the next steps. It doesn't mean the journey will be easier, but you now know where you are going and can make changes, measure your success, modify your plan, know when you arrive, and, if necessary, reset or change your destination.

Having said this, it is worth noting that we do this regularly, especially when something is important. If you take a quick look back on your life, you will see that your most important accomplishments, your most successful strides, were made when you determined a destination. In school, each grade had determined outcomes, things you had to accomplish before completing a grade and being promoted to the next. Once you accomplished the objectives of the first grade, you were eligible and passed along to the second ... and so on and so forth until you reached your ultimate high school destination, graduation. In college, the destination was graduation after completing a predetermined set of requisite courses. You moved from one level of education (freshman, sophomore, junior, and senior) to the next, after completing the requisite hours or courses until you graduated.

This process has been used again and again throughout your life—playing sports or learning a trade or new skill, for instance, how to play a musical instrument, use a specific toy or tool, or master a task or technique. Growing up, we were placed in systems (schools, sports, or clubs) that had defined destinations. We were able to succeed in the various systems because we were told the expected outcome and then given the specific tasks to accomplish it or we figured something out.

Either way, our success was determined in large part because we knew our destination, the desired outcome. Half the battle is knowing where you are going. In school, as in university, these steps, goals, and objectives were clear and defined, black and white. If you do *a*, *b* will happen. If you do *b*, *c* will happen. If you pass grades one, two, three … ten, eleven, and twelve, you will graduate. It is really that simple when it is black and white and all parties involved follow the rules as written. It is my position, belief, and reason for writing this book that it can be that simple when you are walking in the gray if you are aware of the requirements and act responsibly.

The first thing to be aware of and act on is your destination. If you are going to simplify your walk in the gray, you must first identify a destination and begin to take steps to get there. The steps you take may be complicated, overcome by events, subject to subjective group changes, or have an expiration date (one that was not shared or may not have existed when you started walking), but knowing where you are going and taking steps will put you on the path to get there. Having a destination allows you to make changes and continue when life happens. Knowing your destination could also serve to motivate you to push or encourage yourself, especially when things are not clear or black and white.

My parents instilled this type of thinking in me through their messages on work ethics and their philosophies on what it takes to get ahead. My mother told me that to get ahead, I would need a good education and would have to work twice as hard to get half as much. I never questioned my mom's thinking or tried to ascertain the accuracy of her statements. I simply applied what she taught me: work hard to succeed. Implicit in her lesson is both the destination (success) and the process (work hard). While the validity of this lesson can and will be debated later, I want to point out here the benefit of knowing where you are going and having a plan to get there, even if it changes.

In this case, my success is the destination and will be accomplished by working hard. Syllogistically speaking, if working hard yields success, "If I work hard, I will be successful." This seems simple enough. It may be complicated to accomplish as the work may be hard, but the process to accomplish my goal is simple and easy to understand. If you have a destination, a place, a point, or a position you are trying to get to, you can begin to identify the steps required to get there. In my case and the lessons taught by Mom, the destination was success, and the steps or process was really hard work (twice or four times as hard as my competition). Without a destination, you are unable to determine the input required or if your input is yielding your desired outcome. If you don't know where you are going, you don't know what to do to get there.

Having a destination (somewhere you are going [place]; a mark you are trying to hit [point]; or something you aspire to [position]) makes the difference. Your destination gives you a reason for being, doing, suffering, and taking the next step. When on a journey that is filled with circumstances, chaos, and change, having somewhere to go will keep you pushing forward. Talented people have tossed in the towel because they were tired of working with no end in sight, that is, no defined destination. You probably know people who have quit because they did not have a destination they were committed to. Or maybe you were that person.

Generally these individuals start out excited about using their skills, talents, and abilities to accomplish something, but after some time they give up because they do not see the benefit of their contributions or have no real idea why they are doing what they are doing. They lack a destination that is not here and now, which means they have either arrived or are going somewhere they have not identified, chosen, or determined. In either case, they lack the reason to stay true to themselves and the task at hand. It would be so much easier for them if they had a destination they could target.

A destination serves several purposes, for instance, to cause or pause. It helps you to understand why you are doing what you are doing. This could provide motivation and inspiration to put your best foot forward, or it could inform you that you could be of better service on a different initiative. Either staying on a task motivated or leaving one that you are not committed to is better than just wasting your time. We can see an example of this truth in the success or failure of marriage.

If you examine the divorce rate, you will see that the primary cause for divorce is the lack of commitment to stay together for a lifetime. Yes, there is a compelling reason that drive married couples to divorce, for instance, fidelity, finances, family, fights, faith, and foes. However, if you examine the issues more closely, you will see that the couple became convinced of a different outcome than the one they signed up to. Their focus shifted from a life together to one of irreconcilable differences.

On the other side, if you examine the reason people stay married, you will see that they are committed to the institution of marriage. They have a destination of a lifetime together and are determined to stay together to see it through. One could argue that the difference in success and failure in a marriage is the defined destination. I would like to believe that all marriages start out with the same destination in mind. Unfortunately, however, while most couples go into marriage focused on the destination of getting married and being together for a lifetime, some go into marriage focused on getting married to have a wedding. When the focus is on getting married to have a wedding, after all the planning and the ceremony has been accomplished, they have arrived.

Now married life becomes a challenge because they have invested in the wedding but not the marriage. The result is that each challenge they face after the wedding will appear bigger that it should because they signed up for the wedding but not the problems of being married. In the case of those planning to be together for life, the problems they experience, or encounter, are small because they are working for something bigger, a lifetime together.

We see empirically the impact of a destination on those planning to lose weight. We all know people who planned to lose and lost weight but did not keep the weight off. They put their bodies through hardships, difficult workouts, and limited food choices and their minds through challenges of choice and directed desires. After much temptation, time, and torture, they hit their numbers, the pounds they were trying to lose, and the weight number they were working to get to. But then, within weeks or months, they weigh more than they did before they started to diet.

Why? The destination was to lose weight, not a commitment to a healthier lifestyle. They arrived at their destination. They lost the weight. Now, with nowhere to go, they begin to gain the weight back. Because they have no destination beyond losing the weight they have already lost, when they are faced with new challenges of food choices, portions, calories, and exercise, they have nothing telling, motivating, or encouraging them to choose smartly or to assist them to make good and healthy decisions.

That said, if after reaching their weight-loss goal they decide to live a healthy life and make healthy choices for the next six months or in six-months intervals, they would face their bad choice challenges with a renewed focus. With a new destination, they can make informed choices and take planned steps to move forward while being tempted, tried, and tested. The impact of having a destination cannot be overstated. It is often the difference between success and failure, moving forward, standing still, or going backward. When the destination is not determined, it is not likely you will get there because there is not known. This is also true of your success.

If you are going to be successful in life, in a position, or on a job, when taking advantage of an opportunity, you must identify your destination. Where are you going from here? It is like writing a paper. You determine (or at least assume) the topic, your thesis, before you write the beginning. When you identify your outcome, you can determine your research strategy, survey sample, and outline and then proceed with writing. Too many people wonder through a career with hope as their strategy. They hope they get promoted, obtain a certain assignment, and make the right decision. They hope the right person takes them under their wings and they get seen and are recognized for their hard work. They hope they get a fair evaluation.

Hope is a good motivator, but it is not a good strategy because it does not provide or require next steps. If, however, we understand that implicit in hope is a destination and we can identify the destination, we can be well on our way.

Hope is a desire for something, someone, or somewhere. Desire motivates, encourages, and "does not make ashamed, disappoint, or deceive." If you know what you are hoping for, what you desire, hope allows you to believe in the outcome. Hope motivates you to see beyond your circumstances, believe when there is nothing supporting your belief, and take the next step even when your landing is unclear. Hope provides that added ingredient that keeps you moving toward your destination in spite and in the face of circumstances, change, and chaos.

Having a destination is critical to your success. You cannot get there without it. Having said that, the destination you identify or determine today does not have to be. Nor should it be final. Quite the contrary, your destination should be firmly fixed and flexible. This is my way of saying your destination must be determined, but it also must be subject to change. While we know who holds the future, it is impossible to know what the future holds. Tomorrow is neither determined nor guaranteed; however, we must plan for it. The book of James supports this concept.

> Go to now, ye that say, To day or to morrow we will go into such a city, and continue there a year, and buy and sell, and get gain: Whereas ye know not what shall be on the morrow. For what is your life? It is even a vapour, that appeareth for a little time, and then vanisheth away. For that ye ought to say, If the Lord will, we shall live, and do this, or that. (James 4:13–15 KJV)

James makes it clear that we have no control over tomorrow, as even our lives are not our own or permanent. He, however, does not go as far as telling us not to plan, but rather if we are going to plan, we should submit our plan to the One in control and say, "If the Lord will ..."

The adaptation of a line in "To a Mouse" by the eighteenth-century Scottish poet Robert Burn is correct, "the best laid plans of mice and men oft go awry." No matter how careful we plan, something will always happen or go wrong, causing us to deviate from or change our plans. We have become so adept to this phenomenon of changes to our plans that we have identified laws, axioms, dictums, and principles to explain when it happens.

We are all familiar with Murphy's law[3], which says, "Anything that can go wrong will go wrong." This is just one of the many prominent explanations we provide for things beyond our control.

---

[3] by MRx
June 2, 2015
http://all-funny.info/laws-similar-to-murphys-laws

There are many, many more covering the ranges of our activities. Some similar to Murphy's law include, for example,

- Aigner's Axiom: "No matter how well you perform your job, a superior will seek to modify the results."
- Allen's Law: "Almost anything is easier to get into than to get out of."
- Aristotle's Dictum: "One should always prefer the probable impossible to the improbable possible."
- Banana Principle: "If you buy bananas or avocados before they are ripe, there won't be any left by the time they are ripe. If you buy them ripe, they rot before they are eaten."
- Baruch's Observation: "If all you have is a hammer, everything looks like a nail."
- Basic Law of Exams: "The more studying you do for the exam, the less sure you are as to which answer they want."

Often to prevent the appearance of or to avoid failure, we create excuses or explanations. While they may be warranted and worthwhile, they are generally not required (or would not be) if we acknowledged the reality and impact of change and things outside of our control that directly affects things in our control. If we accept change as a part of our reality, there is no need to make excuses for it. Change happens.

We can make plans to go somewhere, but our chances of getting there successfully are increased if we are flexible. That said, knowing where you are going or having a destination is even more important. If you set out on a road trip with no destination, what determines if you arrive? Even if you had a metric—that is, you needed to arrive before running out of gas—you would have no way of knowing that you have arrived. Yes, you ran out of gas, and yes, you arrived somewhere. But is this where you want to be? If you repeated this several times and each time ran out of gas, you still will not know if you have arrived. Why? You did not have or determine a destination. You were going with no place to go. Now you are left with accepting where you are as the place you were supposed to be. Maybe you are happy with where you are, your hindsight destination. The questions abound: Is this really where I am supposed to be? Am I settling? Did I take the right roads to get here?

For the sake of understanding, let us say you end up in Florida. You could live with this. The weather is nice, and there are a lot of things to do (including Disney World). This would not be a problem unless your real destination was California where the weather is also nice and there are a lot of things to do (including Disney Land). Now you know you are about as far off as you could possibly be. Yes, each state has comparable weather and things to do, but Florida is not California, and California is not Florida.

To give you another example, let us say you start your trip in WDC with your destination being San Diego, California. You are now able to map out your trip, and if you so choose, you may select the shortest route. With circa 2,680 miles to travel, if you plan to make this a five-day trip, you will have to travel an average of 536 miles per day. If you averaged sixty-five miles per hour, you will drive almost 8.25 hours per day. In a perfect world, you could tell from the time of your departure on the first and last day of your trip, the time of your arrival.

However, we do not live in a perfect world. There's no utopia here. Therefore, it is likely that inclement weather; unplanned traffic interruptions—accidents, road construction, or detours—or personal biological needs, urgencies, and emergencies, for instance, rest stops, hunger, and bio breaks will interrupt your trip. You can still make your destination on time if you increase your average speed, change the amount of travel time per day, or make other changes as needed to accommodate unplanned events.

There are many benefits to having a destination, knowing where you are headed. One key benefit is the ability to respond to changes that affect the journey to your destination. In these travel examples, you can make changes without giving up on your destination. You may have to change routes, make more stops, spend more or less time than planned on certain days, or revisit your travel plan to include modifying the date of your arrival. These are all doable when you have a destination, but unavailable if you do not. When you do not know where you are going, you are unaware that adjustments need to be made.

Have a Vision

Having expressed the importance of having a vision, a destination, or somewhere to go, I want to reiterate how important this is to your journey and how critical it is to your success. Without a destination, a vision of your future, you will follow the path of least resistance. While this path may ultimately and perhaps accidentally get you to your destination, it offers no guarantees and creates the potential for wasted time, energy, resources, and possibilities.

Water will flow from the mountain into the rivers below without being controlled, channeled, pushed, guided, or steered, but it will do so along the path of least resistance. This path may not be the most direct or desired, particularly if there is something you want the water to accomplish along the way or upon arrival. For example, if water is channeled and led down the mountain into the river, the route it takes would accomplish the desired outcomes, that is, quenching the thirst of villagers, watering plants in a local garden, powering a plant that supports other needs, and flowing into the river at a desired point. Your life and path to success is not drastically different.

If you have a destination, you can plan your approach. Maybe you want to make some stops along the way, run a while and then walk, slow your pace to deepen your knowledge base or avoid an impending pitfall, or accelerate your pace to get there as quickly as possible. When you know your desired destination, you can identify and select how you want to proceed. While your choices will not guarantee your success, they will have a direct and real impact. Knowing your destination, at a minimum, will inform you if your choices will improve or impede your possibility of success. This allows you, given the information available at the time, to make informed decisions to put yourself in the best possible position to succeed, if that is your goal.

The scripture says, "Where there is no vision, the people perish ..." (Proverbs 29:18 KJV). In this passage, vision refers to the revelation (the Word) the prophets receive from God. Without God's Word spoken to the people through the prophet, the people would abandon their purpose and follow their own sinful ways, the path of least resistance. If people do not hear from God, they are left to discover what they already know, which leaves them where they are with nowhere to go. But when they hear from God, they hear from the One whose foolishness is wiser than humans and whose weakness is stronger than humans (1 Corinthians 1:25 KJV). They hear from the One who gives them somewhere to go and something to do and look forward to. This provides them purpose and meaning and gives them cause and courage.

It is worth noting that your path (whether to success or failure) will be filled with challenges, struggles, hardships, haters, ditches, doubters, or resistance. If we do not have a destination, we will abandon ourselves (our purpose and our destiny) and follow the easiest route. This is evidenced in our approach to education. If we were not required to learn and were not expected to show evidence of our learning from out test results, what would the likelihood be that we would ever pick up a book?

If I am honest, one of the primary reasons I was a good student was because of my mom's expectation. I knew the teachers expected us to do well, but my mom expected us to do better. When we brought our report cards home, she would examine them, and if we had less than the expected grades (Ss or As), we had to give an account. If our account of our actions were not enough, we would be disciplined to ensure that the next grading period reflected our effort and not our excuses.

My wife, Sheila, and I did the same for our children. When they brought their report cards home, we reviewed them and questioned all their grades, including their As. We would ask them independent of grade, "Did you do your best?" If they said yes and their grades did not match up to what we believe was their best, we questioned, "Did you give it your best effort?" We realized that all classes were not made equal in complexity or simplicity. We also realized that some subjects for them were not as complicated or easy as others.

As a result, we did not assume that an A reflected an A effort or a C a C effort. So when we asked the question, we posed it for all their grades. After all, it was not just about the grades. It was about them giving their best. We wanted our children to give their best effort, and then we and they could live with the results. We also recognized that they may not have known what their best effort was or how their best looked. So we gave them a vision of themselves beyond their current grade. We told them that they could be the best student if they put in the best effort.

We repeated to them a quote I recall reading before I was a teenager in a set of books my mom purchased for us, "Good, better, best. Never let it rest. Until your good is better, and your better is best." (I later discovered this was a quote from St. Jerome, Father of the Latin church.) We wanted them to give their best and expect the best of themselves. Like my mom, we were giving them something to aim for—a target, a goal, or a vision. Be the best you that you can be by giving your best effort. We let them know that they were special, gifted, and talented and had what it took to succeed. We wanted to make sure they were taking advantage of their opportunities. We presented a vision of themselves that pushed them to want to be better than they were already, to make growth and improvement an integral part of their life, and to never settle for being their average selves.

God told Habakkuk, "Write the vision, and make it plain upon tables, that he may run that readeth it" (Habakkuk 2:2b KJV). Essentially God told Habakkuk to write the vision (His revelation) so they could be preserved and publicized. He wanted the messenger to have access to and read the vision and then run and spread the good news.

This was our intent with our children. We wanted them to understand our expectations of them—our vision for them—so we made it plain. We explained it in words and laced it with consequences. We gave them a vision of our expectation of them. Be the best you that you can be. We did not seek to compare them to their peers, nor to each other for that matter. We wanted them to be the best they could be individually. So we asked the question, "Did you do your best?"

I share this to let you know how important a vision is to your journey. Without a vision for your journey, you will be on a trip and will likely spend a lot of time tripping—tripping over yourself, tripping about what other folks are doing or not, or tripping about what you do or do not have—just tripping. However, with a vision (destination or somewhere to go), you can see your future state despite your present situation. In fact, you can see through your gloomy days and dark nights. You can see past your mountains and over your valleys as well as through your sunshiny days and your darkest hour just before the break of day.

With a vision, you have something that you can preserve and publicize—something you can hold on to; something that will propel you beyond the moment and the difficulty of the task, problem, or challenge; or something that gives you a reason to push when you seem to have nothing left. A vision will give you something to focus on and a reason to press on.

Companies, organizations, teams, churches, civic groups, schools, and public and private industries develop, craft, and promulgate vision statements to ensure that a path is communicated, understood, and followed. Vision statements are developed to motivate and inspire those under its umbrella to accomplish the strategic plan, strategy, mission, or goals. Vision statements are established to guide decisions, actions, policies, procedures, and people. They are there to provide the future state, the destination, to serve as the guiding light and principles to help define how things will take place, that is, how the company will grow, who should be a part of the company, and what the company will and will not do.

The vision statement does not provide the step-by-step guide to get things done. It provides the destination and, with any success, the motivation. For example,

- Walmart's vision statement is "to be the best retailer in the hearts and minds of consumers and employees."
- Microsoft's vision statement is "empower every person and every organization on the planet to achieve more."

Each provides a future state, something to aspire to, and neither provide the step-by-step guide on how to get there. That said, when reading them, employees of the companies have the guiding principles that will help them make decisions that will assist the company reach its destination.

The same is true of your vision, your destination. When you know where you are going, you may not know the details on how to get there or the specific steps to take. However, knowing where you are going provides you the guiding principles to assist you to make the right decisions. If your destination is Arkansas and you are in WDC, you would not be wise to get there via California … unless part of your vision is to arrive in Arkansas after having travelled to the remotest states in the continental United States.

In summary, for your life and profession, you must have a vision, a destination, but you must be flexible. Things, people, and situations change. On the journey to your destination, you will learn something that you did not know before you started out. You will grow and mature. You will get new thoughts, techniques, and tools as you move forward. Be flexible. Be a learner. Be willing and open to change.

Now that we have a destination, it is important that we begin to assess whether we have what it takes to make it. Is this my vision, or does this vision belong to someone else? The first step to make this assessment is to begin with "the man (generic) in the mirror." What do I bring to the table?

CHAPTER 2

KNOW WHERE YOU ARE

WHILE IT IS ESSENTIAL THAT YOU HAVE A VISION, IT IS equally important that you know where you are. Knowing where you are helps you determine the proximity to your destination, identify the tools or talent required to make your dream a reality, and ascertain additional requirements to ensure your success. If you are planning to navigate a course that will get you to where you are going, your vision, you must know where you are.

Archimedes, a Greek mathematician, physicist, engineer, inventor, and astronomer, said, "The shortest distance between two points is a straight line." Two points are essential keys to your success: your beginning and your end, your current position and your future location. It is important to know that these two points are independent. You must know what they are, but you must also know that one does not determine the other. More specifically, where you start is no indication of where you will end up, and where you end up is no indication of where you started.

How many stories have we heard of people who started out poor but ended up rich or began with nothing but ended up with something? We love the Cinderella stories, that is, the story of unjust oppression and triumphant reward, the tale of the unknown becoming known, the unrecognized being recognized.

We love a story of humble beginnings ending in success and riches. We love to see the defeated win; we love to see the underdog defeat the big dog. Truth be told, we all would love this to be our story. We would love to be the hero, the conqueror, the winner, the champ. The only thing that would make this even better is if we "started from the bottom" and made it to the top. What if I told you that this could be your story?

You could be that person who walked on the scene with nothing but walked off the stage with your dream realized, your vision fulfilled. It could be you. However, to make this a reality, you first need to have a vision, and then you need to know where you are in relation to that vision. Are you at the beginning of your journey? Have you already made some progress? Are you on or off course? Are you close or far away? Do you believe you have what it takes to make it, to succeed, to turn your dreams into reality? Are you in the right place, position, or location? Do you know where you are? Knowing where you are is as critical to your success as knowing where you are going. Lewis Carroll stated correctly, "If you do not know where you are going, any road will get you there."

We said it this way, "If you don't know where you're going, any path will do." While this statement is true, if you don't know where you are, it will be difficult to determine if you can get to where you need to be. Knowing where you are is not just about location. It is also about qualifications. How many people start out in life wanting to be the next Michael Jordan? While they may know their vision or destination, what may hold them back is their qualifications. Do they have Michael Jordan's skills or work ethics? Do they have what it takes? Let's examine this because if we are ever going to be successful, we must know where we are right now.

ORGANIZATION

In organizations, it is important that you know where you are. Are you at the top, bottom, or middle of the organization? Are you a new hire, a mid-career hire, a journeyman, or a seasoned officer? Are you an employee, supervisor, team lead, manager, leader, senior executive, director, or head of an organization? Did you just enter on duty, or are you eligible for retirement?

Knowing where you are will help you determine what the next steps are toward your goal, if you have what it takes to get to where you need to be, and how much energy and effort you need to exert to get to where you aspire. Even more critically, knowing where you are will determine almost everything about you—your actions, words, behaviors, connections, new connections and contacts, clothing, conversations, next steps, work plans, goals and objectives, and strategic plan to get to where you want to be.

Individuals typically fail in organizations because they do not know where they are. As a result, they make mistakes. They do things that are inappropriate or unacceptable based on where they are. They expect outcomes that are inconsistent with where they are. They work inappropriately, that is, not knowing when it is appropriate to change from being an employee, supervisor, manager, or leader. They execute tactically as employees and managers. They work hard, expecting hard work to pay off at all levels. They expect what got them where they are will get them where they want to be. They make people and political mistakes at the wrong times. They enter on duty, wanting to lead the organization and, after many years, desire to execute and not manage or lead. Knowing where you are is critical to your success.

The first thing you need to know is the organization you are part of. How do you plan to succeed in an organization when you have no knowledge of the organization's mission, vision, goals, rules, regulations, policies, or procedures? Is hope your strategy? How do you plan to lead an organization if you do not know where the organization is going? How can you manage successfully if you don't know what resources, people, and dollars you are managing to accomplish a goal? How can you lead people and organization when you don't know where the organization is headed? Knowing where you are is essential to your success.

When accepting a new assignment, position, or task, an understanding of what it is you are to accomplish is required. This is no different in organizations. Before accepting a position, you should know what the organization does. This allows you to better perform at whatever level you happen to be. If you are just entering on duty and you possess the skill set required to do the job to which you are assigned, you have what it takes to be successful in that position. Your knowledge of the organization will only strengthen your ability to excel.

Individuals who began a job and have no knowledge of what the organization does can be good performers, if they have the skills for the position and no knowledge of the organization. There is nothing to prevent an individual who has the skills required to do the job from being successful as a performer. What separates the successful person (defined as one who desires to manage or lead the organization) from the average individual is the understanding of what the organization does.

If an organization hires an accountant and the individual possesses the requisite skills as indicated or supported by their résumé, educational background, GPA, qualifications, experience, or test (psychological, physical, etc.) results, the organization has a right to expect that the individual will be successful in that position. If the skills of the individual match the required skills of the position, this should be a match made in heaven. This would be correct, true, and perhaps axiomatic, if all that were required to succeed was skills to master the position. This is rarely the case.

In organizations there are things called hall files, unwritten rules, intangibles, unknowns, potentials, and so forth that suggest and inform us that there are things other than just the required skills of the position necessary for a person to be successful. Assuming this is true, and it is, it would be reasonable to expect that the importance of these other things is not consistently applied throughout the organization. That is, the other things that contributes to an individual's success are not the same at every level and unfortunately are not consistently and equitably applied.

When an individual enters on duty, it is critical that they possess the requisite skills for the position. They must know their job. However, as they move up in the organization, other intangibles become even more critical to their success—perhaps even more critical than the execution of their duties in a position. More specifically, at times, different sets of skills take prominence. That is, at times, it is the individual's skill set; other times it is their will set. Sometimes it is their people set. Knowing the organization and knowing where you are in it is critical to understanding when each of these sets of skills should be at work, when one is more critical than the other. If you know where you are and understand the timely value of the different skill sets, you can leverage them to maximize your return on investment. Too often, instead of leveraging this reality, people ignore and complain about their impacts on them. We discuss this more in detail later. Let's return to discussing how important it is for you to know the organization.

Knowing the organization will help you understand your position and how you should perform to best serve the mission. Having only the knowledge to do your job is not enough. Knowledge to do your job alone provides you, as it is suggested, the know-how. To be effective and have a real impact on the organization and your success, you must know how to apply the knowledge. That is, you must have an understanding, which comes from knowing the organization—its vision, mission, goals, and objectives.

How many times have you known individuals who allowed or used the rules to get in the way of accomplishing something? The law as specific as it is, at its best, is gray, subject to interpretation. If you do not know or understand the organization that you serve, even if you possess the requisite skills to do your job, you can misapply your skills and hurt the organization. Even more significant, you will limit yourself and your success because of your limited knowledge. Yes, you will have a more significant impact on the mission of an organization when doing your job if you know what the mission is. You can do your job without knowledge of the organization. This is accomplished by matching your skills with the requirements of the job. The question this raises is: are you doing the best possible job to serve the mission of the organization, and is the organization serving you the best? It is highly unlikely if your knowledge extends to your job only.

You will not be able to ascend as high in the organization as your skills may allow if you do not have an adept understanding of the organization's mission, vision, and goals. Organizations have a way of rewarding those who are connected to the current vision and have a vision for the future. Those who lead are there because they have communicated, demonstrated, or promulgated their belief in the direction the organization should be headed. Those who ascend to the highest ranks in the organization may not be the most skilled, but they have demonstrated their ability to take the organization to the next level. This can be you.

I think Andy Warhol was correct when he said, "In the future, everyone will be world-famous for fifteen minutes." While clearly applicable to social media, I tend to believe this applies to our opportunities in life. Each of us is given opportunities to excel, shine, be famous, make our mark, have an impact, or succeed. When opportunity knocks, it behooves us to be prepared, ready to answer. Those who have gone before and answered have taken advantage of their opportunities and reaped the benefits. If you desire to lead, you must be prepared to maximize your fifteen minutes. I even recommend you go one step further and not wait for the opportunity to knock. Where possible, create your own opportunity. Be proactive. The fifteen minutes of fame that Warhol prophetically proclaimed that would be available to us are not connected to opportunities given. They could just as easily be connected to opportunities created.

Are you going to build a better mouse trap in the woods and not use the internet to market it? Yes, there is truth in Ralph Waldo Emerson's original quote, "If a man has good corn or wood, or boards, or pigs, to sell, or can make better chairs or knives, crucibles or church organs, than anybody else, you will find a broad hard-beaten road to his house, though it be in the woods."

And there's the quote he was credited with having said after his death, "If a man can write a better book, preach a better sermon or make a better mouse trap than his neighbors, though he builds his house in the woods, the world will make a beaten path to his door."

Or as my mother would say, "Your gifts will make room for you." (I believe she was quoting Proverbs, "A man's gift maketh room for him, and bringeth him before great men" [Proverbs 18:16 KJV].)

If you are gifted and talented, someone or people will find you. However, they may only know the extent of your gift as it affects them. You may be a master craftsman, but they may only know that you make crafts. So they come, and they come in large numbers for your crafts. None, however, come for your training. So while it is true that your gift will make room and create a beaten path to your door, you may have to expand the size and the space. Maximize your fifteen minutes.

People may know that you are a good employee and worker, but do they have any knowledge of your ideas or thoughts on the future of the organization? Have you communicated this? Have you made it known? Have you been a part of the leadership team to determine its future? Have you been a part of groups, teams, or efforts to lead the organization to the next level? Or are you assuming that someone will know somehow? Are you assuming that your gifts alone are enough to get you in the conversation, class, corridor, or C-suite?

Knowledge of the organization is critical to your success and access. This statement cannot be overstated. Not only will your knowledge of the organization aid you in doing your job, but it would also aid you in allowing those who make promotion and assignment decisions to know that you are interested in leading the organization into its future. It is not likely that you can lead something if you do not know what that something does. Even if you plan to take the organization in a different direction, knowledge of its current state is important, as this will help you determine your next steps. You lose nothing by knowing something about the current direction of the organization. This foundational knowledge will prevent you from making mistakes, stepping into pitfalls, or repeating past errors. It will help you determine what you need to keep, what's working, and what the core business of the organization is. In later chapters, we will discuss how you can gather this knowledge, but right now I want to emphasize to you the importance of possessing it. Let's discuss the details of what you need to know about an organization to be successful.

MISSION, VISION, AND GOAL

You must know the organization's mission, vision, and goals. These three things determine the strategic and tactical direction of the organization. Whether you agree with what the organization is doing, how it is doing it, or where it is headed is not the issue. The issue is your knowledge of these things. You may decide that you want to change all of them, and I believe that is your prerogative; however, knowing what they are right now will aid you in identifying what should be changed and how to make the modifications. Besides, if you do not know the organization's mission, vision, and goals, how will you know if they are being followed? Maybe what you are experiencing is an organization that has gotten away from its core. Perhaps the organization you wish to change is the way it was or should be. Possibly the current organization is the reflection of a strong personality in leadership. Unless you know, you don't know.

Sometimes change is easy, as it really is no change in its truest sense. It is going back to the future. It is refocusing on what we should be doing, not on what people believe we should be doing. I have been amazed at how often people have sought to make changes with no history of what has been done or knowledge on what is being done. I have seen history repeated under the umbrella of change; I have witnessed people be excited about their new idea, one that happened long before they took the position. Your lack of organizational knowledge creates problems for the organization and you. You will be served well if you do some homework and get to know your organization.

You also need to know the rules and regulations of the position you hold. Your knowledge and understanding of these rules and regulations determines your ability to provide the best possible service and do the best possible job. Policies and procedures drive the day-to-day activities and decisions of the organization. They may not be conducive to the organization's success or make it agile and high performing, but they are its guiding principles.

If it is your intention to be successful, you must know what these rules and regulations are. Normally this information is accessible online or available in hard copy; it is not hidden from the organization's employees. You can generally access it if you want to. If you plan to move up in the organization, you must make this a priority.

When you have access to the organization's policies, procedures, and regulations, you have access to the road maps and guidelines to succeed. With a command of this information, you will know how to operate officially and unofficially. Equally so, if it is your plan to make changes, which is likely if you are a future leader, your command and mastery of the rules, regulations, policies, and procedures are a must. Think about it. If you are going to change or lead something, you must know how it operates.

It is not uncommon for rules of an organization to change. In fact, change is required and constant. Organizational leaders are generally the ones who understand this, leverage guiding principles and policies to affect change, and are rewarded for their success. Having an inside track on how things get done puts you in a position of strength. You are at your best when you know what determines how your organization operates.

What surprises me is the number of people who fail, make critical mistakes, or are derailed because they do not know or understand the organization when the information is right at their fingertips. They stumble over rules, regulations, policies, and procedures available to everyone, have been around for years, and are subject to change. Instead of breaking the rules, why not change them?

This is like getting a ticket for driving seventy miles an hour in a fifty-five-mile-an-hour speed zone because you did not read the signs. The signs are posted frequently. Your refusal to read or ignore them because you do not agree with them will not lessen your penalty—maybe the contrary. A better option would be to make a case the get the speed limit changed. To do so, you will first need to understand why the speed limit was set at fifty-five miles an hour.

If the promotion system of an organization is well documented and for the sake of argument your desire is to get promoted, the first place to look for whether you are eligible or not is the current written official documentation. If it is stated that your promotion is dependent on a timeline and you have not met the requisite requirement, it is not likely that you will be promoted. So if your aim is to be promoted in less than the documented time and you are not willing to wait, some other course of action must be taken.

For example, if the regulation states that the minimum time of requirement for promotion is two years, as this is the time required to build the requisite skills, if you have not met the two-year requirement, you will not get promoted. This is a painful point for a lot of people, as they fight with the written rules because it does not say what they want to say. If you are unhappy with the results of the rules, it is best that you at a minimum know what they say. At least then you have an option for action—comply, complain, or challenge. Without this information, you will be hoping or wishing for something that is not likely to happen. However, with this information, you can determine a course of action that will serve your goals or ambitions. If you are not willing to wait the requisite two years, maybe a change of organization is your best choice. If you are willing to wait, you know what you need to do to position yourself to be promoted when you meet the minimum requirement of two years.

Please note, the above assumes that promotions are dependent on written rules and regulations—black and white. We all know this is not the case. There are always exceptions to the rule. Just because the rule is in black and white, it does not mean that it is always applied across the board. If you understand the organization, or more accurately, the more you understand about the organization, the more likely you can identify ways to become the exception.

For example, even though the rules state a requirement of two years minimum time for promotion, there will be evidence of those who have been promoted because they were viewed as exceptional, that is, demonstrated promotion criteria by performing in an assignment at the next level or performed at a level above their current level, thereby proving their potential and demonstrating their abilities. When you know the rules, you know when they have been complied with. You also know when the rules have not been complied with and can identify what separated those who were the exception. With this information, you can position yourself to be the exception. The fact is, the more you understand the black and white of an organization, the more effective you can determine when it is performing in the gray and identify how you can "walk in the gray."

UNWRITTEN RULES—NORMS, CULTURES, AND POLITICS

When we agree that promotions are not based on written rules and regulations—black and white—we are agreeing that there are other things to consider. For the sake of simplicity and clarity, I will call these the unwritten rules: norms, cultures, and politics. If success—promotion, assignments with increased responsibilities, or influence—is important, understanding the unwritten rules is a must, a nonnegotiable.

In every organization there are unwritten rules, for instance, the time the workday actually ends, the real meaning of flex day or a flexible schedule, an open-door policy, dress codes, when to take vacations, when to talk in meetings, expected response time to emails, the meaning of customer service, and when and how to complain. For the ease of reference, I want to lump these into three categories: norms, cultures, and politics.

If you think about it, every organization has abnormal norms, creative and different cultures, and plentiful and unique politics. The better you understand the unwritten rules, the more likely you are to succeed. The sooner you grasp what these unwritten rules are and how they are utilized, the better positioned you will be to make informed decisions and take proper actions.

Although I worked at IBM for a very short time, it was clear to me that their norms were different from Xerox, their competition. It was the early 1980s. IBM had a very formal culture as it related to dress codes. Its employees wore dark suits and white shirts, while Xerox allowed shirts and suits of different colors.

I had a meeting with one of the senior executives of IBM to discuss my future with the company. While he informed me of my options, he zeroed in on my attire and in no uncertain terms told me I needed to make some changes. He said, "You need to prostitute yourself."

I was fresh out of college, and my best suit was a double-breasted beige one that I wore with a matching beige shirt, tie, socks, and shoes. While this look may have been reasonable, acceptable, and perhaps suave at church, it did not seem to receive the same traction at IBM.

The senior executive stressed to me the importance of fitting in and not standing out. He told me, "If you want to be taken seriously for any of the options I have discussed, you need to invest in dark suits and white shirts. If you are going to sell IBM's products, you must first sell yourself."

Given that he did not mince words, I knew exactly what he was saying and suggesting. I will have to say that upon hearing this, I was not the least bit happy as I was convinced that what I was wearing was beyond dressed up for business. It was my "Sunday go to meeting" clothes. I even wondered why a senior executive would waste his time talking to me about my clothes, especially when they were presentable and professional.

Having said that, I found it difficult to be upset or frustrated because upon consideration and reflection, the senior executive was wasting his time so I would not waste mine. He knew that even with the best supporting documentation, I would stumble or fail if I did not make the right presentation.

To some, it may seem petty and insignificant to discuss what one wears, but when it is a part of the norm of an organization, it is worth taking note. So like it or not, if my plan were to be a significant part of IBM and be successful, it behooved me to address the concern presented and get a dark suit and a white shirt.

For the record, my next significant purchase included dark suits and white shirts. While my new attire fit the corporate culture, it was also comfortable and professional. What I discovered when I made the change was that I felt better, more like I was a part of IBM. In honesty, it did not take the senior executive to tell me that I stood out to know that I did. I knew that every day I walked through the company doors.

However, it did take his comments to help me recognize that I was being seen but not the way I wanted to be. It did take his comments for me to understand why my attire was important and the impact it would have on my aspirations to succeed and be a leader in the company. Sure, clothes do not define a person and their ability, integrity, and know-how, but they can detract from a person's skills, knowledge, and abilities. Dressing for success was not new to IBM.

IBM had a unique norm associated with dress, dark suits and white shirts. While Xerox, their competition, did not have the same culture, they did value professional attire. I adopted the IBM way as it related to attire. I changed my clothes, and in some ways, my clothes changed me. I no longer saw myself standing out in a way that needed to be justified or explained. I was no longer concerned about others seeing me differently because of what I was wearing. I felt better about myself and was therefore better able to do my job and focus on the task at hand and my plans, not on my clothes.

When I joined the government, I continued wearing dark suits and white shirts. This was not a requirement, but I made a conscious decision to take my attire as a negative part of the conversation off the table. I did, however, make a modification in my approach to dressing. I began "dressing for success," "dressing for the position I aspired to, not the one I was in." Over the years, the focus on attire has diminished. In fact, comfort seems to be that norm in most organizations. However, if you aspire to lead in your chosen field of passion or expertise, I highly recommend you pay attention to what the leaders in your field are wearing and when. While your attire may not prevent you from succeeding, knowledge on what works may position you to make a good impression and could contribute to your success.

My thoughts on attire is that clothes do not change you, but they can modify how others view you. If changing your clothes makes your journey to success easier, then change your clothes. It is easy to change your clothes without altering who you are. Something as small as a change of clothes could contribute to a modification in your atmosphere, attitude, and altitude.

Norms are the standards, patterns, or social behaviors of an organization. They show up in many different forms and ways and are often distinct across organizations and organizational lines, businesses, centers, directorates, offices, units, groups, and teams. Recognizing, understanding, acknowledging, and leveraging them are important to your success.

With that said, accepting or agreeing with norms is not a requirement. Whether they should remain or be removed should not drive your decision to learn of them. Their existence alone is reason enough for you to be aware of them. Whether they should be changed or you should work to have them removed is up to you to decide once you know them.

While norms are difficult to change, they can be. If you believe the norms should be changed and you choose to do so, knowledge of the organization and their part or impact on the organization will only serve to aid you in your efforts. For example, if you are going to even attempt to change a norm, you must make a case to justify the change. Once you identify the reason for change, you will need to build your network and identify your support group and a champion who will help you facilitate the change. Then the real work begins.

Norms are in place for a reason. Knowing what they are will enable you to move seamlessly and with purpose and can keep you from being held back, taking actions that will derail you, or doing something that will cause you to incur a negative label. Knowing the norms will keep you from becoming frustrated and upset because you are doing everything you believe you should be doing to get ahead, but you are not making any progress. You will know if what you are doing is being recognized or overlooked because while it is outstanding, it stands outside of the things that are warranted for your progress.

Norms are, as the name suggests, that which is normal. They are what is normal for a given organization, team, group, staff, directorate, individual, and so on. If it is normal for your executives to wear suits and you desire to be an executive, you should consider dressing for success and wear a suit. If it is normal for your organization to promote employees at your level who are part of the technical side of the organization and you desire to be promoted, it behooves you to acquire some technical skills. In the latter example, you may be an exceptional officer and doing outstanding administrative work, but without some technical expertise, you will be hoping for promotion considerations. Additionally you may become frustrated when you see others who possess technical skills get promoted when they appear to be performing at a level below you. It is important that you know the organization's norms if you are going to succeed and thrive. With this information, you can better focus your efforts, energies, and expectations.

While important to your success, please note that what is normal in one organization may be abnormal in a different one. You should not assume that a set of norms in a previous organization, business, team, unit, or location will exist or be the same in a different area. While they may be, there are no guarantees, even if everything else is the same. It is important that you make it your business to learn and understand the norms in your current organization/location. With this information, you will be better positioned to have the impact or make the impression you desire to make.

Culture is an organization's shared set of attitudes, beliefs, customs, values, goals, philosophies, practices, written and unwritten rules, and expectations that make its environment (social, psychological, and philosophical) unique. The culture is shown in how the organization operates; makes decisions; treats its employees, clients, and customers; accepts or rejects change; aligns the authority; and recognizes and rewards employees. Organizational culture is developed over time and not easily or quickly changed.

Instead of changing, the organization inculcates its culture into the minds (thinking), hearts (beliefs), and actions of its employees. The culture is reinforced by stories and words of its benefits and by actions and deeds proving its existence and value. It is not uncommon for an organization's culture to take precedence over its vision, mission, and goals. The organization's vision, mission, and goals change and are recrafted to reflect the internal and external environment. The culture, however, is the environment and is engrained in the people, purpose, and production of the organization. If, for example, an organization's culture is to focus on the bottom line, even if the mission of the organization is to produce the best product, the quality will suffer in order to yield the requisite bottom line.

There is no denying that the organization has different cultures and they exist everywhere. Some cultures are more engrained; others are more rigid. A few are more defined. They exist and are perpetuated because people believe in them and speak of their value and importance to the organization and its mission, vision, and goals. While one could argue the veracity of these claims, one cannot deny the culture's existence. If you are going to succeed, you must know them, honor them, and, if you disagree with them, identify the appropriate approach to change them. Knowing the culture, much like knowing the norms, will help you maneuver and ensure that your thoughts and behavior yield your desired outcomes.

I recall being told about an organization where contributed time was expected. The rules on the books were clear on this subject. If you work, you get paid. No one forced you to contribute time, verbally said you had to contribute time, or documented your unwillingness to contribute time. However, everyone leading the organization, being recognized or rewarded or being promoted or positioned, were contributing time. It was no secret to anyone serving in the organization. While there were no records or recordings to support this, everyone knew about it and assumed it was the "price of doing business." If someone got promoted, generally they fit the mold of those who were contributing time, as they were recognized as time contributors also. As a result, it was difficult to argue against them deserving their promotion. After all, they put in the time, and their performance (and potential, as seen in their recognition of the culture) supported it.

You may not like the culture, you may not agree with it, and you may even want to change it. I am a firm believer in change and would not disagree with your position. However, at issue here is not your cultural dislike, disagreement, difference, or indifference; rather it's your cultural deference. If you plan to be successful, you must know the organizational cultures. People have stumbled in organizations because of their inability to understand the culture, lack of appreciation for it, willingness to ignore it, assumption that it did not apply to them, assumption that it was the same as in their previous assignment, or underestimation of its impact on them and their success.

Organizational life and the employees' life cycle are more difficult when things occur that the employees are not aware of, ignore, underestimate, or misapply. If you fail to recognize, choose to ignore, or do not understand the organizational culture, you will be unable to leverage it to affect the organization and your career and could be placing yourself at a disadvantage.

People struggle when they do not understand or acknowledge that an organization has a unique culture. They also struggle when they move and assume that the culture of their new organization is consistent with or the same as their previous organization. While this could happen, I would caution you on this assumption, as sometimes "nothing could be further from the truth." The best option when you join an organization is to make it a point to get to know, study, and understand its culture. This knowledge will prove critically important and helpful to you. Your understanding of the organizational culture as it relates to work hours, overtime, contributed time, assignments, promotion, training, and travel, to name a few, will aid you in being a high performing and productive employee, team member, supervisor, manager, or leader.

This is like understanding and applying what Gary Chapman calls the five love languages of marriage: words of affirmation, quality time, receiving gifts, acts of service, and physical touch. If you know your spouse's love language, you can be productive, timely, and accurate in your application of it. This would make your spouse and you very happy. However, if you don't know their love language, you can spend a great deal of time, energy, and effort investing in the other languages and still not make them happy. If you understand the culture of an organization, you can prepare, perform, produce, predict, and position yourself to succeed.

The organizational norms and the cultures are critically important when desiring to understand how you are to conduct, comport, conform, and carry yourself to affect your cause and career.

Politics is a bit of a different beast. The definition of politics in an organization vary in meaning and an application and has a negative and a positive connotation. For our purposes, I will define politics as the art or act of interacting with or influencing people, practices, or policies to accomplish something. Some of you believe politics is negative because to be effective, you must act (play a part) and be different from who you are or manipulate people.

If you want to be the best you that you can be and have your greatest impact, I believe the opposite is true. That is, you must be your best self and identify the best in others. To do this, however, your understanding of the politics of the organization is critical. You do not have to manipulate others, be a yes-man or woman, or be someone other than who you are to be politically effective. When you understand how the organization operates and how the people interact to accomplish the mission, you can leverage your skills and talent to get the best out of yourself, the people you interact with, and the organization.

An organization has two significant parts: organization and organisms. The organization consists of the rules, regulations, policies, and procedures; it is the administrative and official guidelines that govern the organization. The organism is the people, the individuals who make up the organization and determine its outputs and outcome by their individual actions and collective interactions. Politics is about accomplishing the mission of the organization in a professional, organized, and orderly manner (organization) through people (organism). In order to do this, you must identify what is valuable to the individuals you serve, work with, and serve you. Being politically savvy—knowing how, when, and where to interact with who and for what—will propel your progress. To that end, you may have to attend various functions, be a part of certain meetings, remain engaged in a sundry of activities outside of your day-to-day duties and responsibilities, know who's who in the chain of command, and be known by those in leadership for your impact and contributions. Each of these efforts and activities will provide you insights into the organization and organism and better position you to make a lasting impression or impact.

Some people disagree with the fact that they should get involved with politics because they think it is going above and beyond the call of duty. They do not see it as a requirement of the job. They may even point to the fact that it is not spelled out in their job or position description. For the record, nothing could be further from the truth. The unwritten rules of politics will make or break you. Your disagreement with the role that politics plays in the organization and how it affects you does not change the fact of its existence or impact. Organizational politics is real, and your participation with it is required, if you plan to succeed and lead.

Denying or complaining about the existence of politics will not change its impact. Your denial and complaints could, however, have a negative impact on your aspirations and you. If you understand the rules of a game, you are in a better position to play the game. It is like playing a game of Monopoly, chess, cards, checkers, Scrabble, or whatever. You may be successful playing without understanding or agreeing with the rules. You may experience beginner's luck; draw the right hand; make the right play, call, or move; choose the right word; or make the right decision by happenstance. However, you will be challenged to duplicate your success if you do not know the rules, especially if your competition is a skilled player who has mastered the rules of engagement. You may not win against a political master, but you would clearly be more successful, if you knew, understood, and leveraged the rules, even if you were lucky.

Think about the benefits of knowing the rules and being able to apply them to get the desired outcomes. Imagine if you walked into a room and a game was being played that you have never played before. If you watched the game played for a while, even without knowing or reading the rules, you may figure out how to play and identify the norms, cultures, and politics, that is, if you are studying the players and the game with the intent of being successful when you play.

On the other hand, if you picked up the rules of the game, read them, and started to watch after you understood how the game is supposed to be played, you could now identify what was consistent with the written rules and what was unwritten. You may notice that while the rules are generally applied, the players who have mastered them may seem to be playing by a different set, as they are very crafty in their application of them. That is, they never seem to break the rules, but they are stretching them to the max or interpreting them very loosely. They seem to have found some loopholes or gray areas.

With your knowledge of the rules, you want to call them out, but the ones around the table who have been playing for a while are silent. Perhaps their silence is consent to the interpretation of the rule, lack of knowledge on what the rules say, or apathy, or they know something that you do not know. Whatever their reason or motive, the game continues. You may also notice that the winner of the game may not be the most knowledgeable, practical, or prepared. They may even appear to you to be lucky. Upon closer examination, you may discover that while the winner was not the one expected, they seem to keep winning.

If you entered the game and decided to play by the written rules, you find yourself at a disadvantage because you do not know the unwritten rules that have a direct and meaningful impact on who wins. While the rules are the norms to you, the application of the rules may have created a new norm for the players. Maybe the rules stated that players were not allowed to share information, but to speed up the game, the players decided to share info during certain points in the game. It is a new normal.

If you are not aware of this, you are at a disadvantage. Maybe the players decided to gang up on the potential winner for political reasons, for instance, to increase their chances or to extend the game. If you are not aware of this, again, you are at a disadvantage. Essentially the written rules have not changed, but what has been allowed is the new normal. The culture or politics has directly affected the application of the rules. What was black and white is now gray.

Please note, norms, cultures, or politics, in and of themselves, are not negative unless they are applied negatively. Your knowledge and utilization of unwritten rules do not taint you, but they can inform and assist you.

The unwritten rules of organizations often place individuals at a disadvantage. The written rules, those in black and white, are hard enough to understand, master, and leverage. When you apply the requirement to know and understand unwritten rules, things become increasingly more complicated.

1. There is no place to get a list of the unwritten rules that are being applied.
2. There is no official documentation on the utilization or application of the unwritten rules and how they relate to yours or others' successes or failures.
3. Who would really say and can factually support that someone was awarded, recognized, or promoted because of unwritten rules?

The rules are not written; therefore, they do not exist, right? Wrong! You must know that unwritten rules exist and how to apply and leverage them. If you choose to refuse or acknowledge their existence or not to understand, apply, and leverage them, you will be doing yourself a disservice.

For example, in most organizations, there is an unwritten rule about something called corporate giveback, charity, contributed service, corporate contributions, or giving of your time. Whatever the name, it means giving of your time and talent above and beyond your daily duties and responsibilities to affect the organization's (organization and organism) mission. It is generally welcomed and valued from all employees. However, for supervisors, managers, and leaders, it is expected and often rewarded.

If those in the expected categories do not provide corporate giveback, they will pay an opportunity or alternative cost. Please note, I did not say that they would pay a cost, as this can only officially be done if they are not doing their job. But an opportunity or alternative cost is the price they will pay for not choosing to give back. Opportunity or alternative cost is the price they will pay for losing or missing out on what they could have gotten. It is the loss of potential gain they would have gotten from choosing to give back. This could come in the form of the loss of pay, promotion, position, reward, recognition, or opportunity. Those who give back create potential opportunities unavailable to those who do not.

You may argue the equity, fairness, legality, or simple humanity of this, but you cannot refute its existence. As to whether it is equitable, fair, legal, or humane is difficult to prove. Think about it. On paper, individuals are recognized, rewarded, promoted, positioned, or given opportunities because they earn it. That is, they distinguish themselves from the group, as the person who is entitled to something different. Corporate giveback does exactly this. It separates individuals from the group, as it represents them going above and beyond, doing the "and then some," to ensure the health and welfare of the organization.

If you are going to be successful, you cannot be like everyone else. You must distinguish yourself. You must stand out. This becomes even more important as you move up in the organization. You may fight this and argue that it is wrong and unfair and disadvantages a lot of people who do their jobs and do not have time to give back.

I submit to you that this argument makes the case for using something unwritten like corporate giveback as a separating factor. Generally, most people are doing their jobs, and as a result, most people collect a paycheck for what they are doing. A small percentage of these individuals go above and beyond to ensure that the mission of the organization is being met and people are being served. They do their job "and then some." They follow the rules; the rules follow them. That is, while they know and understand the written rules, they do not work for the rules. They make the rules work for them. This behavior puts them in the gray space where the rules are not written but are understood, utilized, and leveraged. They know corporate giveback is not a requirement to get their job done, but it is a requirement if they want to have an impact on the organization and stand out.

As an aside, before you fight the existence of the unwritten rules or seek to change them, I recommend you do two things: get to know what they are and identify the value of their existence. Knowing what they are—and we cannot overemphasize this—is an absolute must. If you identify their value, you are positioned to argue for change or understand why they exist or begin to make them work for you.

For example, if you examine the value of the case for the unwritten rule of corporate giveback, you will discover that while the organization benefits from your contributions, you benefit as well. When you give back, the organization benefits from your contributions, commitment, and corporateness. The organization gets your expertise, thoughts, and ideas for free. You, on the other hand, are required to work away from your position, purpose, and performance description. In return, you gain knowledge and build a larger network.

By working outside of your job description, you learn more about the inner workings of the organization. By working with people on projects that are not your day-to-day responsibilities, you learn more about the organism: how they perform, play together, and produce; what they view, value, and are vocal about; and what they say, do, and think. In return, they gather the same information about you.

If you perform well, this opportunity will create other opportunities, ones unavailable to those who do not participate (opportunity cost). Keep in mind, two keys to your success as a leader, manager, and supervisor are knowledge and networks. Through the giving of yourself, you gain in both areas.

The details on organizational norms, culture, and politics are seldom written for your reading, review, revision, or approval. They are generally unwritten. However, they are as important as, and sometimes more important than, the written rules, regulations, policies, and procedures. You may disagree with them, you may not like that they exist, and you may not support the impact they have on the organization and the organism, but you must acknowledge and agree that they exist. Yes, they could make your progress in the organization more complicated, but they could also help to facilitate your progress.

The choice is yours. If you choose to disagree with and fight their existence, they will impede your progress. However, if you acknowledge and understand them, you can leverage them to assist with your progress. Please note, unwritten rules are real in industry and in life. If you are going to be successful, do not fight their existence. Identify, understand, and leverage them to get your desired outcome.

Organism: Know Who's Who?

An organization is a group of persons organized for a purpose. This definition alone would lead one to believe that an organization is about people. Now while I believe the definition is completely correct and it should be about people, I think it is important to note that an organization is an organization and an organism. That is, it consists of two primary parts: its processes (organization) and its people (organism).

First, the processes or organization ensure smooth, consistent, and continued operation. In large part, these are the rules and regulations, policies, and procedures that govern and guide how the organization functions to accomplish its mission, vision, and goals. They provide its people the official steps they are allowed and required to follow. They define how the business of the organization is to run and what to do when there are deviations. Essentially the organization includes everything involved in and required to execute what the organization does. As we noted earlier (under the caption "Know Where You Are") your knowledge of the organization, how it operates, and what governs and guides its operation is key to your success.

There is no shortage of information on the operation of an organization. Much time is spent in universities, books, articles, manuscripts, and writings on organizations and how they function. They note that organization consists of everything required to make a business run: people, policies (rules, regulations, procedures, norms, cultures, and politics), places (properties and brick-and-mortar), things (resources and dollars), and so on.

When choosing a place to work, one can easily access valuable information about how an organization operates. This information is generally documented and fully accessible via the web, books, brochures, fliers, and word of mouth. It can be found in soft and hard copy, printed in black and white. If your goal is to succeed, you must fully grasp the details of the organizations.

You should not wait until you are an experienced employee with several years under your belt to gather this information. You should make it a point to gather as much information about the operation of the organization before or when you enter on duty. Generally the rules and regulations, policies, and procedures can be found in books, hard-copy files, or in soft copies online. These rules and regulations are the official guiding principles that provide the organization with information and details on what can and cannot be done and how far you can go to get things done.

If you are planning to be successful and operate at a level required to move up in the organization, your grasp of these rules is mandatory. You should locate the best source of this information and begin immediately to read, review, research, and remember as much as is possible, as this will guide you in the execution of your duties. The more you know about what you can and cannot do, the more effectively you can perform your duties and outperform your competition. Equally so, the more you know about what you can or cannot do, the more equipped you are to determine what needs to be changed and how to go about making the alteration.

As an aside, the constant in an organization is the same as the one in life, change. Change is not an option; it is a requirement, a must. That said, you should know that a key to your success will be your ability to accept, acknowledge, and advance change. However, you should also know that if you want to lead, your acceptance of change is expected. Leaders are not selected for their ability to accept change. Instead they are selected for their ability to acknowledge and advance change. The acceptance of change is done by 90 percent of those in the organization simply because it is required. Those who accept change may do so willingly, aggressively, passively, passively aggressive, or under duress. This response to change is expected. Leaders or potential leaders, however, are identified or positioned because they saw the need for change and took steps to make it happen. Being able to identify what needs to be changed suggests that you are paying attention and value what is best for the organization. Being able to advance change demonstrates your leadership ability. It shows those looking for future leaders that you are one to consider.

To strengthen your potential and position for consideration, you must know how the organization operates. You should make it your business to know the business of the organization, the ins and outs, the ups and downs, the rules and regulations, and the people and policies (written and unwritten).

While the requirement of knowing how the organization operates may sound daunting when considering the task and time required to master this information, I would encourage you to be a student. It is not required that you know everything at once, but it is necessary that you know some things. As a student, your learning is continuous, cumulative, and challenging. Learning how the organization operates is very similar, as it is also continuous, cumulative, and often challenging. The difference is the higher you go up in the organization, the more you are graded on the unwritten curve. That is, the higher you advance, the more your knowledge of the written is presumed, and your knowledge of the unwritten is assumed. The higher you go up in the organization, the more you are graded on your interactions with people and policies and less on your individual actions. This really is logical, as the higher you go up in the organization, your responsibilities are dependent on more people and affect more persons and larger projects, programs, policies, and procedures.

I cannot overstate the importance of you knowing and understanding the rules of the organization. However, I will caution you that understanding the rules means all the rules, written and unwritten. The first place to begin your learning is the books (offline or online). The organization has written rules, guidelines, policies, and procedures. They are there for everyone to see, study, know, and use. They provide the standards of behavior and the official documented support for the organization's operation. They are written down in black and white. I recommend, if possible, you secure a copy of these for yourself and get to know them thoroughly and intimately. They will provide you marching orders, operating guidelines, and fallback plans. Since they are written down, it is easy to point to them for support in time of crisis, change, or caution. When all else fails, you can begin and often end the conversation with what is written down. Generally, if you cannot find something in writing to support what you are doing, it is an indication that you are doing something new. If you are doing something new and you have no official documentation to support your actions, you should create your own documentation and secure the requisite approval.

The written rules are generally your official guide. They provide you supporting documentation and cover for actions. In them you will find details on the employees' life cycle, business operations, property, support, and so forth. Anything officially supported can be found in the organizations' written records. Your knowledge of this can help you identify, accomplish, and exceed the standards. With this information, you can determine what actions you need to take to assist the organizations and advance your career goals. Armed with this information, you can accelerate your competitiveness by strategically having a greater impact on the organization. You are less likely to make mistakes and embarrass yourself if you know what you can and cannot do and what should or should not be done.

For example, if your organization has a travel policy and a set of travel guidelines, it would benefit you to know these in order to know how to spend your organization's money while traveling. The worst thing you can do is be in violation of official guidelines when you should know what they are, especially when the error is not the result of erroneous interpretation. On the other hand, your knowledge of the travel rules could save you and the organization money.

Simply put, your knowledge of the rules can make you look good or bad in the organization's eyes. How you look will affect how people see and interact with you and where and how fast you advance.

Going one step further, an organization generally has its vision, mission, and goals identified. A key to your success is being able to assist your organization realize or exceed them. Not knowing them will place you at a disadvantage. How can you truly affect what you do not know or understand? Maybe you will get lucky. However, it is highly unlikely that you will be able to sustain positive (and impressive) impacts this way. It is also difficult to have a sustained impact on something when you are not familiar with how it works.

We have all experienced playing a game for the first time with competitors more experienced and winning. The feeling of accomplishment was difficult to put into words. We earned bragging rights. We beat the one expected to win. We probably should have let good enough alone and walked away with the feeling and the win, but instead we put our winning to the test. We took another shot from the same spot and missed. We played the same game on the same table against the same opponent and lost. We pulled the same handle on the same machine (several times) and lost (giving back everything we won plus).

We encounter a phenomenon frequently experienced by novices called "beginner's luck." It is a good feeling. Unfortunately, beginner's luck, as the name suggests, only happens when you begin. It does not continue or last. This is the same with your effort to leverage luck to repeat your impact on the organization or advance your career. It is not likely to continue. I would be naïve to suggest the luck does not play a part in your success. However,

I would have to modify its meaning. Luck, as we denote, is success occurring by chance, not your actions. I would caution hoping to get anything from this type of luck.

I remember a definition placed on the blackboard in my sixth- or seventh-grade classroom that I believe is more applicable to what I mean when I say "luck plays a part." The definition read, "Luck is when opportunity comes your way and you are prepared for it." This type of luck recognizes an appreciation for things you do not control (opportunity) and an acceptance of a thing you can control (your preparation). When you put in the time and the effort to know what the organization is seeking, expects, or values, you are positioned to take advantage of an opportunity when it comes. You are waiting for your chance to smile on you, and you are looking for the opportunity to smile on your chance. You are positioning yourself to affect the organization and secure the recognition necessary to excel.

A key reason why some employees will not excel in leadership is because they fail to understand the whole picture. They fail to see how the organization connects, the pieces fit together, and organizational success depends on the collective movement of the individual parts. When you understand how what you do connects with the rest of the organization, you understand your value and the value of those around you. Your knowledge of the organization's vision, mission, and goals contributes to your understanding of these connections. Working in a vacuum may allow you to get your job done and make you an exceptional employee, that is, assuming exceptional is measured by your individual output and production. In a production-oriented environment, where the increased size and amount of your individual contributions directly and positively affect or influence the total contribution to the overall unit's production, this may be the case. However, when production is sequential and action a is dependent on action b and b on c and so forth, one's action must be accomplished in a timely manner to ensure the welfare and safety of the whole.

If one produces too fast, excess inventory is created, and cost is incurred. If one produces too slowly, a backlog is created, and cost is incurred. Knowing how your organization operates is key to you knowing how to maximize your contributions. It is also key to you understanding how to apply the guiding principles (mission, vision, and goals; rules, regulations, policies, and procedures) of your organization to your actions.

Knowing how what you do connects with the organization positions you to maximize your organizational contributions and impact. For example, if you are a finance officer and have the fiduciary responsibility of auditing and certifying your organization's funds, generally you abide by a specific set of laws, rules, and regulations. To that end, what is written in black in white determines approval or disapproval of funds. If the request or action in questions satisfies the five Ws (who, what, where, when, and why, the basic questions to gather information or solve a problem) and are in compliance with the laws, rules, and regulations governing the organization, it is allowable and therefore approved. One could argue that this is the easiest decision to make, assuming you know the guidelines governing your decision. If the rules say yes, it is yes; if the rules say no, it is no. The rules are black and white. What they say go.

In this example, if you're looking to just do your job, knowing the rules makes deciding on the lawful execution of funds considerably easy: yes or no; can or cannot; or may or may not. After all, the rules are the rules. In a perfect world, this may be how decisions are made. However, a perfect world or a utopia rarely if ever exists in an organization, even for a brief time or in a small place. More often than not, things are at best gray. When things are gray, your ability to do your job depends on your understanding of the organization mission, vision, and goal as well as rules, regulations, policies, and procedures and how to apply them.

When things are gray, and they are, the black-and-white written rules do not always provide the answers that the organization needs to get the job done in the time allotted. As a result, the rules appear to get in the way, impede progress, or slow things down. This has prompted some to dispense with, break, ignore, or work around the rules. Some have gone even as far as to say that "rules are made to be broken." These reactions and explanations are expected from someone who is trying to do their job, but the rules seem to be or are preventing them.

In most cases, those complaining about the rules are not the ones making them. The complainers are those required to abide by the rules when performing their duties. The rule makers seldom complain about the rules, as they are rarely negatively affected by them in the execution of their duties. This separation of reactions as it relates to the rules is an example of what happens when members of the same team fail to see and appreciate their unique but collective functions. They see the value in what they are doing and pride themselves on maximizing their outcome with their efforts. Unfortunately they fail to take into equal consideration the value of others' contributions and requirements who share in their efforts to accomplish the overall mission. They see and value their part of and impact on the mission. They do not see how what they do could negatively affect the overall mission. After all, they are doing their job and doing it well. This is due in part to the fact that they are walking in the gray. They know only their part of the mission and can see only a part of the picture. They fail to understand and see how what they do connects to others in the organization. So while they may excel in their individual task, they fail as members of a team. While accomplished in their own area, they create backlogs or complications for others. It may be the finance officer's job to approve the expenditure of funds and the logistics officer's job to spend the funds, but it is both of their jobs to accomplish the mission of the organization. To that end, they must work together to clear the gray. The finance officer must leverage his fiduciary knowledge to assist the logistics officer to make the right and legal purchases. The logistics officer must leverage his knowledge to secure supplies consistent with the financial rules and regulations and in a manner where the five Ws can be answered.

The laws and rules of an organization have been established to ensure the legal execution of actions. They are not there to prevent actions, but to ensure that actions are legal, consistent, defensible, and in compliance with stated guidelines. The only time these guidelines are questioned is when they seem to or clash with actions required to get things done. Guidelines rarely get questioned if they support or allow actions that need to be done to accomplish something. Unfortunately, much of what is required to ensure organizations meet or exceed their vision, mission, or goals is not written in its entirety in black and white. Most times this can be found in the spirit of what is written, but not specifically stated in writing or defined by law. That is, there are times and cases when executing the mission of the organization that the written guidelines are simply that, guidelines. They provide us the approval to accomplish something without the specific details of how it will or should be done. The guidelines provide us the beginning and the end but leave the middle for interpretation. They leave a gray area for those walking in the gray. If you understand the mission of the organization and its corresponding laws and rules, you can leverage these to ensure that the mission is accomplished lawfully, timely, and in a manner consistent with the goals and objectives of the organization.

When you understand the mission of the organization and its corresponding rules and regulations, you can anticipate and interpret the rules to assist others with their requirements, especially those that seem out of bounds but critical to mission success. That is, when you receive a request for an action that the written, or black and white, rules do not support, you can review, interpret, and translate the rules to allow those needing support to accomplish the desired outcome without breaking the law. Your knowledge of the mission of the organization allows you to examine the request and review the rules to determine not only whether the action is right or wrong, but, more importantly, if there is a way to execute the action legally. It is not difficult to determine the legality or lawfulness of a requested action when it is clearly documented in the rules in black in white. The difficulty is encountered when dealing with actions that are not clearly supported by the rules, in black and white.

Most people can read the rules and determine the written legality of something. It takes a true professional, a leader, to answer the mail when the written rules do not support the action in question. This is not to say or suggest that you should break the rules, but it is to express the importance of your knowledge to your growth and development. The individual who answers the mail when the rules are not black and white must provide convincing documentation to support or deny the action in question. If you want to succeed, you must be prepared to move the mission when a simple "no" or "yes" is not an option or will not suffice. You must demonstrate your knowledge of the mission and its corresponding rules and regulations and your ability to orchestrate and coordinate the two. You must know how to apply the rules when the answer is not so obvious. You will not only gain the respect of those looking to you for the answer, you will gain their support, a critical piece to your success.

As mentioned earlier, an organization consists of two primary parts: its processes/structure (organization) and its people (organism). With so much written on and attention given to the organization, it is easy to lose sight of the value and importance of the organism, the people. This has been the failure of many organizations. They lose sight of what is most important to their existence, their people. Wisdom of old has told and taught us that people are the most important resources of an organization.

However, while this has been stated repeatedly, in execution, the organization places its people near the bottom rung of its importance ladder. Please note that this is a failure that you cannot afford. For you to succeed, you must understand and appreciate the importance of people (the organism) to your and the organization's success. In fact, you must go one step further beyond this and get to know who's who in your organization.

People are the driving force behind an organization's accomplishments. They apply the rules, honor the structure, and abide by the processes to accomplish the mission. They also revise rules, change the structure, and develop new processes when it is necessary to accomplish the mission. If an organization is going to exist, be effective, succeed, thrive, and grow, it will be the result of decisions made and actions taken by its people. The most effective organizations are not those following the rules, complying with the chain of command, or following a set of operating procedures. Quite the contrary, the most effective organizations are those in tune with and responsive to their environment and environmental changes. They are flexible. This flexibility comes from the organism, the moving parts of the organization, the people.

When you consider what happens in an organization during a crisis, you can see the true value of the organism. During a crisis, organizations have been known to ignore the rules, dispense with protocols, and do whatever has to be done to ensure the success of the mission. After the crisis, they review their actions and outcomes to determine if the organization (rules, structures, and policies) worked to support the organism in their efforts to accomplish the mission. If the organization impeded the organisms' efforts, changes are considered. The rules, structures, and policies are reviewed, revised, or rejected.

Crisis seems to bring out the best in the organization. In crisis, successful organizations thrive and are generally more effective during and after the crisis. In crisis, the organism takes control of the organization to ensure that it does not get in its own way. The organism focuses on the desired outcome and does not let what they have put in place, what they have established, and what actions they have agreed to follow prevent them from getting the job done. In crisis, the people become the central focus, not the organization and not its rules, structure, or policies. In crisis, the people work to accomplish the mission and try to do so within the confines of the organization. However, putting the mission in front of the mandates, the math/measurements, and the methods, the people identify what in the organization does and does not work and what expedites and what impedes progress. As a result, the crisis reveals what needs to be revamped, revised, and redone.

An organization does not exist without the organism. It is the organism, the people who make up the organization, that executes the vision, mission, and goals that ensure that the day-to-day operations, the short-term goals, and long-term objectives are accomplished and that monitor the organization's performance to keep things on track and going as planned. The people establish the objectives and metrics that measure the success of the actions taken to accomplish them. The people move the organization forward, maintain the steady course, pull the organization down, or put it in a holding pattern. The people manage and utilize the organization resources, including themselves.

If you have the right people leading and steering the ship, the ship will sail or move to its destination seamlessly. However, you may have the best ship, best equipment, best tools, and best rules, regulations, policies, and procedures and still fail because you do not have the right people steering, supporting, servicing, or sailing the ship. The people, the organism, make it all work and work together. The people are your most important resources. As has been alluded to when discussing what happens in crisis, you may have a bad structure, poor equipment, and unclear guidance and be in a horrible situation, but if you have the right people, they will manage and meet or exceed the mission. The right people "can sleep through a storm."

I remember a story a supervisor and friend shared with me years ago about the importance of being prepared. His story emphasized not just being ready when things are going well but being prepared for the worst. The story was about "sleeping through a storm"[4] and went as follows:

> A young man applied for a job as a farmhand. When the farmer asked for his qualifications, he said, "I can sleep through a storm."
>
> This puzzled the farmer ... but he liked the young man. So he hired him.
>
> A few weeks later, the farmer and his wife were awakened in the night by a violent storm ripping through the valley. He leapt out of bed and called for his new hired hand, but the young man was sleeping soundly.
>
> So they quickly began to check things to see if all were secure. They found that the shutters of the farmhouse had been securely fastened. A good supply of logs had been set next to the fireplace.
>
> The farmer and his wife then inspected their property. They found that the farm tools had been placed in the storage shed, safe from the elements. He sees that the bales of wheat had been bound and wrapped in tarpaulins.
>
> The tractor had been moved into its garage. The barn was properly locked tight. Even the animals were calm and had plenty of feed. All was well.
>
> The farmer then understood the meaning of the young man's words, "I can sleep through a storm."

When you have the right people on the job, you and they can sleep even when the storm is raging. They will use what they must

---

[4] Sleeping Through The Storm
A Parable-like Story -- Author Unknown
http://www.inspire21.com/stories/faithstories/sleepingthroughthestorm

to ensure that things get done, on time, and right. If necessary, they will make adjustments, corrections, and changes, and they will ensure that the changes are part of the actions going forward. They will not let external forces, a storm, determine the outcome.

In an organization, the people ensure that the organization is prepared, progressing, or pausing. If they find themselves in crisis, where their preparation proved insufficient, they adjust actions, realign resources, revise rules, skip structures, and commit to change. They do not allow what they created or control that is not working to control them. Instead they do what they must do.

The organization may be static, mired by its rules, structure, or policies, but the organism is not. The organism, the people, can change and make modifications, and they do so to ensure not only the mission gets accomplished, but the organization grows or is sustained. Given the importance people are to the organization and its mission, you can begin to understand why it is important that you know who's who. People get things done, and individuals do different things to make things happen. If you know who's who, you know who knows and does what, which will be critical to you being able to have a real organizational impact.

Knowing who's who in the organization is important for number of reasons, not the least of which is providing you the opportunity and ability to accomplish the mission and excel. People at all levels in the organization will afford you the opportunity to get things done. People are your most important resource. They accomplish the mission. They are the living stones, the flexible force multipliers, and the mission managers. They are the life of the organization and the reason it exists, remains, and thrives— not the rules, regulations, and policies or procedures. The fate and future of the organization is not determined by the brick-and-mortar, the staffing structure, the obtrusive order, nor any thing. The people, the organism, determine it.

People make the rules, interpret the regulations, and write the policies. People, the organisms, move the organization. You knowing who does what to make the organization move is as critical to your success as you knowing the organization. If you plan to be successful, move up, lead, or have an impact on the organization, you knowing who's who is not an option. It is nonnegotiable. It is mandatory.

It is worth noting that your knowledge of the organization and the organism will affect you differently at different times and levels during the life cycle of your career. For example, in the early stages of your career, you must understand the organization—the rules, regulations, policies and procedures, mission, vision, and goals. As you move up in the organization, when you pass the journeyman level, your midcareer level, it is more important that you are in tune with the people, understanding the organism.

With that said, while your interpersonal skills are more important at the journeyman level, you cannot wait until you arrive to utilize them. There must be evidence of these skills before you reach the level required to utilize them; otherwise you may never be given the opportunity. Additionally the proper display of knowledge of organization and organism at the appropriate level is equally important. If your interpersonal skill surpasses your organizational knowledge as a junior officer, you may be viewed as unproductive and too social. Knowing when to say what is as important as knowing what to say. Knowing when to do what is as important as knowing what to do. After all, timing is everything. This is equally true when it comes to the utilization of your knowledge of the organization and the organism.

NETWORK

A key to your knowledge of the organism is your network. The higher up you go in an organization, the more important your network becomes. However, you cannot afford to wait to develop your network when it becomes most important. You must do so as soon as possible. Your network should be well established and growing by midcareer. By definition, a network is a group or system of interconnected people established to exchange information and develop professional, social, and political skills. The most important word in this definition is *people*. The people are your keys to success. Therefore, your interaction, or how you interact with them, will determine whether you succeed or fail.

While people are the organization's most important resource, they are also your most important resource. So what do people provide you that makes them so important to your career? First, most organizations have noted the importance of networks to the success of their mission. The sooner you realize this, the quicker you can capitalize on it, tap into this most valuable resource, and accelerate your success. Your network will affect how far you go, how connected you are, and how much you can get done. Organizational impact is not about who you work with, who you work for, or who works for you. It is about your network. Your network provides you that extra something you need to succeed. It provides you height, depth, and girth. Your network should consist of people in your inner circle who provide you insightful information about you; people outside your job who provide advice, guidance, and direction; people in your profession who provide insight, knowledge, and understanding on how to execute your work; and your friends who provide you emotional equity.

Your network should be inclusive. It should consist of individuals throughout the organization: up and down, juniors and seniors, young and old, and different cultures and nationalities. Their collective input will provide the insights on how to get from where you are to where you aspire to be. They will provide you insights on how your colleagues and peers view you, honest feedback on your actions and their corresponding consequences, and information on the organization not readily available to you as well as serve as a base of power to support and assist your efforts to have significant impact.

An individual needs power to move something, to affect or change the organization. Power is simply the ability to get something done, determine an outcome, and produce an intended effect. While power is derived from many sources, your position and people are the two sources that will most definitely affect you. Your personal power, the true source of your strength, is determined by and derived from your position and the people. Given that the more power you possess, the greater impact you can have, you must make it your business to increase your power.

Position power is, as the name suggests, determined by a person's position. Position power is as old as the ages and is obvious in hierarchical organizations, those with an organizational chart. They are very common in American culture and society. This type of power comes with the position the individual holds. Generally the higher you ascend in an organization, the more position power you have and can wield. To that end, the president, CEO, CFO, managers, or supervisors have more position power than their employees do. Position power is not people sensitive or dependent; it is determined only by the position of the individual.

If you are in the position, regardless of age, nationality, training, education, association, affiliation, friendships, or enemies, you have the power of that position. Having said that it is worth noting that while the position comes with power, not everyone uses the power the same way. If they did, it would be so simple to determine who is in control, assuming the level of power determines who is in control, and if position power were the only power in question or to consider. It is not.

Since organizations are organisms, access to and influence of individuals comes with a second type of power, people power, which is derived from the number of followers you have and determined by the number of people you have access to or influence. People power is not position sensitive; it is not determined by your tenure, expertise, or know-how. While these may contribute to your ability to garner people power, they are not required.

You may have worked in an organization and noticed what appeared to be a displacement of power. That is, you may have served in an office where the person in the most senior position did not run the show. The show was being run by someone else in the office who did not have the position but did have the power and were in control.

This dynamic provides proof and evidence of people power and its importance. A person in this situation may not hold the position or may not officially run the office, but unofficially they are in control. Their reason for being in control but not in position vary, for instance, their strength of personality, tenure, expertise and knowledge, and network. Whatever the reason, when the people follow you for other than the position you hold, you have people power. Your strength comes from your circle of influence, people who trust you, believe in you and your skills, or believe you represent a better alternative to the person in the position of authority.

When you exercise the authority or power of a position, you are doing what is expected. This is not the same for people power. As a result, your ability to garner and leverage people power is one of the first indications to the organization of your potential. While a psychological test, a survey, or a questionnaire could be used to determine your potential, your people power is a testament to its existence. Potential is latent qualities or abilities that may be developed and lead to future success. When you display people skills with the ability to gain access to or influence people to do or accomplish something when you have no control over them, you are displaying potential, making potential practical. This being true, it is incumbent on you to expand your territory, to build and grow your network, your power base.

Your network is your base of individual power. It is your way to influence and affect the organization beyond your job. Yes, you may have a direct and positive impact on the organization because of your job or position. However, it will never be as impactful and meaningful as the one you will have with and through your network. Your network provides a way for you to introduce yourself to people throughout the organization without you having to be present and accounted for. Your network is the most effective way to expand your territory. Remember it is not just about who you know, but more importantly about who knows you. Organization leaders are less inclined to promote or position someone, especially into their ranks, without knowing who they are and how they can and will affect the team. Your network is your means to that end.

If you have an effective network, it will cut across organizational lines. As a result, you will have someone who knows you, of you, or your work ethic when it matters most. With this knowledge, they can speak up for you at the table where decisions are being made and you are not around. Leaders look for people who can get things done. Your network can serve as proof that you are the person for the job because you get things done. Your network is akin to a dictionary. You may not know all the words in the dictionary, but the fact that you have access to it gives you access to the information in the dictionary. All you must do to get the meaning of a word is open the dictionary and look it up.

If you have an inclusive and effective network, you have access to people who have access to information about you, the organization, and the organism. With this access, you can secure the requisite information you need to be a high performer and display potential. You may not know it all, but through your network, you have access to all they know. All you must do is contact them for the information. So it stands to reason, the more people you know and the more people who know you and what you bring to the table, the better, that is, assuming what people know about you will support what you are selling, your positive and impactful self. As an aside, if you are not positive and productive and do not have potential, the fewer people who know you, the better.

People are the key to your progress. Therefore, expanding your network is a must. You should get to know as many people as you can in as many different professions, disciplines, positions, or areas of expertise as possible. The more people you know, the broader your territory—the larger your vocabulary. The more people you know, the more access you have to information.

The best organizations are committed to giving back to the community and society. It is their way of showing their appreciation and saying thank-you to those who make it possible for them to exist. While their goal is giving, as by-products, the organization receives customer loyalty, commitment, and goodwill in return. The best employees, like the best organizations, should be committed to giving back as well.

The truth is that learning organizations do not wait for the employees to get the memo. They make corporate giveback a requirement. These organizations realize that if they are going to maintain their edge internally as well as externally, they must ensure that their employees, especially their leaders, are committed. When employees are doing what they are being paid to do, no matter how outstanding, it is their job, duties, and responsibilities. To that end, their job performance is only a small indication of their commitment to the overall health and well-being of the organization. However, when an employee goes above and beyond their call of duty and does something not in their job description that benefits the organization, they show evidence of corporate commitment.

While an employee's corporate giveback benefits the organization and shows the employee's commitment and appreciation, it also profits the employee. When employees get involved in the organization beyond their job description and desk responsibilities, they benefit in two ways: network and knowledge. Being involved beyond their desk allows the employees to first expand their network—increase the number of people they know and know them. As mentioned earlier, your network is key to your success, and the more people you have access to, the greater your influence and the impact you can have on the organization.

The second benefit of involvement beyond the walls of your desk is increased knowledge. Anytime you are given the opportunity to work or get involved in the organization outside your assigned responsibilities, you will learn something. You learn something new about the organization and the people. When placed in a new environment, through your contact with the task and the people, you gain new insights on what the organization does and who does it.

People you engage when giving back corporately provide you additional information and insight. They offer different perspectives, thoughts, ideas, solutions, concerns, approaches, and angles. If you only work within your area of responsibility, you limit what you know and can do. When you expand your network through corporate giveback, you reduce your limits. You introduce more diversity and options into your thinking. This increases your flexibility and positions you to handle more complex issues, concerns, challenges, and problems. The broader your network, the broader your influence; the broader your knowledge base, the broader your ability to understand and affect the organization. By connecting with others when giving back, you gain additional knowledge on what others do and how what you do connects with them and how they connect with others. By giving of yourself and connecting with others, you gain others' expertise, years of experience, and know-how. You expand your vocabulary and ability to access a larger dictionary of information. Now when you are faced with a challenge unique to your experience, you have someone to consult, contact for support or action, or call. Maybe the person you call does not have the answer but someone in their network does.

Your network and the network of those in your network grows as you give corporately. I cannot overstate the importance of having a network; nor can I overemphasize the importance of growing this network. Giving back is one way to do this. Take advantage of the opportunity. Your network is your lifeline to the organization. You should do everything in your power to extend and expand your lifeline. Giving back is a small price to pay.

Given the significance of having a network, the following are some steps to take to build your network, your organizational lifeline. The first step to building your network is understanding your current network. Ask yourself a sundry of questions relating to the existence, makeup, and health of your network:

- Do you have a network?
- Is your network effective?
- How effective is your network?
- Is your network broad enough to affect you and position you to influence the organization?
- Is your network inclusive?
- Does your network consist of individuals from around and across the organization?
- Does your network consist of only people within your profession?
- Does your network represent a broad contact list?

You must have an effective network to successfully climb the corporate ladder. There is no way you can be successful by yourself. "People need people." Yes, you may get some things done and done well, but without others' support, you will never maximize your potential, to be the best you that you can be.

After Moses received his job description, to teach the people the commandments of God, he proceeded to do everything on his own. He handled every issue, small and great, as best he could. I imagine he felt productive and accomplished as well as tired, as he was giving his all to what he was assigned to do. After observing him for a while, his father-in-law, Jethro, saw how ineffective he was trying to do it all by himself and advised him to get some help. Jethro told Moses that he needed to identify individuals to take care of the smaller, less complicated issues, as this would free him up to handle the bigger, more complex issues. The following text taken from Exodus details the incident and shows the value of having help from others and, more importantly, guidance from a mentor:

The next day Moses took his seat to serve as judge for the people, and they stood around him from morning till evening. When his father-in-law saw all that Moses was doing for the people, he said, "What is this you are doing for the people? Why do you alone sit as judge, while all these people stand around you from morning till evening?" Moses answered him, "Because the people come to me to seek God's will. Whenever they have a dispute, it is brought to me, and I decide between the parties and inform them of God's decrees and instructions." Moses' father-in-law replied, "What you are doing is not good. You and these people who come to you will only wear yourselves out. The work is too heavy for you; you cannot handle it alone. Listen now to me and I will give you some advice, and may God be with you. You must be the people's representative before God and bring their disputes to him. Teach them his decrees and instructions, and show them the way they are to live and how they are to behave. But select capable men from all the people—men who fear God, trustworthy men who hate dishonest gain—and appoint them as officials over thousands, hundreds, fifties and tens. Have them serve as judges for the people at all times, but have them bring every difficult case to you;, simple cases they can decide themselves. That will make your load lighter, because they will share it with you. If you do this and God so commands, you will be able to stand the strain, and all these people will go home satisfied." Moses listened to his father-in-law and did everything he said. He chose capable men from all Israel and made them leaders of the people, officials over thousands, hundreds, fifties and tens. They served as judges for the people at all times. The difficult cases they brought to Moses, but the simple ones they decided themselves. Then Moses sent his father-in-law on his way, and Jethro returned to his own country. (Exodus 18:13–27 NIV)

While I realize there is much to take away from this passage, I want to focus your attention on two areas: Jethro and his advice to Moses to get some help. First, I want you to see how important it is to have others around you, in your inner circle, to provide you guidance, advice, and support. You simply cannot succeed alone. Success does not happen in a vacuum. Individuals succeed because others noticed their potential, performance, skills, knowledge, or abilities and decided to work with them or for them to ensure their success. Whether you know it or not, someone is always there for you when you are successful.

Jethro, while now a relative of Moses, saw Moses's potential and production and offered him advice so he could be more effective. Moses was getting the job done, but he was doing so rather ineffectively. The queue to secure Moses's judgment was long. The issues were broad, and the importance of these issues and decisions varied. While he was working long hours and getting things done and done correctly, one must wonder if this was the best use of his time. Was he handling things in the order of their significance, or were important things falling through the cracks? Clearly, there was a better way, and he did not see it.

Jethro did. Jethro, while awed by Moses's work ethic, was concerned about his approach. He did not know the details involved in and intent behind what Moses was doing. He had to ask him, but he was certain that the approach Moses employed was not the "best in class." Moses's approach not only wearied him, it wearied the very people he sought to help. So Jethro asked him to listen as he advised him on a different approach. The benefits of having a network and someone a part of it that sees what you do not and is willing to advise you is invaluable. Even if you do not take the advice, you are at least aware of it.

Does your network include someone who is willing to be honest with you when honesty is not requested or desired? Does it include individuals who can provide you information, knowledge, insights, understanding, and simple support that you may not even know that you need? Your network is so important to your success that you cannot leave its composition to chance. You should include individuals who can provide you information on who's who in the organization. Who are the players, the leaders, the decision-makers, the power players, the power brokers, the influencers, and the individuals who can make your life or journey to success more manageable?

You should include individuals who know and understand your specific business and area of concern. However, you should also include individuals who know nothing about your area but something about everything else. Remember, the higher you go up in an organization, the more you are required to know. While you should increase and expand your knowledge, you should not rely on it solely. Instead you should expand your knowledge territory through the expansion of your network. The more your network knows, the more information you have access to and to knowing. So be creative when building your network. Make it diverse and inclusive.

As an aside, some people believe that the higher they go up in the organization, the more of their soul they must sell. That is, they believe they must sell out in order to be successful. This stems from a misunderstanding of the requirement of an organizational leader. The title of Marshall Goldsmith's book, *What Got You Here Won't Get You There*, speaks to the origin of this problem. People believe that if they work hard and harder, they will and should be rewarded, recognized, and remunerated regardless. This may have been the case when they started out in the organization, as their responsibilities were limited and their competition was known and limited. As they moved up, their responsibilities and competition expanded. This expansion came with an inability to do it all by themselves.

The higher you move up, the more dependent you become on others to assist you with accomplishing your duties and responsibilities. With this change, a new way to grade and rate your impact and success is warranted. Instead of being rated on your performance alone, you are rated on your ability to get things done through people, interpersonal skills, leadership, and organizational engagement. For each of these categories, rate your interaction with or influence of others. After all, you need others to get things done. So you go from being rated on your individual performance to being rated on your ability to leverage, influence, and get things done through others.

GET YOUR LEADERS TO KNOW YOU

Some people refuse to take steps to be successful because they think you must be a suck-up, brown-noser, boss-pleaser, yes-person, or someone other than who you are. This is absolutely not true. Having the leadership know who you are is the next critical step in your leadership development. This must not be discounted. Some people feel that they can and should make this journey and will be fine if they do not do anything special to come into the focus of the leadership. And there are those who make it without taking any special steps because what they do commands the attention and focus of the leadership. This is not always the case. What is consistent is the fact that the leadership must know who you are. Please note, very few people will or frankly should be promoted into a leadership position without being known by the leadership.

This is a very simple concept. If the leadership does not know you, how can they trust you? How will they know what skills you have and what you bring to the table? How will they know what impact you may have on the organization or the organism? Your promotion to the leadership ranks is based on what you have done and what you can do, your performance and potential, and your conversation and conviction, as evidenced by your consistency. If the leadership does not know you, how will they know this?

If you are doing an incredible job in your current assignment and believe that you will be the next promoted, you are likely mistaken if the leadership does not know you. A key basis for promotion is trust that the individual will deliver. If they do not know you, how can they trust you or know that they can trust you?

Think about it. When the current organizational leaders are looking for employees to induct into the leadership core, they are looking for individuals with people skills, as they are required to influence, lead, manage, supervise, get along with, or leverage others to get things done. They are looking for someone they can team up and partner with to continue to move the organization forward. For this reason, the current leaders need to know you. Very rarely will anyone become a leader in an organization that the current organization leaders do not know. It is not important how they become aware of you. This will vary by individual and the leader. Future leaders may come into focus of the current leadership because of their expertise, briefing skills, leadership management or supervisory skills, exceptional people skills, business savvy, or any other sets of skills, knowledge, and abilities.

How they get to know you is not as important as them knowing you. To that end, it behooves you to take measures to ensure that they know you. This may mean stepping outside your comfort zone and doing things that you typically would not do, that is, getting involved in activities outside your specific position duties. This may include being a significant member on working groups or temporary evaluation management teams, taking training classes or attending conferences, volunteering for new initiatives, or simply identifying or leading efforts that are important to your organization. You may also consider something as unique as contacting the leaders to have a fifteen-minute conversation about their plans for your future or your qualifications as they relate to the specific mandates, directives, or initiatives of the leadership. During this meeting, you can discuss your performance and what you bring to the table to assist the leadership.

Instead of leaving your consideration to chance, you can provide the details that they need to consider. That is, you should not leave it to others to determine your fate or success. You must take matters into your own hands and take the necessary steps to ensure that at a minimum the leadership know you and what you have to offer. That said, please note, when you approach a leader for your fifteen minutes to discuss their plans and your future, you know their plans for the organization. It would not look good on your résumé to have a meeting with a leader to discuss your leadership consideration and options and you only talk about what you want and what you want to do. You should know what you want, but even more important, you must know what the leaders are doing and how your desires fit with the direction the leadership is going and how your skills can advance the leader's initiatives and programs. This lets the leader know you understand and know what is important to them and the organization and believe you can be of assistance.

Additionally you should always have your fifteen-second elevator speech ready just in case. Each of these steps in addition to expanding your network brings your skill sets, abilities, and potential performance into the focus of those who are looking for future leaders. To some degree, this is where the concept of sucking up originates, having to go above and beyond your norm, if your reach is not far enough to get you recognized. I question: is this sucking up or reaching up?

Having your leaders know you is critical. However, equally critical is you knowing who's who. That is, you must know who the leaders are in your organization. This is important for several reasons. When you know the leaders, you know what makes them tick, what is important to them, and which direction they plan to take the organization.

With this information, you can better position yourself to leverage your skill sets against their requirement so you can have a significant and noticeable impact. It can also inform you that your skill set does not fit and prevent you from wasting valuable time as a square peg in a round hole. With your knowledge of your leaders, if you have an new initiative that you want to advance, an effort that you need supported, or a direction you want to take the organization or believe that it should be headed, you can better determine how to approach them with this new idea, concept, initiative, or direction. Without this information, you are hoping that what you plan to do or are doing works.

Knowing who's who in your leadership will help you determine how they make decisions about promotions and advancement opportunities. This will help you ensure that you are focused on the right things to advance your career. Too often, individuals spend a great deal of valuable time working hard doing a specific job, only to discover later that what they were doing had little impact on the direction the leadership was trying to take the organization. As a result, their hard work had little impact on their next-level consideration. This becomes unfortunate because everyone is being paid to do a specific job that clearly needs to be done, one that will help maintain the status quo. However, not everyone is doing the specific task that's going to move the organization forward, have a next-level impact, or bring them into the focus of the leadership. So one must ask: is there something I can do to better position myself against my competition? The answer is yes.

Yes, you can develop an approach or take steps to ensure that you are doing something that does not go unnoticed by the leadership, you are doing something the leadership values, or the leadership knows you want to be a part of the leadership team.

An organization is an organism; it is people. People make the decisions and the plans; set the rules, regulations, policies, and procedures; and determine what is right or wrong, who gets promoted, and the organization's direction, mission, vision, and goal. People are the living organization, the organism. You are an individual in an organization and therefore part of the organism. You succeed or fail based on your interaction with the other individuals who make up the organism.

It may be true that as a junior officer you may be able to manage being successful based on your performance. However, as you move up in the organization and begin to lead larger projects and are expected to deliver on major initiatives, you cannot succeed alone. You will have to rely on others, other people, other organisms. How you interact with others becomes key to your success. Your ability to influence other organisms, utilize your interpersonal skills to get along with and work productively with others, communicate to get your message across to others, and leverage your people skills to influence others to tactically and strategically affect the organization are keys to your success.

The higher you aspire and ascend in the organization, the more you and your success is dependent on other organisms. Therefore, if you desire to be a leader, you must make other organisms at all levels in the organization your business. The more effective you are at depending on and directing others, the more extensive your impact and the more likely you are to make the current leadership's short list of candidates for promotion.

In conclusion, a key to determining where you go from here is knowing where you are as it relates to who's who in the organization. An organization is an organized body of people, guided by regulations, policies, and procedures to accomplish a mission. People are the organism of the organization. It takes people to run the organization. If you are properly aligned with the right people so you get the right advice and guidance at the right time, if you have an effective network to assist and inform you, you are positioned to succeed.

Having an effective network cannot be overstated. An effective network informs you of decisions that are being made, how they are made, and the impact they may have on you. This is critical if you are going to be a leader. If your network is effective, you will be informed of things that are typically not in black and white, things in the gray, and things you need to know to keep you on the path to success.

People aspiring to succeed do not generally fail because of what they know. They fail because of what they do not know or are unaware of. Even if their failure is due to them knowing and ignoring, that is normally because they fail to understand the impact of the "ignore-ance." That is, they failed because they did not know that ignoring what they knew would have such an impact on them. Having an effective network can help you with this as they will inform you of how your decisions and actions will affect your career.

Your network will ensure that you do not stumble or fail because of something they are aware of being said about you or done to you that you may not know about. As much as we like to think that we are in the know, there is just too much to know to know it all. Having an extensive and diversified network can assist with this. You cannot be in two places at once, and you will never be in all places important to your success. In fact, when the most important decisions are made about you, it is more than likely that you will not even be in the room. When these decisions are being made, you may be intentionally, lawfully, legally, rightfully, or wrongfully excluded. Additionally, there are realities in the organization that do not permit you to be in the know, that is, secret meetings behind closed doors, hall files, and perceptions.

As much as we would like to deny it or wish that it did not happen, secret meetings are still being held behind closed doors that have direct impact on people's careers. Career management and assignment boards often discuss and decide the fate of individuals' careers without the persons' best interest in mind. These decisions, while career influencing, are being made without accurate information, based on feelings, with limited details, subjectively, for the good of the career service to develop and grow some officers (not all) and often just to fill a vacancy or a requirement.

Unfortunately, sometimes it is something as simple as, if they like you, you succeed. If they do not, you fail. Other times, the information about you is incomplete, slanted, unclear, one-sided, misinterpreted, misunderstood, based on limited interaction with you, or inaccurate. Think about your understanding and meaning of the hall file. This is a combination of words you cannot find meaning(s) in the dictionary or on the internet. Yet, if you have been in or around an organization for any small amount of time, you have heard about it.

And more significantly, it has affected more officers negatively than any other activity or decision in the organization. Think about the number of times you have heard of someone's negative hall file, the impact a person's hall file has had on them, the discussions you have had about the impact of a hall file, and how important it is that you not have one or at least know what it is so you can, if not control the narrative, manage the impact. Careers have been altered, and assignments have been denied, curtailed, or reassigned because of the dreaded hall file. It does not exist in the official record. There is no documentation on hand advising how individuals should handle the hall file to ensure consistency and equity. In fact, to make matters worse, the hall file on an individual may vary. It depends.

That is, even if the information in the hall file is the same (and it is not), how the information is used by the recipient, given there are no guidelines, varies depending on the desired outcome. For example, if the recipient of the hall file wants to help, they may tell you what is in it and develop a plan to help you overcome it. If the recipient wants to hold you back, they may come up with official verbiage to support their decision not to select or advance you.

You may say that this is unfair and unreasonable. You may be right, but unfair or unreasonable, it is real. It happens, and it occurs a lot. Your emotional response, sense of right and wrong, belief system, or feelings on the subject do not change the fact that it happens. Given this reality, the question that needs to be asked and answered is, "How do I handle this?" Because of the diversity of the individual possibilities of the hall file and its use, the answers to this question varies and depends. However, having an effective network and being aware of your hall file and the potential impact it could have on you are good starts.

As mentioned earlier, having an effective network is one way to stay informed on things said about you when you are not around. With this information, you can make informed decisions and take decisive actions. You may contend that the information in your hall file is not correct, dated/outdated, inaccurate, never happened, or fake. Again, I must caution you that as it has been repeatedly quoted, "perception is reality" in the absence or denial of reality. Your hall file is real when it is the only available, acceptable, or allowable information.

Yes, there may be some other truths/the real truths. However, if what they have in your hall file is all that there is, whether it is through choice or command, it is all there is. Your reality, what you know to be true about yourself, may be known to you and a select group of people. If you and those who know you are not in the room or conversation when decisions are being made about you with information from a hall file, for the time being, your hall file is your reality, at least to those in the room or conversation. Their perception of you becomes your reality. It does not have to be this way.

You can take steps to ensure that your hall file reflects your reality. It starts with you knowing who's who. Yes, you should know the names of the individuals on the organizational charts, as they are the official organizational leaders. However, if you are going to affect your own career development, you must go deeper. You must know something about the decision-makers, and you must ensure that they know something about you. If you are going to be a part of the organizational leadership, the current leadership must know something about you.

To that end, it is incumbent upon you to ensure that what they know about you is as accurate a depiction as possible and the information you want them to have. Also it is not just your hall file or perception, but is your reality.

In fairness to the decision-makers/leaders, they only have pieces of information about you or anyone in the organization. Generally, those pieces are relevant to them, their business line, or their area of concern. Other pieces of information about you is given to them by other affected or interested parties, and it too is limited by their interest or involvement. This is not being arrogant, vicious, uninterested, or detached. It is just being human.

You likely remember the story of the blind men and the elephant. The story is about a group of blind men (three was the number I remember being told), who had never seen or come across an elephant before. They were tasked with describing the elephant from what they could learn and conceptualize by touching it.

Each blind man approached the elephant and felt a different part of the elephant's body, but only one part. They then described the elephant based on their partial experience. As you could easily conclude, their descriptions of the elephant were in complete disagreement. Their descriptions were not wrong but limited by the part of the elephant they felt.

In some versions of the story, the blind men suspected that the others were dishonest, and they came to blows. The moral of the story is that humans tend to project their partial experiences as the whole truth and ignore others' partial experiences. Given that each of the blind men were right about their individual experience, they would have been best served to consider each other's partial information.

Even with accurate facts and details about individuals, decision-makers only have partial truths. Without the facts or proper information, with partial truths, we expect and rely on individuals to make good decisions and determine our fate. And through no fault of their own, they are doing so with limited details of the relevant facts. With limited information, details, or facts, decision-makers' truths or perceptions become the reality (theirs and ours). Perception is a powerful thing. Therefore, it is important that you take it upon yourself to ensure that the perceptions of you are laced with truths that align with your true reality. You cannot leave this to chance.

Much like the story of the elephant and the blind men, people make decisions about you based on incomplete details. They may know only what they have heard, seen, experienced in one area or on one day, or simply believed. This becomes problematic when these partial details become the facts that people use to draw conclusions and consider you for promotion or leadership. Unfortunately, this is a reality that you must deal with, but you do not have to leave it to chance.

Given this fact, it is incumbent upon you to ensure that the partial information those making decisions about you have is consistent with your reality. Data you want them to have should be more truth than perception. You are your own and best career manager. Own it.

CHAPTER **3**

COMMIT TO A COURSE OF ACTION

MAKE IT BIGGER THAN NOW

ONCE YOU HAVE AN IDEA OF WHERE YOU ARE GOING, have committed to a destination, know where you are in the organization, and who's who (the organism), you must commit to a course of action. It is not enough to gather information, to get the facts. You must do something with the information. Information alone can tell a story, but it cannot create an outcome. Quite the opposite, information has been known to create paralysis. Even with the right information in the right amount, you can become paralyzed trying to predict the outcome, paralysis by analysis. We live in the Information Age (Computer Age, Digital Age, New Media Age), and the one thing we cannot seem to get enough of and yet seem to get too much of is information.

In this Information Age, we have access to all the information we could possibly need to make decisions. Instead of this equipping us to make more informed, accurate, and timely decisions, it has caused us to want more information. We want to know everything before we do anything. Unfortunately there is no way to know everything, as everything changes. A better course of action would be to decide and take an action that represents respect for the best information available to you at the time. Be advised. Information's job is not to make the decision. Its job is to inform the decision. Once you have gathered enough data and details to call it information and it is enough to inform your decision, it is your job to decide. When you have done your homework on the organization, committed to a dynamic destination, and figured out where you are and who you are with, you are more than equipped to act.

Action has been defined as doing something, and yet a choice of action is to do nothing. My point here is whether you choose to act (do something) or not (do nothing), you are taking an action. The question you must answer is, "Will my choice of action—do nothing or do something—get me to my destination or achieve my desired outcome?"

The reality is life happens whether we are engaged or disengaged. Time passes whether we are having fun or not. The show goes on whether we are participants or spectators, and the game will be played with us or play with us. That is, you either play the game or get played. Your refusal to decide to take an action does not excuse you from what happens next. It only excuses your choice in how you participate. You can be an active participant or a passive participant, but you will be a participant. You must note, however, that the outcomes from your choice to participate or not are quite different. Elizabeth Gilbert correctly describes the lack of benefits passive participation provides when she said, "No experience in this world has ever been cathartic without the willing participation of the individual. Life does not automatically bestow wisdom or growth on anyone just for showing up."

You miss so much when you simply occupy a space. You miss out on opportunities and the benefits gained from being actively involved—the lessons learned, the contributions made, and connections developed. Active participation has personal and professional benefits, for example, confidence building, dream realization, growth from challenges, skill and talent displays, and self-fulfillment. Given the reality that active involvement yields increase, for instance, experience, expertise, or exposure, those desiring to lead or succeed cannot leave next steps, decisions, or actions to chance when it is within their control.

When you have the information that you need to make an informed decision, do not sit by the wayside waiting for someone else to decide for you, lead you, or tell you what to do. Step up. Take a chance. Commit to something and see it through. Decide and act. A key challenge you will face when you decide to commit is how to handle the information overload. With the access and availability of information combined with your desire to know as much as you can, if you are not careful, you will put yourselves in a no-win situation. While you want the information to decide, with each new piece, you see the benefit of another piece of information. Eventually you find yourself really informed but more about stuff that has no relevance to the decision you must make.

Alternatively, your discomfort with the risk of making the wrong decisions forces you to continue to ask for more information. It is worth noting that too much information is as dangerous as too little. One key ingredient of a good leader is the ability to decide and commit to the decision's outcome. This does not mean or suggest that every decision a good leader commits to is correct. Far from it.

Good leaders know that commitment comes with consequences. The consequence depends on the audience, accuracy, popularity, purpose, success, failure, intent, impact, goal, or outcome of the commitment. Good leaders know this, and after they gather the requisite details, they move forward knowing that no one decision will satisfy 100 percent of the people involved, impacted, or interested.

While a commitment will drive good leaders to make 100 percent approval a desire, after given it their best possible effort, they will make decisions without this level of approval and live with the consequences. Please note, it is important to get to a point in your research where your commitment outweighs your need for information. Once you are committed to something, the value of information may increase, but it will not determine your decision. The information will serve to inform you of the value and outcome of your commitment. It will let you know that you are right, wrong, on or off track, doing the right thing, or not be further from the truth.

Information gathering is like collecting pieces of a puzzle, and your commitment to a desired outcome is the puzzle. If the goal is to just gather information, it is like collecting puzzle pieces from different boxes. This would include puzzle pieces that go together with other pieces in their box but have no relevance when put with other puzzle pieces. While the unmatched puzzle pieces could serve the purpose of letting you know what does not belong, they have little service beyond this.

The same could be said of puzzle pieces that go together if they are thrown together with no intention or vision on how they connect. However, if these pieces were gathered, with some knowledge that they go together and you are committed to put them together, even without the final picture available, the uniting of the puzzle pieces becomes possible. At first glance this would appear to be a daunting task, but as each piece of the puzzle is put together, one piece at a time, the picture becomes clearer. As the picture becomes clearer, the missing pieces and how they fit become more obvious. This is true of you getting to your destination.

While you may not have a clear picture of the outcome, once you commit, you accept the challenge of putting the pieces of information together that, while in abundance, seem to have no connection. Once you commit, you accept the challenge of having to figure out how the pieces fit together; taking the next step even when you do not know exactly where it will lead; and walking in the gray and putting the puzzle together one piece at a time, moving to your destination one step at a time. Your commitment will give you what you need to see it through.

You have done your homework. You know the organization; its mission, vision, and goals; the rules, regulations, policies, and procedures; the organism; and who's who and what they do. You know you want to succeed and lead. I submit that you know all you need to know to know that you must do something. You must commit to something. This is the next step required for you to move in the direction of your destination, a commitment to a course of action. If you want to be successful, you must commit to success. You must live it, walk it, talk it, study it, focus on it, test it, try it, prove it, chance it, breathe it, believe it, and be it.

While your definition of and destination to success may differ from others, your commitment must not. Your commitment will drive your thoughts, behaviors, communications, presentations, preparation, expressions, engagements, endurance, patience, and persistence. Without a commitment, you will fail the first challenge, and you will be unable to take the next step. With a commitment, you will be able to see through, past, over, under, around, or despite the challenge.

Your commitment to a course of action shows you are dedicated or obligated to seeing it through. It does not come with a timeline, only a finish line. It shows that you understand the value of sticking to something, however long it takes. It should be noted that lasting results require a lasting commitment; long-term results require a long-term commitment. Success gotten quickly may be lost quickly. Take the information you have. Do an analysis on where you want to go against where you are. Do not wait until your desire, destination, or dream becomes a reality. Act now. Take one step at a time and learn with each movement. Do not expect every step to be a success, but do anticipate every step to be a teacher. Take each step with a committed confidence that right or wrong, good or bad, or ugly or pretty, you are going to keep moving and learning.

Given there is so much that you will not know or understand while moving, your best option is to believe and keep moving. The step you take may feel awkward, mistimed, out of sync, and painful. Take the step. Do not give in to the action of doing nothing unless that is your choice option.

Remember as you take each step that not every day is sunny, warm, or perfect. Four seasons mark the passing of each year, and each has its purpose and place in the grand scheme of things. In the spring, the seeds root, and plants begin to grow. In the summer, it's hot, and plants come to full bloom. In the fall, the temperatures cool, and plants begin to grow dormant. And in the winter, it's cold. Plants grow deeper roots, and animals find ways to warm themselves. Your steps along the path to your destination, like the seasons, will be different and serve very distinct but valuable purposes. Expect it and value each step.

When you value your steps, whether they appear to be good or bad, you position yourself to learn the lesson each step brings you. Additionally you reduce your frustration caused oftentimes by your desire to be in control. When you can commit to a course of action and keep moving despite what you see, how you feel, or what your current situation is, you are truly walking in the gray. When you take steps because you are committed but tired or cannot see the black and white of it, you are walking in the gray. Your commitment from the start will be a key to your success. Your commitment will drive you when you cannot see where you are, nor where you are going. There will be days, weeks, months, and sometime years on your journey that you will be unable to see where your steps are taking you, what all your hard work is getting you, and why you are doing what you are doing.

Even when you saw the end at the beginning and it was so clear that you knew you had what it would take, could do it, and was ready for whatever, there will be times after your own and others' doing and undoing that you will lose sight of your destination. The clarity will return, much like the picture of the puzzle becomes clearer with the putting together of each piece as you take another step. You must stay committed and keep stepping.

I recommend one more critical step that will aid you in your commitment. That is, when you make your commitment, make it bigger than now. When you are focused on here and now, the present moment, and allow it to become, or see it as, the only thing that matters, it is easy to get off track. It is easy to become completely frustrated, upset, confused, and disoriented and want to throw in the towel.

When now becomes your focus, you lose sight of tomorrow and the possibilities that come with it, for instance, a new chance, a turn of events, or other possibilities. As a result of this narrow focus, when you experience a setback, it is viewed as failure and final. When you are focused on now, you have a very short time frame to realize success, now. This can result in you losing faith in the system, the organization, and yourself far too soon, too often, and too easily. When something goes wrong when you are focused on now, you wonder, *Why me? How could this happen to me? What was I thinking about?* You see each setback as terminal and make statements that suggest you believe you have no more opportunities or chances, that this was it.

When you focus on now or an event as the only thing that matters, you set yourself up to fail and to do so quickly. You should instead focus on your destination and allow life to happen as you continue to move. When life happens, there is a possibility that you will have now moments that are inconsistent with your plans, those that will set you back to set you up, or those that by themselves look like failure but in the grand scheme of things will prove critical to your development and success.

Please know that while a failure, fault, error, setback, or mistake is negative, their outcomes may not be. There is an often-quoted passage of scripture that speaks to this in Genesis 50:20. "As for you, you meant evil against me, but God meant it for good, to bring it about that many people should be kept alive, as they are today."

Having experienced evil at the hands of his brother for his dreams, Joseph, seasoned in age and life, now sees and shares with his brother that for his dream to be fulfilled he had to experience the evil that had happened to him. God used Joseph's evil experiences to position and reposition him, to get him to the place where his dream could and would be realized.

Not every failed attempt, negative experience, or everything that happens that is inconsistent with your good plans will have a negative outcome. Sometimes things happen to you to divert you from where you are headed to put you on the track you need to be on in order to get to where you are going. You do not have a crystal ball that tells you what the future holds. Therefore, you should not get caught up thinking you know what actions need to be taken to get you to where you are going.

As you are walking in the gray, your best course of action is to accept the fact that things are going to happen that you did not, could not, or should not plan for. This does not mean that you are lost or off track or will not be successful. It may only mean that you are experiencing a setback. Maybe this impediment is designed the way Willie Jolley saw it and titled his book, *A Setback Is a Setup for You to Come Back*.

Many things that happen today will have their value revealed tomorrow. That is, when you look back on your experiences, you will see that they were parts of all that contributed to making you great, producing you who you are. You will see that each of your experiences contributed to your growth, potential, and purpose. You do not have this same feeling when you are going through your challenges. It is difficult to see or feel good when so much bad is happening.

When you experience challenges, struggles, trials, tribulations, happenstances, mishaps, and rough spots, if you could see them for what they are, that is, steps, building blocks, and teaching moments, while you are going through, you will be better equipped to continue your journey.

Sometimes the only action required is continuation. If you continue, you do not lose. You learn. If you continue, you do not stop. You strive. If you continue, you do not stay where you are. You proceed on your journey. With each continued step, you get closer and closer to your destination. When you make your destination bigger than now, when you are shooting for something that requires you to grow in order to achieve it, when you know now is only part of something larger, you can see now for what it is. Now going forward is the present time or moment. However, when you look back on now, you can see that it is won (the reverse of now). Won, the past tense of win, is what happens after now is past, but with now's contributions.

When making your plans and committing to a course of action, make sure your destination is long term and requires you to stretch, grow, learn, and to be more and do more. Your destination or dream must be out far enough and big enough to stretch and force you to see more than you are looking at right now. With this in your view, you will not allow yourself to get caught up in the minutia of the moment.

When I mow my lawn, I aspire to have lines so straight that it appears I had assistance from a measurement or alignment tool. To accomplish this, I do not look at the alignment of the lawn mower or the ground right in front of me. Instead I fix my eyes on an object in the distance, at or near my destination. If you want to move in a straight line, you cannot afford to look at the ground in front of you. You must look at your destination and push to it. This allows you to stay on track and aligned. Like a runner in a race, they do not look down at the line. They look forward at the line and to their finished line. The destination/finish line gives us something to shoot for that is not here, something to aspire to.

When you have something to shoot for, somewhere to be, or somewhere you are going, it affects your response and reaction to things that happen right now. You are more able to cope with the daily challenges knowing this is not where you are supposed to be. When you have your eyes on the prize, you are more equipped to move forward because here and now is not your destination. You will move more easily because you realize now is just a step required to get there.

When you have the bigger picture in focus, you know that this is a war and not a battle. As a result, you know that you can lose a battle or two or three, but you can still win the war. When you are focused on the bigger picture, the war, the little pictures, or the battles seem doable, part of the process. These parts may be significant, but they are only parts. You will have days, months, or even years of challenges on your journey to your destination.

These challenges, if taken alone as the only thing that matters, will defeat you.

If you are unable to overcome them, they will end your journey. However, if you can keep things in context and know that each step, while significant, is just a step, you will know that whether your step is successful or not, it does not determine your outcome. When you approach life with a bigger view in mind, you know that what matters is the process. Each step, whether good or bad, equips you for the next step and brings you closer to your destination. So if you have a bad step, you learn not to take that one again, but you keep moving because it is just part of the process.

Given that you are walking in the gray, you must assume and know that there is much that you do not know. You may know the black-and-white rules, but you do not know the outcome of their application. There are just too many unknowns and too much information lacking. Given this reality, you would do yourself a service to take your day-to-day medicine, moves, moments, momentum, mishaps, missteps, and misses for what they are, steps that take you into tomorrow more equipped, experienced, and educated.

I know people who have committed to doing a great job, and they do. They dot every I and cross every T. The moment something difficult happens, they hit a bump in the road, or something does not go the way they plan, they are off and running. They feel underappreciated, unprepared, unloved, or unwanted. That is, on a given day, they expected something to happen, an assignment, an award, a recognition, a promotion, a praise, an opportunity, or a favor.

However, the day passes, and what was expected did not come to pass. So they were ready to go. What if these individuals had a different perspective and decided to persevere? What if they decided what they expected today was only for today but "come what may, I am moving on"? Wouldn't life be different? A different perspective could make the difference.

When setting your plans for your future, make them bigger than your abilities, larger than you believe you can accomplish. This will cause you to see the need for and value in continued improvement, self-development, and growth. Additionally it will cause you to see that regardless of what is going on right now, you have plans for a bigger and better future. Stretch assignments stretch you. They challenge your strengths and weaknesses. They teach you to value successful outcomes as they prove evident that where you start is not as important as where you finish.

When you look back over your life, you will see that not every day went the way you planned or turned out the way you hoped. You will notice that you had some ups and some downs. Some smiled, and others frowned. There were some challenges and a few opportunities. And yet you are still here better than you have ever been. When you look back, you will see how you grew from infancy to childhood, juvenile, adolescence, and adulthood (young adulthood, middle age, and old age). You will notice that as you grew, despite the growing pains and pains of growing up, you got smarter and stronger.

When you look back, you will see that you went from kindergarten to elementary school, middle school, high school, and postsecondary education (college or university). You will notice that despite the task of learning, the toil of studying, and the trouble you got in and out of, you are no worse for the wear but better equipped for the journey. You will be able to see clearly that not everything has gone the way you planned or desired. In fact, you may notice, as most of us do, that while things have gone quite well, there were days when you felt like giving up and throwing in the towel. You will see that your most difficult times taught you the most as well as positioned and prepared you to face your next challenge.

If you look close enough, you will see that the struggles of your moments were useful in preparing you for things that you are now on the path to receive that you would not be prepared for otherwise. Therefore, instead of getting caught up in the moment, in the now, in the here and now, see this moment in the context of the bigger picture. Commit your thoughts, mind, and actions to your journey—something this bigger and greater than the task at hand—not to just what the day holds.

PART
2

WHO AM I? SELF-AWARENESS

CHAPTER 4

KNOW WHAT YOU BRING TO THE TABLE

TO KNOW WHERE YOU ARE, YOU MUST TAKE AN inventory of yourself and your surroundings. Inventory of yourself gives your qualifications; inventory of your surrounding gives your location. To be successful, you must take an honest and accurate inventory of yourself. In *Hamlet* (Act 1, scene 3), Shakespeare said, "to thine own self be true." This was Polonius's last piece of advice to his son Laertes, who was in a hurry to get on the next boat to Paris, where he would be safe from his father's long-winded speeches.

Now given how Hamlet was written and how often it is read and interpreted, I am certain the meaning of this short passage can, has been, and will be debated. Whatever the conclusion of the debate, for this writing, I am using it to emphasize the fact that to be successful you must first be true to yourself. Given that you know you better than anyone else, being true to yourself should not be difficult. Abraham Lincoln said, "You can fool all the people some of the time, and some of the people all the time, but you cannot fool all the people all the time." While I agree with this quote, I believe additional truth can be found by taking the quote one step further noting, "you cannot fool yourself anytime," or more correctly, "you should not fool yourself anytime."

It is common sense and common practice to be aware of how people see you and make the best first impression. It is not uncommon to put your best foot forward, to let people see your best side in public, or to want to shape the conversation others are having about you. Sometimes to accomplish these things, you may have to change the narrative. That is, you may have to put on a façade, to smile when you feel like frowning, to appear positive when in fact things are negative, or even to dress up when you have been dressed down. This is not uncommon in business, politics, and life.

With that said, you must be true to yourself. To lie to yourself is to set yourself up for failure, embarrassment, or a fall. If no one else knows who you are, you must know who you are. That is, you must know yourself—your weaknesses and strengths, your down sittings and uprisings, and your thoughts near and afar. You must know who you are.

Now I know most of us would say that we know ourselves. I would suggest that this is not totally the case. Most of us are often challenged by our own selves and sometimes surprised by the outcome of our own actions, if not the actions themselves. How many times have you said to yourself, "I cannot believe I said or did that"? How many times have you told yourself or others, "It is just not like me to be this way" or "I do not normally behave that way"? How many times as an excuse or an explanation for your actions have you quoted Paul, "For I know that in me (that is, in my flesh) dwelleth no good thing: for to will is present with me; but how to perform that which is good I find not. For the good that I would I do not: but the evil which I would not, that I do?" (Romans 7:18–19 KJV).

I think to a certain extent that we know ourselves empirically based on past experiences. To that end, we can predict our behavior in response to similar situations. (We have been there and done that, and we can do it again.) On the other hand, new situations or experiences, where we have nothing from which to draw, we make it up and hope we can keep it in line with who we say we are or desire to be. An Old Testament scripture in Jeremiah reads, "The heart is deceitful above all things, and desperately wicked: who can know it?" (Jeremiah 17:9 KJV). This passage questions our ability to even know what is in our own hearts. Maybe this explains why we fall in and out of love or why the word *love* is tossed around so frequently that sometimes we find it hard to believe the actions of love equates with the term *love*.

While this is a discussion for a separate book, my point here is to note that to know ourselves we cannot assume self-knowledge. We must ascertain it. To ascertain self-knowledge, we must examine ourselves. Through self-examination—thoughts, motivations, actions, deeds, desires, skills, knowledge, and abilities—you get a good picture of who you truly are.

It is worth noting that self-examination is not a new thing. It has been done throughout time. We could go back to the beginning of time to see where self-examination was evident and active. When Adam and Eve tasted of the forbidden fruit in the garden, their response to God calling for them speaks to their awareness of self.

> And the LORD God called unto Adam, and said unto him, Where art thou? And he said, I heard thy voice in the garden, and I was afraid, because I was naked; and I hid myself. And he said, Who told thee that thou wast naked? Hast thou eaten of the tree, wherefore I commanded thee that thou shouldest not eat? (Genesis 3:9–11 KJV)

Prior to this passage, it is stated that Adam and Eve "were both naked, the man and his wife, and were not ashamed" (Genesis 2:25 KJV). With nothing to be ashamed of, no wrong, no guilt, no stain, and no outside influences, Adam and Eve were completely exposed/ naked and not ashamed. After being deceived and disobedient, doing something they were told not to do, having no intention of doing, and were being tricked into doing, they became ashamed of their nakedness. With nothing to hide, they were naked and not ashamed, but with something to hide, they became aware of their nakedness and were ashamed. And they hid.

While Adam and Eve's awareness of themselves did not excuse them from their punishment, it is interesting to see how their error heightened their awareness of their situation, their nakedness, and they became embarrassed. So God asked, "Who told you that you were naked?"

That is, He called for them to examine themselves to determine what caused them to disobey His command. In short, they each accused someone/something else, an outside influence. If left alone, we would not be ashamed of our nakedness. However, we are never alone. The impact of outside influences continues to warrant that we examine ourselves. Outside influences caused Paul to tell the church at Corinth to "examine yourselves" (2 Corinthians 13:5a KJV).

Paul was afraid that those at the church at Corinth had been deceived, and given the importance of their Christianity, he encourages self-examination. Given the impact of outside influences, competition and challenges, to your corporate welfare, it behooves you to examine yourself. Know yourself. Know how you stand against and alongside the competition. Know if you have what it takes to face and overcome challenges. There is no need for you to be surprised or embarrassed.

You have everything you need to know you at your disposal. The benefits of this knowledge warrants that you take the necessary time, inventory, and examination to know yourself. Your success is dependent on you knowing your present status, standing, situation, or state of affairs. Some people are afraid to take inventory, fearing what they may find or discover. If it is any consolation, know that where you are does not determine where you will be. If used properly, knowing where you are only represents a starting point, a previous location, an experience, where you were, a testimony.

However, your lack of awareness of where you are resulting from assumptions or ignorance could prevent you from making progress toward your goal. If you assume you know more than you know, what is your motivation to learn more? If you assume you have arrived, where else do you need to go? If you assume you have done everything, what is there left for you to accomplish? However, if you ascertain your location and determine that you have not arrived, that you have not apprehended, or that there is room for growth, you create a starting point on your journey to success.

Someone said it correctly, "The more I learn, the less I know." Another way this was stated, "The more things you know, the more things you know you don't know." If you never attempt to learn how to play the piano, you would not know how much more you do not know or need to know about playing the piano. Perhaps basketball would be a better example. If I play basketball by myself, at my house, or in my driveway, to myself I may be the best player in the world. However, if I take my game to the local court and begin to play against competition, I may realize that I am not as good as I thought I was. If I become accomplished at this level and decide to push my skill to the next level by getting a coach and playing on a team, I may further understand how little I know. If I become accomplished after joining a team and decide I want to be a professional, I will again become familiar with how little I know. Wanting to be like Mike is not enough to get you in the game. You must put in the time.

However, if you think you are as good as Mike and have never played against Mike or anyone almost as good as him, you may cheat yourself of the opportunity to be like Mike, thinking you have already arrived. That said, if you see and ascertain the difference in Mike's talent and skills and yours and are driven to be like him, you will push yourself to improve. If you are good, the more you push yourself and learn, the better you will become, and the more you will realize that you have so much more to learn.

STRENGTH

If you are going to be successful, you must know yourself, which means you must know what you do not know. To accomplish this, you must examine yourself and understand your strengths and weaknesses. Being self-aware, knowing yourself, means knowing what you do and do not know. When you know yourself, if necessary, you can recalibrate your compass. You can take stock of where you are and where you need to be and better position yourself to get to where you want to go. Self-awareness allows you to take inventory of what you have, what you do not have, and what you need. The importance of self-awareness is reflected in the book of Luke.

> Suppose one of you wants to build a tower. Won't you first sit down and estimate the cost to see if you have enough money to complete it? For if you lay the foundation and are not able to finish it, everyone who sees it will ridicule you, saying, this person began to build and wasn't able to finish. Or suppose a king is about to go to war against another king. Won't he first sit down and consider whether he is able with ten thousand men to oppose the one coming against him with twenty thousand? If he is not able, he will send a delegation while the other is still a long way off and will ask for terms of peace. In the same way, those of you who do not give up everything you have cannot be my disciples. (Luke 14:28–33 NIV)

As you can see from this passage, while planning is a key component to success when building or when going to war, knowing what you have in your possession to build or fight with is key to planning. It is not likely you will plan accurately when you do not know what you possess to carry to the table or have at your disposal. For example, if it takes $100 to complete a task and you are not in possession of the total amount but plan to borrow the balance, how will you know what to borrow if you do not know what you have? If you know how much money you have, you can make an informed borrowing decision. If you have $50, you know you only need to borrow $50. If you have $25, you know you only need to borrow $75. If, however, you have $95 and you borrow $10, you incur a debt 100 percent larger than warranted.

The importance of you knowing what you bring to the table is even more evident when your physical safety is at stake, when considering going to war. After all, the first law of nature is self-preservation. Perhaps T. F. Hodge said it correctly, "The first law of nature is self-preservation. Cut off that which may harm you. But if it is worth preserving, and is meaningful, nourish it and have no regrets. Ultimately, this is true living and love of self … from within."

We go into a fight with the goal of winning. To that end, it behooves us to make informed decisions about our own skill set or the requisite tools or weapons we will need to position ourselves to win. Someone (perhaps Sean Connery in *The Untouchables* [1987]) said it this way, "You do not take a knife to a gunfight."

If you are planning to win the fight, before starting it or getting involved, you must consider yourself and your opponent. For the record, it is not enough to just assess your opponent's strengths and weaknesses. You must also assess your own. Know yourself. If you know you are lover and not a fighter, it may be best you talk your way out of the situation. How many times have you seen or how many people have you known who have used their communication skills to get out of a physical fight? They realized that they did not have what it would take to win physically, so they chose another option, utilizing their strength and communication. To avoid a physical fight, some people talk their way out by talking tough, others stare their way by looking tough, and still others walk their way out by acting tough. Whether you talk your way out, stare your way out, or act your way out is determined by who you are going in. The only way you can determine which tactic to apply is by knowing who you are.

Because knowing who you are represents your first step on your journey to success, it cannot be overstated. Lao Tzu said, "The journey of a thousand miles begins with one step." I learned this quote incorrectly. I thought it said, "The journey of a thousand miles begins with the first step." Having said that, I like the way I mislearned and misquoted it. Yes, the one step could be the first step, or the one step could be any step along the way that calls your attention to your journey. The first step, however, is just that, the first step.

There is no denying it. It represents your beginning, your start. The emphasis on your first step is significant to me because it emphasizes your first action. You will take many one steps on your journey, but you will only start once. You may choose to start over or initiate a new journey, but your first step will always be your first step. Your first step is important because it represents your first move on the way. It does not determine how things will go and where you will end up. It simply says that you have started. You will have bumps on your journey, hills and mountains to climb, valleys to go through, and crooked and straight places to traverse. You will have ups and downs, good and bad days, and successes and failures.

Things will change around you, under you, over you, behind you, and in front of you, and you will change. However, what will never alter is your first step. Regardless of what happens, you took your first step. This you can and should use as your inspiration and motivation when it seems that you are not going to make it. Know that you took the first step. Now all you should do is keep taking one step at a time.

Given the importance of your first step and the impact it can have on creating for you a good beginning, an excellent foundation, you should take precautions to ensure that it is your best first step by beginning with you. You are the common denominator to your success. While you may not control the stimuli, you manage your response. While you may not control the outcome, you regulate the input. This being the case, do you know who you are? Knowing yourself is your first step. Your journey begins with you.

The questions are: Are you a left or right step; a forward or backward step, or a side, down, or up step? Knowing your stepping tendencies will ensure that each step works for and not against you. It would not prove productive to go backward when forward is key to your success. So if your tendency is to go backward, not to face confrontation, and not to face the issue head-on, knowing this could assist you with the timing of your step to ensure that your tendency does not work against you. That is, if the situation warrants confrontation, hitting the issue head-on may be waiting until it blows over or someone else tackles the issue as your best option.

Alternatively, you may have to step up. To have stepping tendencies that would work against you does not mean that you will be unsuccessful; however, it may mean you need to change your normal behavior. My point here is that it is important for you to understand yourself. If you know your strengths and weaknesses, you can ensure that they work for and not against you. Having a weakness is not a bad thing. Not knowing that you do or what it is is a bad thing. You can take the necessary steps to either equip yourself to succeed or simply ensure that your weaknesses do not cause you to fail. The only way you can do this, however, is to know yourself, to know that you have this weakness.

While a vision to know where you are going is important to your success, the first step to accomplish this is knowing who you are. If you know who you are, you can get a true assessment of where you are. However, if you do not know who you are, your assessment of where you are is not likely to be accurate.

Let me explain. If I am Superman and I do not know that I am, if I am placed in a challenging situation where superhuman skills are required, I lack the knowledge or vision to see my way out. My vision of my possibilities is limited by my knowledge of self. As a result, while I am equipped with everything, the superhuman skills I need to handle the challenge I am facing because I do not know myself, I will succumb to the challenge.

The same is true if I lack superhuman skills and I am called upon to exercise them. While I may have an inflated sense of self and think I can do what a superhuman does, my attempt will end in failure because I do not have what it takes. Again, not knowing myself works against me, except this time it leads me to an action that I cannot accomplish. Knowing yourself can ensure that you leverage your abilities to face challenges appropriately.

I must emphasize the importance of you knowing what you bring to the table, your strengths and weaknesses. Most people are familiar and comfortable with their strengths. They thrive in conversations and dialogues about them and in life when they can use them. There is no shame in knowing what you are good at. Quite the contrary, you should know your areas of strength in details. These are things that generally come natural or easy for you. These are things in life that you enjoy most because not a lot of effort is required for you to stand out or excel.

Generally your areas of strength separate you from the pack. That is, when you are using your gift, your area of strength, things you take for granted, others, not gifted in this area, struggle to do, or accomplish. For example, if public speaking is your gift, you are not challenged by standing in front of and speaking to crowds of people. For someone not gifted as a public speaker, they may find it very difficult to even think about the possibility of doing this. They may get nervous; experience illness, sweating, and loss of thoughts; and refuse to have anything to do with it.

With knowledge of your strengths, you can position yourself to have the greatest impact on the organization while exerting the least amount of energy. You can leverage your strengths against the most important requirements of your organization. In other words, you can get the most output with the least amount of input. This is called a good investment. Alternatively, you can spend a lot of time working on projects that require you use your weaknesses. You may accomplish the task, but the time and effort put into accomplishing it may not be the best use of your time and talent.

Allow me to digress and note that organizations spend a great deal of time, resources, and efforts on individuals' weaknesses. We will discuss this more in detail later. Despite the organization's focus, your primary emphasis needs to be on understanding your strengths. If you are good at something and can leverage that to have an impact on the organization, your input and output is both fun and productive. If you have a strength in a certain area, why not use it? There is nothing wrong with taking advantage of your strengths and doing something that you enjoy, an activity that comes comparatively and competitively easy for you.

When you know your strengths, you can position yourself to maximize your output and outcome by being where the organization needs you most. If your strength is numbers and you are on the people side of the business, you may be doing yourself a disservice. You could have a more lasting and productive impact on the organization, if you worked in an area where you could use your strength, that is, finance, accounting, budget, audit, and mathematics. Your strengths can be what propels you forward and positions you for advancement. Your strength could separate you from the pack. The organization is in constant need of people with specific skill sets, certain strengths. At times people are needed with interpersonal skills to lead the organizations and its organisms to the next level. Other times people are needed with technical skills to enhance technical tools and equipment to improve production. Sometimes people are needed with technological skills to improve the speed, accuracy, and output of the organization. And at other times, people are needed with a combination of these skills to work in and across the organization. You knowing who you are and what your strengths are will go a long way to ensure exposure and position you for promotion considerations.

When you have mastered the knowledge of yourself and your organization and have taken an inventory of where you are and know where you want to be, you can begin to leverage your strengths to accomplish the mission of the organization. This will put you in the best possible position for high performance and potential, reward recognition, and promotion or assignment considerations. Most people working in the areas of their strengths are happy or enjoy what they are doing. It has long been said that, "A happy employee is a productive employee." Studies have shown that employees work harder when they are happy. Their happiness results in increased productivity, creativity, and earnings for the employee and the company.

When you can identify and determine your strengths and match them up with the organization's requirements, you are more likely to have a lasting and noticeable impact on its mission, vision, and goals. When you enjoy what you are doing, you look for ways to make improvements and have an impact. While knowing your strengths will directly benefit you, it could also benefit the organization—improved policies and procedures as well as increased output and productivity.

While an organization spends the larger portion of their employee training and development budget and resources on their employees' weaknesses, you would be wise to ensure that your and their investment in you are on your strengths. Yes, you should spend time and resources investing in the development of your weaknesses. However, the bulk of your time and investment should be in your strengths.

Many of us have strengths that we have not yet discovered or tapped into. This is due in part to the fact that we focus on what we do not have and avoid or run away from challenges that make us uncomfortable, like most challenges do. You should identify your known strengths, areas that you are obviously strong in. You also work to identify strengths that you have that are not as obvious. Sometimes our strengths are discovered through our struggles, which often reveal or allow us to see that we have what it takes. Our challenges or struggles give us the opportunity to exercise our muscles in ways we never considered and may, in like manner, reveal that we have strengths we never thought about. This being the case, we should never run away from opportunities that present themselves as challenges. Instead we should step up.

Having a destination that is bigger than now gives you something to shoot for. It gives you something to stretch for, and it provides you something to focus on. Reaching for something bigger than now challenges you to leverage the strengths you know, to recruit the strengths you may have but are unaware of, and to test yourself and not get caught up with what you are doing or experiencing now. The more you take on, the more challenges you face, the more opportunities you take advantage of, the bigger your journey, the more you will and should rely on and discover your strengths. Your strengths will become your go-to plan, your how-to process, and your way-out strategy.

No one should shy away from their strengths. Quite the contrary, you should seek every opportunity possible to leverage your strengths to your advantage. Get to know yourself, identify your known and unknown strengths, and use them to directly improve and affect the organization's mission, vision, goals, regulations, policies, and procedures. Your strengths, your gifts, will create opportunities for you. "A man's gifts make room for him and brings him before great men" (Proverbs 18:16 NASB).

If you are looking to be successful, you are looking for opportunities. Your strengths can be your opportunities. "Use it or lose it." Use the gifts of your strengths to get the footing you need, to have an impact on the organization and your career.

WEAKNESS

In being true to yourself, you must also know your weaknesses. The inability to admit or acknowledge one's weakness is one of the primary causes of individual failure. Solomon wisely noted, "Pride goes before destruction, and a haughty spirit before a fall" (Proverbs 16:18 KJV).

People are generally unwilling to admit their shortcomings. Even though there is nothing wrong with having weaknesses, people are shy when it comes to sharing or admitting theirs. People want to be viewed as a renaissance or universal man, a man who can do all things, an individual who is the master of all trades. Please note, for the record, the universal person does not exist, at least not in real life. The average person is a jack-of-all-trades, someone who is versatile and able to do passable work at many different tasks.

While people have their strong suits, their strengths, and things they excel at, they also have some tasks they can do well, a few activities they just get by on, and other things they struggle with, their weaknesses. We all have things we are good at and those we are no good at. Having a weakness is natural, not negative. Or at least it does not have to be.

Much like having something that we appear naturally good at, having a weakness is just a part of our reality. If we know and acknowledge what our weakness is, we can ensure that it does not hinder our progress or take necessary steps to strengthen this area. Ignoring it or assuming we do not have any weakness could work to our disadvantage. The worst thing you can do is to believe that or act like you are strong in every area. Unfortunately your denial or disbelief does not excuse your weakness. They only make you blind to them. Your blindness displays itself as refusal to accept your weakness or self-denial. Either display (refusal or self-denial) can prove detrimental. For example, when given a task, a project, or an initiative to accomplish that falls in your area of weakness, if you are in denial, you will take on the task and succeed through hard work or fail and start to place blame.

Let's first assume that you succeed because you were able to figure it out. If you calculate the amount of time and effort involved in accomplishing this with your weakness, you must ask yourself, "Was this the best use of my time and energy? Could this have been accomplished by someone with the requisite skills and abilities more efficiently and effectively? Do the benefits gained outweigh the cost?"

Alternatively, you accept the task, project, or initiative, and you fail because you do not have what it takes to succeed, as this requirement falls in your area of weakness. Likely responses given that you have already chosen to accept the requirement without the requisite skills are to start the blame game, deflect, or make excuses. This approach is not likely to yield you the desired success or outcome you seek.

Far too often, people do not want to share their weakness because they believe this will disadvantage them. They believe that if they share their weakness, they will be excluded from opportunities or will be called out for what they lack. Unfortunately, there may be some truth to this. That is, they are not totally wrong. As mentioned earlier, most organizations expend the larger part of their growth and development budget on strengthening or improving the weaknesses of their employees.

If the budget were the only issue, there would be no problem. However, the budget is focused on developing employees' weaknesses because most of the assignment, promotion, development, and growth decisions are based on employees' strength. Conversely, the elimination of employees from consideration of promotion, assignment, and growth opportunities is determined by their weaknesses. Organizations spend a great deal of time and effort identifying, highlighting, and calling out the weaknesses of its employees to explain, justify, or support their employee decisions' rationale to themselves and the employees.

For example, when panels are being held or career or assignment boards meet to discuss employees' opportunities of advancement through assignments, training, and promotions, feedback given to the employees focuses on things they need to do to make themselves more competitive. Even the employees who rank in the top 10 percent or are promoted are given feedback on things they need to improve or assignments they need to consider for development.

The feedback suggests to the employee that their failure results from their weakness. Armed with this information, the employee believes that their success depends on their weakness rather than their strength. This is not a bad conclusion, given the fact that clearly their strengths have not afforded them the opportunities they seek and have not been the topic of the feedback they receive.

This concept of the employees' weaknesses defining or limiting them is further perpetuated when competing for an assignment. The employees apply for an assignment that they believe they can do or receive an opportunity to develop in an area of their weakness that they have been given feedback on, only to be denied the opportunity because of their weakness. When given feedback on the reason they did not get the assignment, they are told that they did not have something, they were weak in a certain area, or their competition was stronger or had more experience.

The feedback essentially says, "We appreciate your application, and while you had a strong interview, we are looking for someone with XYZ years of experience, who demonstrated leadership having led a large and a diverse team."

What really happened was, after interviewing all ten candidates, nine of them were competitive for the position, but two had led a large, diverse team, and one had XYZ years of experience. So while you could do the job and would have been selected, if you were the only candidate, they had options. However, you needed to know why you were not selected, and they are required to tell you why. The real why is that your competition was stronger, not that you were weaker.

It has been quoted, requoted, phrased, rephrased, stated, and restated that "feedback is a gift." A gift is simply something given willingly to someone without payment. So, yes, in this regard, feedback is a gift. The question is what type of gift. Not all gifts given are good, appreciated, wanted, preferred, useful, fun, or liked. Some gifts, while free and given willingly, are for gags, useful as a white elephant, trash, or unwanted.

The type of gift, as is true with feedback, is determined by the recipient. You get to determine the type of gift your feedback represents. It is important to note, as suggested earlier, that feedback given when competition is involved may be more about the competition than about you.

In summary, you did not win the position because the competition was stronger. This is an important qualifier because in most cases your wins or losses are a result of your competition. If I am playing basketball against Michael Jordan and lose, what would you believe was the cause of that loss: my age, height, or my or his skills? All of these could be the correct answer, but the one that stands out as unequivocally true is Michael Jordan's skills. Even in my youth, on a tall day with my best skill, I will lose that game. Why? Michael Jordan has mastered skills in basketball that I have not and some I know nothing about. If the two of us were competing for a position on a team, I will lose out every time. My feedback would focus on what I lack, but I lost out because of the competition, Michael Jordan. If I were competing for the same position against a player who was not as skilled as I was, I would get selected. Why? Because I am more skilled than my competition.

My point is that often feedback is focused or received incorrectly. Yes, it is true. You did not get the position, and yes, you were weaker than your competition. However, if you are qualified for the position and you did not get the position, the real reason is the strength of your competition, not your weakness.

The feedback you receive about how you fared against your competition for an assignment, position, or promotion is too often focused on your weakness and not on the competition's strength. This leaves you to think about your weaknesses and how they are holding you back or impeding your success. As a result, you are left with a need to take an action to address or ignore your weaknesses. To the credit of some, they take this gift and assess its value to determine whether it was the competition or their competence that determined their outcome.

Unfortunately too many employees take the feedback for face value and determine that they lack something. Then they either surrender to their weaknesses, wave the white flag and give up, or take it to heart and begin to work on themselves, strengthening their weaknesses. We know how negative an impact it is on the employee to give up, but I submit that it is just as negative to have a person focusing on their weaknesses, assuming this will get them the advancement they seek next time. It might, but that really depends on the competition.

If you are competent but have a weakness, investing too much energy into developing your weakness may not yield you the results you desire. Additionally, dedicating too much time and effort to strengthen weaknesses could prove feckless and detract from opportunities to use and leverage your strengths. To that end, before accepting feedback as a good gift, make sure you understand the context, content, and consistency of the feedback. If you do your homework before applying for a position, the feedback you receive should come as no real surprise. That is, when applying for a position, assignment, or promotion, you should already know what the panels are looking for, as this will aid you in the assessment of your competence or readiness. With knowledge of what the panels are looking for, you can determine if you have the requisite skill, knowledge, abilities, experience, or strengths to be successful in the position or assignment or if you are prepared for promotion. If, in your assessment, you realize that you do not have the skills to be competitive or the competence to do the job, it is incumbent upon you to be true to yourself and address your weaknesses.

To be true to yourself, you must continue to take an honest look at your knowledge, skills, and abilities. You must continually assess whether you have what it takes to do the job to which you are assigned, take on additional task, or secure the assignment or development opportunity you desire. You must not assume that yesterday's successes resulting for the use of your skill are an indication of today's or tomorrow's successes. To that end, you must repeatedly review yourself against your task. Your skills, knowledge, and abilities may have been more than adequate to get you to where you are today—the promotions, positions, publicity, and place. They may not be enough to get you to the next level, but they may be. You must determine if you have what it takes or you need to add something else to your toolbox.

Having done your homework and determined that you have what it takes, if you apply for and do not secure a position, you must again take inventory of yourself. You must determine if you have what it takes or if there something else at work. It is important that you secure, review, and assess the value of the feedback on why you were not selected. Did you overlook something? Was there a skill set required that you did not possess? Was your non-selection competence or competition? Did you get beaten out by someone stronger, or were you not qualified?

You must be honest with yourself when doing your personal assessment. If you determine that you were not selected because of your weaknesses and you aspire to the position, promotion, or place that you were deemed not qualified, you have been given a gift. Your next step should be to determine what you need to do to acquire the requisite set of skills.

Please note, if after securing your feedback, noting that you were not qualified for the position and doing your own assessment to draw the same conclusion, if you determine that this is not something you aspire to do, you will be better served focusing on your strengths. That is, if you do not aspire to the level where this skill set that you lack is required, your time and energy will be better invested on leveraging your strengths. However, if you aspire to move up in the organization and you lack the requisite strengths and skills, you must determine a course of action to secure them or strengthen your weaknesses to make yourself competitive.

Having impressed upon you the importance of knowing your weaknesses and encouraging you to assess the value of your feedback to determine if not being selected is because of the competition or your competence, please be advised that competition is always a part of your assignment, promotion, and placement decisions. While you may be your own worst enemy or critic, your competition can certainly help you with that. When you seek to advance, you will automatically face competition, who will either make you or break you. Your advancement does not depend only on what you do, how equipped you are, or what you bring to the table. Your advancement also depends on your competition. Your success will depend on how competitive you are.

If you want to secure a position, move up in the organization, and take advantage of growth and advancement opportunities, you will have to compete. To be successful, in addition to knowing and understanding the requirement of what you seek (the position, promotion, and publicity), know that an assessment of you and your competition determines the final decision.

Even if you meet the minimum requirements for the position you seek and are therefore qualified to be selected and do the job, you may still not get selected if your competition is stronger. This will likely result in you getting feedback suggesting you were not selected because of your weakness when it was your competition's strength. That said, there is something to be gained from competing for what you want. If you continue to miss out on opportunities because of your competition, you should not take this for granted. Instead you should take an inventory of yourself and the feedback you are being given. It is possible that the feedback that you are being given is valid and should be taken to heart, not to task. Not all feedback is about the competition. Some of it, the best of it, is about your competence.

How many times have you applied for an assignment that you did not believe that you were qualified for? How many positions have you been selected for that you felt that you were not qualified for? Your qualification for an assignment or opportunity or your ability to do the job should be the last things that surprise you. You should know you. That said, you should not presume or assume your knowledge when you do not have all the facts. One fact that is often unknown that determines whether you will be selected is the competition. You rarely know what the competition has that you do not that will prove critical enough to get them selected over you. This information will be revealed after the fact, which is too late to affect the current opportunity, but could prove valuable in the future. As a result, you should take every opportunity serious and review details provided you on the decision made, positive or negative. Feedback in this context is a gift, as it gives you historical insights that could have an impact on your future.

For example, if you have been working as a carpenter, are interested in a position as a carpenter, and have submitted several applications but with no success, the feedback you continue to receive states that you need several years of experience as a carpenter. While you have worked as a carpenter for a year and have demonstrated the competence, ability, and potential to do the jobs you have applied for, the lack of several years of experience continues to hold you back. You may get lucky and secure a position because there is a requirement and you are the only applicant and candidate available. It is a long shot. Knowing this, you can continue to apply for these positions requiring the several years of experience and hope something comes through.

Alternatively, you can do something different. First, you can accept the feedback and acknowledge your one year or lack of experience and the fact that you are not being selected because the competition has, and the requirement is for, several years of carpentry experience. That is, you can acknowledge that you are not being selected because of your competence (lack of qualification) and your competition (having the required several years of experience). Second, if this is something that you want to pursue, you should begin to take steps to get the required experience. This could be continuing in your current assignment or seeking another position that will afford you the opportunity to get the requisite carpentry experience. The point is, if you desire an opportunity that you continue to be denied, you must not adopt hope as a strategy. You should do your research; secure, review, and analyze the feedback; assess your qualification against the requirements of the opportunity you seek; and take actions.

You may also decide that you are no longer interested in these opportunities. If after several attempts to secure an opportunity, you continue to be unsuccessful because of your competence and the competition, maybe it is time to consider something else. If you decide you are unwilling to do what is required to become qualified to meet the requirements or competitive to win the assignment, it may be time to redirect your focus, to change directions.

If you are not willing to take actions to change your outcome, a change of directions to seek opportunities where you are competitive and competent is a good idea. You must take an honest look at yourself, your qualifications, and your motivations and then decide which direction works for you. Develop new skill? Leverage developed skills?

It is easy to sit back and point your finger at and blame others for you not being selected for an opportunity you want. You could say, "They had a preferred candidate," "They had someone they wanted for the position," or "They did not want me because I was not their type." Or you could be honest with yourself and acknowledge you were not qualified and the competition was stronger.

It does you no good to try to explain off your weaknesses when they are getting in the way of your success. It is critically important that you take a serious look at your skill set and be honest with yourself. As we have noted, not all feedback is good. However, some of it is, and for this reason, you should accept and review all feedback. If the feedback you are given is repetitive (that is, if you hear something more than once and from more than one source), you should not take it for granted. If you have been told again and again that you lack a set of skills or need to develop a certain strength, you should take this feedback as a gift, constructive criticism.

When more than one person tells you about something that you lack or need to work on, it is worth hearing and taking a closer look to determine the cause or origin of their commentary. Maybe they are wrong or do not have all the facts. Possibly someone else saying the same thing about you has biased them. Or perhaps they are right. Maybe you have a blind spot about you that others can see clearly. It is incumbent upon you that you determine which is which. "The truth will set you free."

What you do not want to do is continue to do what you are doing and having to explain away your weaknesses because you refuse to face them. We all have weaknesses. Knowing what they are and either acknowledging them or working on them are a key to your success. Having a weakness is like having a problem. You may ignore it, but it may not go away. Taking the first step to solving a problem, acknowledging that it exists, moves you in the right direction to the solution.

The same is true of you having a weakness. The first step is for you to acknowledge that your weakness exists. The outcome you want from it will determine whether you address it, ignore it, strengthen it, work around it, highlight it, downplay it, or whatever you decide to do. However, nothing can be done until you first acknowledge that it exists.

Sometimes, all that is required of our weakness is an acknowledgement, often to ourselves. Knowing your weakness can prevent you from trying to do too much with it; knowing it can prevent you from failing because you chose to do something you were not equipped to handle. For examples, if finance or analysis is your weakness, you will do yourself a disservice if you choose an occupation like accounting, auditing, or finance. Knowing that finance or analysis is your weakness, you are equipped to choose an occupation where you can leverage your strengths. Or if you do secure a position requiring you do finance or analysis, you know you need to spend some time on the job, in the classroom, or online getting up to speed. You also know that by selecting an occupation where you must spend time developing your strength, you may have placed yourself behind the eight ball, the curveball, and the curve. This could result in you losing out on a lot of opportunities to your competition until you become competitive. This does not mean you are at the end of the road. However, it could mean that you are going to spend a lot of time feeling that you are at the end of your rope because you just keep missing out on opportunities to more qualified or competitive individuals.

You must be honest with yourself when it comes to knowing who you are, especially as it relates to your weaknesses. Your honesty to yourself will determine your next course of action. If you choose not to be honest with yourself, you could spend and waste a lot of time doing or trying to do something that you will be unable to do because your weaknesses keep you out of the competition. On a separate but good note, knowing your weaknesses and being honest with yourself positions you to take informed and impactful courses of action. Your truth to self about your weaknesses gives you choices. You can choose to address them or simply acknowledge they exist.

I do not recommend you deny the existence of your weaknesses. We all know that when it comes to decision making, doing nothing is always an option. It may not be the best one, or even a good one, but it is an option. When it comes to your weaknesses, I recommend you take the option of denying they exist off the table. Instead I highly suggest you do your homework in this area, insist you have weaknesses, and make it your business to determine what they are.

We all have weaknesses. Some are more obvious and pronounced than others are; a few are more transparent than others are, but they exist. You should know your weaknesses before anyone else. It is one thing to acknowledge your weaknesses and not do anything about them. It is something totally different to deny their existence. If you acknowledge them, you at least accept the fact that they exist. If you deny their existence, you are saying to yourself and everyone around you, "I do not have any weaknesses."

This could become problematic for you, as it suggests to those around you that you lack self-awareness. When you acknowledge you have weaknesses, you give yourself an opportunity to improve or address them. Please note, a weakness of itself is not a problem; however, denying its existence can be.

All of us have weaknesses, whether we like to admit them or not. However, the person who denies having any weaknesses and behaves as if they do not exist can do nothing about them. You cannot teach an individual something when they know everything already. If you insist that you have no weaknesses (which is what denial does), conversely, you insist you are the best that you can be. If there is nothing wrong about or with you, there is nothing to make right. The problem with this approach is that while you may not be able to see or know that you have weaknesses, others around you do.

Additionally, when you are in denial of your weaknesses, you will not receive well any feedback given to you suggesting you have weaknesses. It appears to you that not only is your feedback wrong, but the individuals who developed the feedback are in error as well. All the signs of weaknesses may be there; the commentary of many on the subject of your weaknesses may be there. Your weaknesses may even be evident in the daily execution of your duties or interactions with your colleagues/peers, but if you cannot see it or choose to deny that you have weaknesses, they do not exist, at least as far as you are concerned.

This is where the problem begins, when your perception of reality does not align with others' reality. With this misalignment, it is appropriate to believe the problem is not you but them, to point your fingers at the ones saying you have weaknesses, and to blame them for holding you back. This lack of self-awareness is extremely detrimental to anyone trying to move up the ladder of success.

Self-awareness is a valuable key to a leader's ability to lead and influence others. When you assume the leadership role (either team lead, supervisor, or manager), you become responsible for others' behavior and actions. Good leaders know when they should take, share, or give credit. One thing is for certain, as a leader, you will make mistakes. If you are in denial of your weaknesses, being unaware of yourself, you are more likely to take credit for the good and give credit for the bad things that happen under your leadership.

This type of behavior undermines the team. People do not mind following someone who makes a mistake and is willing to admit it. However, people are suspicious and skeptical of leaders who do not mind calling them to task for their mistakes but are unwilling to admit their own. If you aspire to be a leader, you must—it is mandatory—have a really good handle on your weaknesses, as you cannot afford to have a weakness as your blind side.

There are many benefits to knowing your weaknesses. For instance, you will know where you fit. As a team member, you need to know what you can do to make the team stronger. Equally, you need to know that some things are out of your lane and do not fit your skill set. When you know your weaknesses, you can leverage your strengths to have the greatest impact on the team's outcome. Each member of your team has areas where they are strongest and zones where they are weakest. Knowing this allows you to construct or build a high-performing team.

While you may be the leader of the team, you are still a member. Therefore, knowing your strengths and weaknesses are critically important to the team's performance. A team works best when each member contributes from their position of strength, much like the functioning of the body. Each part or member of the body is most valuable doing what it was designed to do or does best. While various parts can function effectively doing what other parts do best, it is not optimal. Yes, you can walk on your hands and use your feet to pick up things, but it is not optimal. When you are seeking to optimize your team, to get the most from them, you will accomplish this when they are doing what they do best or using their strengths. 1 Corinthians 12 speaks to this and the value of each member of the body functioning in its own unique way.

> For as the body is one, and hath many members, and all the members of that one body, being many, are one body: so also is Christ. For by one Spirit are we all baptized into one body, whether we be Jews or Gentiles, whether we be bond or free; and have been all made to drink into one Spirit. For the

body is not one member, but many. If the foot shall say, Because I am not the hand, I am not of the body; is it therefore not of the body? And if the ear shall say, Because I am not the eye, I am not of the body; is it therefore not of the body? If the whole body were an eye, where were the hearing? If the whole were hearing, where were the smelling? But now hath God set the members every one of them in the body, as it hath pleased him. And if they were all one member, where were the body? But now are they many members, yet but one body. And the eye cannot say unto the hand, I have no need of thee: nor again the head to the feet, I have no need of you. Nay, much more those members of the body, which seem to be more feeble, are necessary: And those members of the body, which we think to be less honourable, upon these we bestow more abundant honour; and our uncomely parts have more abundant comeliness. For our comely parts have no need: but God hath tempered the body together, having given more abundant honour to that part which lacked: That there should be no schism in the body; but that the members should have the same care one for another. And whether one member suffer, all the members suffer with it; or one member be honoured, all the members rejoice with it. Now ye are the body of Christ, and members in particular." (1Corinthian 12:12–27 KJV)

Much like the body functioning detailed in this passage, a team consists of many members with many unique functions. In addition to the body functioning best when each member is doing what it is designed to do, each member functions best as well. A strong team is indicative of strong team members. When each team member operates within their areas of strength, they and the team are strong. However, if the team members choose to operate within their areas of weakness, they will do the team a disservice. They will weaken the team.

What is also interesting about this passage is the acknowledgement that there are members who require more attention because of their weaknesses. A strong team will have members who are doing their best, but it is not enough. So to ensure the strength of the team, others step up. The weakness of a team member is of little concern, as it is common. That is, even the strongest teams, the highest-performing ones, have weak members. Weak members can and do serve a purpose and a function. In an effective team setting, the weak members have a place.

There is not a team that you can name where every player, every member, is equally strong. What is concerning is not a weak member, but one who chooses to be weak when their strength will have the greatest impact on the team's success.

I want to reemphasize that your weaknesses are not your downfall and are not an indictment on your future. Your unwillingness to acknowledge that you have a weakness could be. Think about it. People succeed with weaknesses. I cannot think of anyone who has been successful without a weakness. All individuals who have been successful have done so despite their weaknesses and not because of their lack of weaknesses. In fact, you may discover that most successful people have achieved this status because they failed enough to identify, accept, and acknowledge their weaknesses. They were able to find their strengths and utilize them to accomplish their goal, and they were keenly aware of their weaknesses, ensuring they did not cause them to fail. If you desire to be successful, knowing your weakness is not an option. It is mandatory. The best way to prevent something from causing you to fail is to know what it is.

Your acknowledgement of your weakness is not failure. Quite the contrary, it could be the key to your success. When you acknowledge you have weaknesses, you open yourself up to the possibility of addressing them and being able to develop that area and strengthen yourself so it will not cause you to fail. Or you position yourself to accept them as part of who you are.

When you know you, you know what you can and cannot do. When you were in high school, you took courses that were easy and others that were difficult. The easy courses you mastered with little effort, but the difficult courses required a great deal of study, time, and effort just to secure a passing grade. Your strengths and weaknesses determined if the course was easy or difficult. The difficult courses, the ones that demanded something from you that you had little to offer, were difficult because of your weaknesses. You may have been able through hard work, dedication, prayer, or support to secure a good grade, but it was not easy.

Generally, most can accomplish a task despite their weaknesses. They just may not accomplish it as well as someone who is strong in this area or may have to work harder. In like manner, courses that were easy to you were this way because of your strengths.

Your weaknesses or strengths do not define you. To acknowledge that mathematics is not your strength is not to say that you cannot do math; however, it does note that this is not your preferred subject or the one you are likely to excel at. However, if English is your strength, you are likely to excel at it with little effort. While you will not be exempt from using math, given the challenge it poses for you, you may choose not to select an occupation or a means to support yourself that requires math as your strength. Perhaps a career that requires you to use English would be preferred.

When you deny having weaknesses, you must compensate for mistakes resulting from them. This comes in the form of pointing fingers, placing blame, making excuses, telling lies, and creating more mistakes. With no weaknesses, you must blame someone or something for faults or failures they caused. This type of behavior may not prevent you from doing your job and getting credit for your personal accomplishments as a junior employee, but it will have a negative impact on you publicly and as you move up in the organization. In other words, you could become your own worst enemy and impede your own success.

You must know that in an organization, your weaknesses will be noticed and highlighted. When this happens, if you are in denial, people will make several attempts to make you aware of your weaknesses (if you are lucky), but if they continue to be met with resistance from you, they will give up on you and communicate the results of their attempts to others. So what was originally an effort to help you, to share information with you about your weaknesses, has now become a hall file for others about your lack of self-awareness. What began as good intentions on the part of someone to help you turns into communications about your bad behavior. What could have been an opportunity for change and growth that would positively impact your career becomes an opportunity cost that could be detrimental to your career.

The denial of your weaknesses contributes to the development or enhancement of your hall file, which becomes a part of your unofficial documentation and affects your opportunities and growth. When you apply for a position or assignment, in addition to the official documentation about your individual accomplishments, those considering you as a competitive candidate may also have your hall file, which speaks to your weaknesses and highlights your self-awareness issue. Now your weaknesses, which may have no impact on your ability to do what you are applying for, takes center stage and becomes a major factor in your competitive consideration.

Weaknesses that were of no consequence become consequential because they are used to support a bigger issue, your lack of self-awareness. Your weaknesses are things that if you worked on or accepted, you could be more competitive for future opportunities. However, because you deny their existence, they have become a character flaw, a lack of self-awareness. For example, your feedback indicated that you needed to strengthen your knowledge of budgeting. The documentation and firsthand experience presented by your colleagues supports unequivocally that your budget knowledge was lacking and weak.

Because of your denial of this weakness, the conversation shifted to your lack of self-awareness. In addition to still having to strengthen your budget knowledge to be competitive for certain assignments and positions, you also need to become self-aware. What started out as a workable weakness (strengthen your budget knowledge) has been compounded by your denial of its existence. This denial has enhanced your weaknesses, become detrimental to your career growth and development, and increased your unofficial documentation (hall file), which could have additional negative ramifications.

Knowing yourself creates options. Perhaps the most notable ones are that you have strengths that you can use to accomplish the task you are assigned and you have weaknesses that need to be developed or addressed to ensure your success. There is some truth to the statement that the first step in solving a problem is acknowledging that there is a problem to solve. This is equally true of opportunities.

The first step in taking advantage of an opportunity is acknowledging that an opportunity exists. Knowing yourself is your first step to solving your problems and taking advantage of your opportunities. If you want to be successful, you must know what you bring to the table, who you are, and what your strengths and weaknesses are. If you deny the existence of either your strengths or weaknesses, you position yourself to fail or have a more difficult task succeeding. Your strengths and weaknesses are easily identified and noticed by you and others. While we would prefer highlighting our strengths only, we would do ourselves a disservice to do so.

It is equally important that we identify our weaknesses. However, you must know that having weaknesses do not mean you will fail. Your weaknesses mean there are areas in this life that you do not excel at or are not the best at doing. Some people are better at some things; a few are better at others. Your strength represents the things you are better at. Your weaknesses represent things you are not as good at doing.

There is nothing wrong or unusual about having weakness. We all have weaknesses. What separates the successful person from the unsuccessful is their acknowledgement of their weaknesses. Knowing what you bring to the table (strengths and weaknesses) will allow you to function at a high performing level. Knowing your strengths allows you to leverage and position yourself to demonstrate what others perhaps cannot. Knowing your weaknesses ensures that the things that you are not the best and doing do not keep you from being successful. "To thine own self be true" (William Shakespeare).

IDENTIFY YOUR MOTIVATION

WHAT DO YOU ENJOY? / WHAT ARE YOU WILLING TO WORK FOR?

KNOWING WHO YOU ARE CANNOT BE OVERSTATED. IT is extremely important that you know your strengths and your weaknesses. However, this is only part of the story, the segment that tells you who you are now. The part that you also need to understand is what determines who you will become, your motivations. Your strengths today could be your weaknesses tomorrow, and your weaknesses today could be your strengths tomorrow.

How often have you seen people change? Basketball players whose strength was dunking become high percentage three-point shooters. Average runners become track stars. Average students become academicians, doctors, lawyers, and teachers. People who start out average can over time become exceptional. It happens, and it occurs often. People are equipped with the ability to choose and change. If you choose to have your weaknesses become your strengths, you can do it. You will have to invest your time, your energy, your resources, and yourself, but you can do it. However, to do it, you must be motivated. Your motivation is a determinant of your future self, of who you are and who you will be. To that end, you will sell yourself short if you only know yourself, your strengths, and your weaknesses. You must also know your motivations.

Understanding what motivates you is as important as knowing your strengths and weaknesses, as your motivation can defy the

135   WALKING IN THE GRAY

odds against them. When it comes to competing for opportunities, at your worst, you do not have a chance. At your best, you may not be good enough. Your motivations will allow you to go above and beyond, to push yourself past what you thought was possible, to tap into your potential talent, and to reach for the finish line. You will need to know what motivates you to get the best out of you. Your motivation is what drives you, gets you up in the morning, keeps you up at night, excites you and makes you want to do more, drives you to say yes when everyone else says no, and pushes you to go a step further when you really feel like quitting. Your motivation brings out the best in you regardless of your strengths or your weaknesses.

You will need to understand your motivations because there will be times when they are the only things that will keep you moving forward on your journey. Life happens, and when it does, much of what occurs does so beyond your control. Life is full of happenings, things that take place that you have nothing to do with, but they have a lot to do with you. When life happens, you must exercise your ability to manage what you can and not lose control of yourself when things are out of control. Paul speaks of life happening: "For, when we were come into Macedonia, our flesh had no rest, but we were troubled on every side; without were fighting, within were fears" (2 Corinthians 7:5 KJV).

Unfortunately, where Paul finds himself is where we find ourselves often. While life happening is common, not an anomaly, it occurs to everyone at different times and locations. And often when it happens, it brings new challenges and opportunities. When life happens and we must engage or deal with new things, we may not have a support base or experience to fall back on. As a result, we experience fears within and conflict and questions without.

During these times, if you do not have the proper motivation, you will be discouraged and surrender or quit. However, if you know your motivations and can tap into them, you can push through these difficult times. When you are motivated to be, become, overcome, achieve, excel, not surrender, and do what you have decided that you are going to do, you can face incredible odds and win, stay in the fight and move forward when everything around you says stop, and stand and speak up for something when others insist that you sit down and be quiet. Your motivation can tip the scale, shift the paradigm, and change the outcome.

Motivation has been defined as our reason for acting or behaving a certain way. Everything we do, we do for a reason. We may not be intimately or remotely aware of the reason, but there is a cause, which is our motivation. Knowing why you do what you do could make the difference in whether you continue to do something or not. If you can identify what motivates you, you can use this motivation when you need it. If you know why you work out, sleep in, go to work, stay home, or thank God for Friday but dread Monday, you can choose to use your motivation to proceed with business as usual or change for the better. As an example, if your motivation is money, you obviously want to make more of it and as much as you can.

To that end, you will make decisions based on how they will affect your net worth. If you have an opportunity to choose between an assignment that will give you more knowledge and experience or an assignment that will assist with your promotion, you will more than likely select the assignment that will get you promoted. While the other assignment may provide you additional knowledge and experience that could better position you for future growth, you will pass on it because you have a better opportunity, one that motivates you.

If you look a little deeper, you may discover that the reason that money motivates you is because you did not have a lot of it growing up, you had a poor upbringing, and you decided that you were never going to be broke. Knowing money is your motivator, you can now understand what drives you and can remind yourself of this when things are not going your way. Additionally, knowing your motivation, you can determine if you need to set boundaries or change your motivation because it is causing you to make poor decisions. While having money as a motivator is not a bad thing when you control it, it can become bad if it controls you. I believe this is partially what Paul had in mind when he wrote 1 Timothy 6:10: "For the love of money is a root of all kinds of evil." Money itself is not the issue, but when you love it and allow it to control you, it may cause you to make unwise decisions to secure it, for instance, stealing, doing something illegal, or breaking laws.

When you know your motivation, you understand your why. When your why becomes detrimental to what you are trying to achieve or proves counterproductive, you know it is time to check it or change it. Too much of a good thing can become a bad thing. You may have the best motivation and be highly motivated, but if it causes you to behave inconsistently with your character, your motivation must be altered.

For example, if you are motivated to become an executive, this will drive the decisions you make about your experiences, assignments, training, contacts, and network. If you become so motivated that you are willing to do anything—for example, take shortcuts, sacrifice your colleagues, take credit for things you do not deserve, or cheat your way to the C-suite—you may have to check your motivation. That is, you may have to set boundaries to ensure you do not get ahead or outside of yourself. The boundaries may include a list of things that you will do and not do to become an executive, guidelines that you will follow, steps that you will take, and a realistic timeline that will govern your expectations and behavior.

If you are motivated to become an executive, the better approach is to use this motivation to take the necessary steps to make this a reality. You may begin by doing some research on the current executives to identify what they did to become executives and what they are doing as executives. You may discover that they all have different talents and abilities. They arrived from different walks of life and are doing distinct things. You may discover that they all have the same type of qualifications, skills, backgrounds, and experiences. Whatever you discover is valuable information you can use to assist you to properly align yourself and your motivations to ensure that you are at least on track.

Please note, having accurate information on the current executives and being highly motivated will not guarantee you a promotion or a ticket to your destination. However, it can serve as a standard and help you to position yourself better to ensure that you are not off track. Even if you can accurately identify how the current executives arrived, I would caution your overuse of this information as times change.

With the passing of time, what was a requirement for advancement may not be anymore, and what was not may have become a requirement. Given the reality of change and the dynamic and diversity of executive skills, knowledge, and abilities, some people choose not to do the research. Instead they choose luck as a strategy. (Please note that luck is not a strategy.) When people use luck as their strategy and things go awry or not the way they expect, they are upset, despondent, discouraged, disappointed, and angry. And to make matters worse, they act out their dissatisfaction in ways that prove detrimental to them and their desired goals. By doing the research, you at least get an idea of what is required.

Your motivation may be properly placed when you have the proper place to place them. (That's a mouthful.) In other words, if you are motivated, but the assumptions about your aspirations are wrong, you will be doing the wrong things and getting comparable results. If you aspire to be an executive, you must commit to at least the minimum requirements to be considered viable. However, to commit to the minimum requirements, you must know what they are. To be competitive, you must be knocking the minimum requirements out the box and excelling at the requirements. To be considered for promotion to executive, you must be knocking the minimum requirements out the box, excelling at the requirements, and surpassing your competition. None of this is possible if you do not do your research. It will reveal facts, fears, fictions, fables, fabrications, and falsehoods. It will provide you with a lot of details and information that you will have to sort through, select, simplify, sell, or shape. Some of what you gather will be useful; some will be useless. Regardless of its use, it is important that you do the research, starting with available information and building upon it.

When you are gathering your data, details, and information, some of what you collect will be black-and-white facts. When the rules are written in black and white, when they are clear and undeniable, they are obvious, and the precedent has been set. It is in your best interest to acknowledge, adopt, and accept them. You may not agree with or like them, but they are facts. Fighting city hall can be hard, feckless, and a real waste of time, especially when you are fighting something that is not going to change. Believing that something does not seem right to you or should not be done does not change the reality of its existence and impact. You may not like the written requirements to be an executive, and you may not like how these requirements are being applied. Unfortunately, your likes or dislikes do not change their existence.

If the documentation states that you must serve five years in an executive assignment for you to be promoted into the executive ranks, you may not like it, but those are the written requirements. If you are serious about your desire to be an executive, you should work to fulfill the five-year requirements. I am not suggesting that you should like or agree with the requirements, but I am saying that if you plan to be an executive, you must fulfill the requisite requirements. If you really believe the requirements are wrong or need to change, work on the change while you fulfill them. This way, if nothing changes, you meet the requirements for promotion and may be given another shot to change the rules as an executive.

When things are at their worst or going in the wrong direction, this is when your motivations will prove most helpful, as they will keep you on track and not allow you to derail yourself. Someone less motivated to be an executive may make excuses or justify why they choose to go in a different direction and abandon their hopes to be an executive.

For example, an unmotivated person may say, "If I have to do all that, then it is not for me," "I am not going to be a sellout," "I will never be a suck-up," or "I do not do politics." There are any number of word options they may choose to describe, define, or defend their logic. They are not wrong. They are just not that motivated, at least not for this. This happens even when people feel they may miss their mark, when, evidenced by their failed attempts, they lack the understanding of what it takes to get what they want, and they must save face. They feel that they must explain and justify to others and themselves why being an executive is not for them.

Before this happens to you, I recommend you refocus on your motivation or identify another motivation. If you are seriously motivated to become an executive, you must understand that it is not going to go your way all the time. At times you will be floating on cloud nine; sometimes you will be looking up to see bottom. When you hit that proverbial wall, you must be prepared to bounce back, push off, get your balance, or jump. You cannot let it knock you out or take you out of the game. To that end, you must know your motivations and ensure they are strong enough to hold you up under the pressures pushing you down.

It would be a lot easier for all involved, if the regulations governing our desires, aspirations, and goals were all written in black and white and were applied consistently. This is not the case. As a result, much of the research you do to determine what is required for you to succeed in the accomplishment of your goals will prove useless. Additionally, you will identify inconsistences in the execution and application of written documentation that outlines requirements for advancement. If you are not highly motivated, your research on how to go up could prove to be your downfall. While you were looking for consistent patterns of behaviors, skills, or actions of past executives to duplicate, you discovered based on your analysis that a lot of folks who should be executives are not and some who are should not be. You discover that promotion to the executive rank is subjective, not meritorious. Instead of your research encouraging you, you are confused and discouraged. You are no longer sure if you can make it to the C-suite. You are doubting the system and yourself.

Again, this is the reason knowing and understanding your motivation is so important. Whether you are motivated to be an executive, to succeed in an organization or in life, you will have experiences that will make you wonder about your desires and question your ability to accomplish them. During these times, you will need to fall back on your motivations and gather the strength to keep moving.

Your motivations will drive you to take the next step when you wonder if it is worth it or not. Your motivations will call upon your strengths to stay in the fight and drive you to strengthen your weaknesses. David found himself against the wall but leaned on his motivation to change his situation in 1 Samuel.

> And it came to pass, when David and his men were come to Ziklag on the third day, that the Amalekites had invaded the south, and Ziklag, and smitten Ziklag, and burned it with fire; And had taken the women captives, that were therein: they slew not any, either great or small, but carried them away, and went on their way. So David and his men came to the city, and, behold, it was burned with fire; and their wives, and their sons, and their daughters, were taken captives. Then David and the people that were with him lifted their voice and wept, until they had no more power to weep. And David's two wives were taken captives, Ahinoam the Jezreelitess, and Abigail the wife of Nabal the Carmelite. And David was greatly distressed; for the people spake of stoning him, because the soul of all the people was grieved, every man for his sons and for his daughters: but David encouraged himself in the LORD his God. And David said to Abiathar the priest, Ahimelech's son, I pray thee,

bring me hither the ephod. And Abiathar brought thither the ephod to David. And David inquired at the Lord, saying, Shall I pursue after this troop? shall I overtake them? And he answered him, Pursue: for thou shalt surely overtake them, and without fail recover all. (1 Samuel 30:1–8 KJV)

In this passage, David looked beyond the experience of his situation, examined his motivation, and received a revelation. David was able to encourage himself in the Lord and take the next steps. That he was encouraged (motivated) to take actions did not change the facts that his wives had been kidnapped and possibly killed, that his men of war wanted to stone him, or that he had been discouraged to the point of wanting to give up. These were his realities, but his motivation drove him to do something others were not doing—to act, stop crying, pursue, overtake, and recover all. David's discouragement is akin to what you will experience as you walk in the gray in life, in corporate America, and in your organizations. You will face odds that seem insurmountable, challenges that seem impossible, and issues that seem unsolvable. When this happens, this is a good time to reacquaint or introduce yourself to your motivations, as they can be what get you up from your bed of do nothing, off easy street, and away from kosher corner.

You can lean on your motivation to get you going when "the road is rough, the going gets tough, and the hills are hard to climb." Your motivation will help you pick yourself up, dust yourself off, and get ready for another round. If leading the organization is your desire, your motivation will drive you to learn about the organization, the organism, the rules, regulations, policies, procedures, norms, cultures, and politics governing the day-to-day interaction of employees. Your motivation will drive you to know yourself, your strengths, and your weaknesses and to push past perceived impossibilities. Your motivation can determine your fate.

When you consider the employees of an organization, the organisms, and yourself, when you examine who you are and what you bring to the table, you can conclude that you possess two sets of abilities: skill set and will set. Your skill set consists of your qualifications, your range of skills, talents and abilities, know-how, training, educational underpinning, and experiences. Your skill set is what you bring to the table that provides you evidential competitiveness. This set of skills is generally supported, documented, and identifiable.

Your will set, however, is internal to and innate in you. It is your motivation. Your will set may be unmatched by your skill set. That is, you may have the will/motivation but not the requisite skills to do what you desire. Your will set inspires you to willingly do what is required to get the job done and to acquire the requisite skills. Your will set makes you eager to step up, take stretch assignments, learn the job on the job, take additional classes to acquire the necessary skills, work extra hours, and go the extra mile. "Whatever, wherever, whenever, however" is the mantra of the will set.

Your will set could prove more useful, productive, and valuable than your skill set. An organization would clearly prefer someone with both skill and will sets, a person with the abilities and drive to do the job. However, if given a choice of skill or will, they would have to examine the situation, as a choice of will over skill may be the right answer. If you had the choice between an individual who has the will but lacks the skill and an individual who has the skill but lacks the will, who would you choose? You probably know several people at work who have the skills required to do what they are assigned to do but lack the desire to do it. They coast along, doing just enough to get by, behaving as if they have retired, resigned, or rested on duty. You probably also know someone at work who is performing exceptionally well in a position that their dossier does not support or suggest that they are qualified to do. There is much truth in the metaphor, "You can't judge a book by its cover."

You really must read through the pages. Your motivation—what is on the inside, the internal pages of the book, or your will set—can position and place you successfully when your skill suggests and says otherwise. If you are highly motivated, you will find a way, as you subscribe to the idiom, "Where there is a will there is a way."

Life is not easy, and it is complicated by the fact that you are walking in the gray and often feeling things are not in your control. While this may be true, if you are introspective and can tap into your motivation/will set, you can shape your perspective and prospective, attitude, and future. Life happens to us all, but not all of us live life abundantly. With the proper motivation, you will take control of what you can control and accept what you cannot.

Your will set provides you with a level of active serenity that shapes your focus and fight. Like the Serenity Prayer written by Reinhold Niebuhr ("Lord grant me the serenity to accept the things I cannot change, the courage to change the things I can, and the wisdom to know the difference"), you fight with all your strength for what you desire, and you accept your losses. You live to fight another day.

When you are motivated to succeed, you will go above and beyond when the odds are against you. You will do the research, learn from your findings, and not be dissuaded. You will not keep bumping your head against the wall. Instead you will make modifications, changes, or adjustments in your attitude, altitude, actions, and thoughts to ensure that you do not continue to make the same mistakes. When you are motivated, you will not allow your methods to succeed impede your progress, as you will increase, decrease, or change them to keep yourself in the game and moving forward.

For example, if you were motivated to succeed through hard work and you discovered a different truth, you would adjust. Perhaps you were taught and believed that hard work was the key to success and that you had to work four times as hard to get half as much. Having success as your goal, you were motivated to put in the work, outwork your competition, and demonstrate your desire to succeed by your work ethics. While you are committed to working hard to succeed, after seeing others promoted who are not working four times as hard and discovering that there are other things of value at work, you will serve your goal well if you make the necessary adjustments. If you pay attention to your surroundings and the impact that others' actions are having, you will discover that while hard work demonstrated in your commitment and exceptional work ethics was warranted and rewarded, it was not enough to secure a promotion—not at all levels. You will discover that when the focus was on your productivity, working hard was a key factor in your promotion. You will notice that as you advance in the organization, the focus shifts from work ethics to people skills, your ability to get along with, influence, inspire, and affect others. That is, instead of being rewarded for your hard work, you get rewarded for getting others to work harder. With hard work as your motivation, you find yourself experiencing a diminishing return on your work investment. You will discover as you advance that working harder, even four times harder, may not get you the desired outcome because there are other elements at work. With this information, you must revisit, reset, or revise your methods. You may still be motivated to work hard, but if you want to be promoted, you need to identify the different drivers that support your promotion and adopt them as your new methods.

Being motivated is a must, and so is knowing what motivates you. Your motivation will determine whether you succeed or fail, give it your all, throw yourself into a job, or just coast. Your motivation will determine if you are working, dreading, or enjoying what you do. Marc Anthony said, I believe correctly, "If you do what you love, you'll never work a day in your life." When you are motivated to do what you do, it does not seem like work. Enjoyment is an outward expression of your inward motivation. Given the impact motivation has on you now and in the future, you must take an introspective look at yourself to determine what drives you, makes you tick, and gets you going.

Maybe you are extrinsically motivated and prefer external recognition, for instance, public recognitions, monetary and nonmonetary rewards and recognitions, pats on the back, or attaboys/girls. Maybe you are intrinsically motivated and driven by something on the inside, for instance, you want to do your best and be the best you that you can be. Maybe you are motived extrinsically and intrinsically at different times. For example, when you had no money to pay your bills, funds may have been your motivator, and you were very interested in securing more of it, getting a larger check, or getting a raise or promotion.

Now that your bills are being paid and a little money is being saved, you are satisfied with your pay and enjoy what you are doing. Whatever your motivation, it is important that you know what it is, because your motivation will affect or determine your next course of action. Again, if money is your motivation, you will make your next career decision based on the amount of money the decision will yield. Alternatively, if you are intrinsically motivated, the job itself or the idea of doing something good for someone else will be enough.

Motivations are as diverse as the people with them. The quantity and quality of your motivations are not as important as having and knowing what they are. When you have and know your motivations, you know yourself and are better able to understand and communicate what is important to you. During my career, I was surprised or, more correctly, shocked when people were not motivated to ascend as high as they could in the organization. I was frustrated when they were offered assignments that would position or provide opportunities for advancement and they refused. They were extended the offer because they had the requisite skills, knowledge, and abilities to excel in the assignment.

After some conversations, I discovered that their motivations were not the same as mine, or they had different aspirations. Therefore, even if they took the assignment with the requisite skill set, what I perceived as a great assignment opportunity may not yield the expected outcome because they lacked the motivation or will set to excel. In retrospect, kudos to them for knowing their motivations and not allowing others to set them up for what could be a failed great opportunity. They did not position themselves for promotion, but they did so with "eyes wide open." They were happy and continued to be good contributors to the organization.

Knowing your motivation is knowing yourself. It is not possible to be true to yourself, if you do not know yourself. Your passion, drive, and will set can separate you from the pack and allow you to distinguish yourself. Without motivation, you will coast along doing what's required or, worse, retire, resign, and rest on duty. With the proper motivation, you will push when others pull, stand when others sit, speak up when others are silent, say yes when others say no, or succeed when others fail. Your motivations give you the X factor. They shape your attitude to see a setback as a setup and would have you believe that with your will you can find a way. Your motivation is a critical key to your success. How motivated are you to accomplish your goal? How motivated are you to succeed despite the resistance? How motivated are you to get what you desire even if you do not have the requisite skill? What is your motivation? Why do you do what you do? If you can answer these questions, you are on your way to your destination. You may know how to get there and will not stopped.

CHAPTER 6

OWN THE OUTCOMES

WHEN YOU ACT TO GET SOMETHING YOU WANT, YOU trigger a reaction. The reaction you get from your action may or may not be what you want, but it is the result of your action. Newton's third law of motion says, "For every action there is an equal and opposite reaction." That is, when an object exerts a force on a second object, the second object simultaneously exerts a force equal in magnitude and opposite in direction on the first object. Or more clearly, whenever an object pushes another object, the other object pushes back in the opposite direction equally hard. Conceptually, every time you take an action, you will get a reaction, a response, a result, or something in return. I particularly like the way the Bible speaks on this subject in Galatians 6:7, "Whatsoever a man sows that shall he also reap."

If you sow corruption, you will reap corruption; if you sow a good seed, you will reap a good harvest. The scripture and Newton support the idea, the concept, the fact that if you put something in, you will get something out. If you invest, you will get a return on your investment. If you act, you will get a reaction. If you sow a seed, you will reap a harvest. If you do something, something will happen. Please note that I did not say something good would happen or that you would get a corresponding return.

While you might like your returns to at a minimum match your investment or your output to match your input and you might surmise that Newton's third law supports this, I must caution you that this is rarely, if ever, the case. The equation calculating your inputs to outputs and actions to results does not support the one-for-one concept. If you put in one, you may not get one out. The laws of replication, or replenishment, may have expired with the law of retaliation ("an eye for an eye" or "a tooth for a tooth), if they ever existed. What you put in is generally inconsistent with what you get out.

There will be days when you receive more for your input and days when you receive less. It is like the stock market; the value fluctuates daily. The short-term value of your stock may not be representative of your investments. It could be up or down depending on the market. Over the long term, if you invest properly, the return on your investment will increase. When examining your inputs or investments from day to day, because of the volatility and unpredictability of things affecting your goals, you will experience fluctuations and shifts, gains and losses, pluses and minuses, positives and negatives, and upturns and downturns. You should not get excited or upset since you are in it for the long haul.

Over time, things balance themselves out. You get the proper return on your investment. You, however, must ensure that your contributions, what you put in, is consistent with what you want to get out. You must be continually aware that your contributions will affect your outcome, as detailed in scripture and by Newton. While not one for one, your results are linked to your inputs, your actions. Having said that, regardless of the fluctuations, shifts, and turns, you must own your results. While you may not get what you want today and your outcomes may not match with your inputs, you must continue to work your plan, ensure that your actions reflect your desired outcomes, and then live with the results.

Regardless of the outcome, whether it is in your favor or not, you must own it and accept it for what it is, a step in the gray, a move in the right direction, or a lesson learned, as it represents a contribution to your desired outcomes. This is the reason your goals must be long term and strategic. When you are working toward something great, bigger than today, something that requires the best of yourself daily, you cannot allow yourself to get caught up in short-term occurrences, or results. For example, if your plan to be the director of your functional area is dependent on your securing an assignment as the chief of XYZ office, you must take steps to make this happen. If your plan to secure the position is foiled by someone else less qualified being selected for and assigned to the position, you must live with this and make another plan. You may have been the most qualified (having prepared yourself to fulfill your plan) for the position and had the best interview, but you were not selected. You could complain, call people out, point your fingers and blame others, pout, lash out, give up, or become bitter, or you could keep it moving, live with the consequences, become better, review and revise your plan to get to your destination, and learn from the experience.

Maybe there is another way that you have not considered. Do you really need this assignment for the position? Has every director of your functional area served as the chief of XYZ office? If so, could you be the first to do so without serving? Do you need to adjust your timeline? When you have invested yourself and done your part, the only thing left is to live with the results.

When you have a goal, a plan, an objective, or a destination, you can only do what you can to make it a reality. There are many factors, forces, and foes at work that directly affect the outcome of your input. You do not control the stimulus that affects the outcome, the situations that occur while we are trying to affect an outcome, or the story that results from our efforts to secure an outcome. However, you can respond—more specifically you are response-able (able to respond)—you are able to respond. Once you have done all you can do or what you have done, you can and do respond.

With so many things affecting the outcome, it would be easy, understandable, justifiable, and perhaps allowable to shift the blame for what happened, to disavow the results, to deny responsibility because of others' involvement. However, you must ask yourself, "What does this accomplish? Does it change anything? Does it get me any closer to my destination? Am I better off being bitter? Will the results be any different? Will I get what I want?" When you answer these questions and others you may pose, you will discover that in most cases it is best to keep it moving.

If you have done all you can do, keep it moving. Do not waste your time, energy, or resources harping or dwelling on the past or the most recent experience. Let your response typify your commitment to your course and represent your ability to not be controlled, coerced, captured, or confused by circumstances or consequences. Own the outcome. That is, acknowledge that having given it your best shot, you hit the mark or missed it. When a golfer sets up and makes a putt after reading the greens, identifying the line, determining the distance, and taking the stroke, the ball will go in the hole or stay out. If the shot is missed and the ball stays out, the golfer could respond by blaming the wind, the pace of the green, others in the flight or group, the sun, the rain, and the gallery. Alternatively, the golfer could accept the fact that he gave it his best shot, or he tried and missed for reasons within and beyond his control. He can take this experience and move on or take himself out of the game. If the golfer continues, accepting the fact that what happened happened, there is a possibility that he will hit his number. Not so, if he quits.

There is no need for you to look for someone to blame or an excuse to make. Sometimes you win; other times you lose. The Controllers were on to something when they sang the following in "Somebody's Gotta Win, Somebody's Gotta Lose,"

Somebody's gotta win
Somebody's gotta lose
Somebody's got to play the fool

Somebody's gotta laugh
Somebody's gotta cry
Somebody's got to almost die

If you accept your loss as a loss, you lose, but if you accept it as a lesson, you learn. This was Paul's experience that he shared with the Philippians.

> I have learned, in whatsoever state I am, therewith to be content. I know both how to be abased, and I know how to abound: everywhere and in all things, I am instructed both to be full and to be hungry, both to abound and to suffer need. I can do all things through Christ which strengtheneth me. (Philippians 4:11b–13 KJV)

You have a choice when life happens to be a student or to be a standout. If you choose to be a standout, your stubbornness will be your downfall, as you will insist on an explanation or an excuse if things do not go your way. For a standout, life is win or lose. If you are winning, life is good, but if you are losing, life is to blame as it happens, and it is not your fault.

However, if you choose to be a student, you are always learning. So when life happens, you know that it is teaching you something that will prove useful—good or bad, win or lose. I recommend you live life as a student, as you will be best positioned to own your outcome, whether you caused them or not, as you did what you could do.

Let us look at this a different way. Do you honestly want an equivalent return on your investment, one-for-one? Would you prefer a higher return, for example, a two-for-one? While you may consider yourself a success and perhaps satisfied if you get a 100 percent return on your investment or a percent equivalent to your expectations, this would be short-lived satisfaction if you discover you could have gotten a higher percentage or more than expected. Your desire for and satisfaction with a one-for-one reciprocity or barter is only applicable, relevant, or desired if there is not a higher return option available. You want more for your investment, not less.

Interestingly, however, you may be satisfied with doing less to get more, and you may even find cause to gloat and teach if you can generate a return higher than your investment. You may call this "doing more with less," "working smarter, not harder," "economizing," or "getting more bang for your buck." You may find accepting responsibility for positive outcomes easy and worth sharing. Conversely, you are not likely to be satisfied doing more and getting less. The problem with this approach is you set yourself up to fail in the long run over short-run results. You start to prefer the quick guide, fast returns, and shortcuts and become impatient with or intolerant of putting in the time and learning from your experiences. You want success, and you want it now at the minimum cost. When that does not happen, you refuse to own the outcome by denial, disavowal, destruction, dumping, or doubting.

If you are willing to accept more for less of your contributions, knowing this outcome was not the direct results of your inputs, why can't you accept less for more of your input, again knowing that the outcome is not the direct result of your inputs? When you make your move toward your destination, investing yourself in your outcome, you may get more or less for your contributions. Having done your part, the only thing remaining for you is your response to the outcome. If you understand and accept that your desired outcomes will be inconsistent with your input, that it could be less than or more than your contributions, you can control your response or, more correctly, be response-able. If you understand and accept that what you do will last, that what you do contributes to your outcome, whether it appears to or not, you can control your response.

You must understand that you are responsible for your contributions to your desired outcomes, not the outcomes. As we have noted, because of the number of things affecting your outcomes, you cannot control them. You can only control your contributions, your reaction. To that end, you must ensure that what you are doing is contributing to or working toward your desired outcomes.

It is worth emphasizing that you should focus your energies on your input and response to the outcome. Too many people have lost their footing, gotten off track, derailed, lost it, given up, or thrown in the towel because round one did not turn out the way they expected. Their short-term expectation ruined their long-term goals and gains. They felt cheated, disadvantaged, overlooked, underrated, and undervalued because their outcomes did not match their contributions. So instead of waiting until next time, until their turn, until the tides turned in their favor, or until their outcome exceeded their contributions, they became frustrated, upset, disappointed, unhappy, angry, or disengaged and opted to act out negatively or walk out.

Before this becomes your story, please note that Isaac Newton was right, "what goes up must come down." Seasons change, life is a cycle, you will get your fifteen minutes of fame, day follows night as sure as night follows day, and you will have some ups and some downs. If you can accept the reality that life is not fair but equitable, that "God causes His sun to rise on the evil and the good, and sends rain on the righteous and the unrighteous" (Matthews 5:45b NIV), that you are a composite of flesh and spirit, good and bad, that "there is a time for everything and a season for every activity under the heavens" (Ecclesiastes 3:1 NIV), and that sometimes you will get more for you input and sometimes you will get less, you are positioned for the proper response to your outcomes. You must be in the business of investing—investing your time, energy, and resources. Investing has inherent risk, but they must be ones you are willing to assume. You must work toward your goal and contribute on the assumption that "if not now, my time will come."

If you really want something, you must be willing to commit, invest, and surrender yourself to work to get it. For example, if you want to write a book, you must put yourself in position in front of a computer/typewriter/notepad and begin writing/transcribing/

telling your story. You must make the investments necessary to make the book a reality. The book will not write itself. However, there will be days when your productivity will be high and days when it will be low. You must not surrender until the book is written.

While there are no guarantees that the completed product will be what you expect, your output will match your input. You can be sure that if you put nothing in, you will get nothing out. Your efforts, input, and contributions matter. Therefore, you must ensure that the actions that you are taking are moving you in the right direction. The same is true if you want to be an executive in an organization. You must get moving and begin to do those things that will position and secure your desired outcomes. Once you have done your part, given it your best shot, and done all that you can do, then you can or should live with the outcomes.

Please again note that you are not responsible for the outcome, but you are accountable for your response to them. When you give it your all, that is all you can do. The thing you must not look to control are the things out of your control. When things out of your control change or affect your outcomes, you must be willing to live with them, knowing you did your part and understanding that when you take an action, you may not be able to generate the outcome you desire in the time you desired and waste valuable time bemoaning, distressing, or crying over the outcome.

If you do not like the results, change them. Looking at where you are and complaining or wining about how you got there will not change your location. Move! You should begin to expect, anticipate, and appreciate things outside of your control, affecting your actions and inputs. When you do this, you will understand that what you expect to happen overnight may not, but you will work to make it happen and live with the results.

Sometimes our view of life is not life's view. Expectations are often unrealistic or realistic but out of your control. You must trust that when you are contributing to your desired outcome, it will ultimately come. In the meantime, you should live with the results as they come. Solomon said it best, "Sow your seed in the morning, and at evening let not your hands be idle, for you do not know which will succeed, whether this or that, or whether both will do equally well" (Ecclesiastes 11:6 NIV).

Solomon urges the people to be constant and be diligent in their efforts and prudent in their investments because the outcome was out of their control, in God's sovereign control. You would do well to heed Solomon's urging. Your input may determine your output, but your output should not determine your input. You must be constant, consistent, driven, and dedicated to actions and efforts that will yield your desired outcome. Then you live with and accept the results. By accepting the outcomes as they happen, you alleviate your frustration. You decrease your inclination to believe that you have been disadvantaged because you did not get what you wanted or expected today, and you reduce your stress because you will live with whatever comes or outcome. Having done your part, you can accept the outcomes that you desire in the long run will ultimately yield themselves or greater goods will yield themselves in their places.

Accepting your outcome is a critical key to you moving forward and should be done whether you get what you deserve or not and whether you did what you were supposed to do or not. While one could understand why people putting in work could be upset if they did not get the requisite return, this behavior is not expected of someone who is not carrying their load, slacking, or doing only the necessary.

If you are not doing your part to make your reality real, you should not expect success. Quite frankly, it should be easy for you to accept whatever outcome comes. You should not be frustrated or upset by what happens, but you should accept the fact that you may not get what you desire because you did not put in the work. Getting something for nothing may be desired, but it should not be a goal, an expectation, or a wish, as it should not happen.

Frederick Douglass, father of African American history, was right on this topic when he said, "If there is no struggle, there is no progress. Those who profess to favor freedom and yet deprecate agitation are men who want crops without plowing the ground. They want rain without thunder and lightning. They want the ocean without the roar of its mighty waters ... Men may not get all they pay for in this world, but they must certainly pay for all they get."

Let's face it. Nothing in life is free. Everything will cost you something. There ain't no such thing as a free lunch. If you want something, you must give something. If you put nothing in, you should expect to get nothing out. Conversely, if you put something in, you can expect to get something out. This is analogous to putting money in the bank. If you put money in the bank, you can withdraw money from the bank. If you put nothing in, you should not expect to get anything out. Besides, the only thing collecting something for nothing is the cemetery.

Life of abundance or prosperity is based on the ideology of giving and receiving, sowing and reaping (harvest). The scripture says it best, "Give, and it shall be given unto you; good measure, pressed down, and shaken together, and running over, shall men give into your bosom. For with the same measure that ye mete withal it shall be measured to you again" (Luke 6:38 KJV).

If you want a return on your investment, you must invest. Outcomes depend on input. To that end, if you want a desired outcome, you must ensure that you input for results. While your desired outcomes are not guaranteed, you will be satisfied with them if you gave it your best shot. That is, you can get comfortable with the results when you give your best. Only when you have done the best that you could will you be able to live comfortably with the outcomes.

If you have watched sports, you have seen the impact a loss takes on a team that did their best. You may have noticed that while they were dissatisfied, they were not disappointed in themselves. Instead they seemed resolved that they had given it their best shot. They left it all on the field, the court, or in the ring. They showed a commitment to continue to work, to go back to the proverbial drawing board, to get better, and to come back next time to secure a different result. Their resolve seemed to stem from them having given their best.

You have undoubtedly heard many times and in many ways, "When you have done your best, you have done all that you can do." Your input, efforts, and actions should reflect the best that you have to offer or contribute. Once you have given your all, you should and can live with the outcome. Do not get distracted or lose focus expecting an equal return on your investment. Doing your best is your responsibility; accepting and responding to the outcome is your responsibility. You are not responsible for the outcome.

Far too many things beyond your control contribute to making this happen. Please know that when you have done your best, you have done all that you can do. Now you should resolve that there is nothing else that you can do; therefore, you will live with the outcome. The issue is, if you have done your best and you do not accept the outcome, you are left making excuses for yourself or blaming others.

No More Excuses (Can You Handle the Truth?)

Excuses, excuses, excuses! An excuse is an attempt to lessen the blame attached to a fault, a failure, or an offense. It is an attempt to defend or justify your action or inaction. Since excuses are not under the microscope of truth or the burden of proof, they are like documents on the internet. They are many and must be true, right? Unfortunately, because excuses are designed to exempt or release one from an action or to justify unwanted results from one's action or inaction, they work against the very thing that is needed to get better, improve, grow. Benjamin Franklin said correctly, "He that is good at making excuses is seldom good at anything else."

Excuses not only justify inaction, they prevent action. Why work on something you have an excuse for? Herein lies the challenge. When you have a desire to succeed, not everything is going to go your way. Nor will you receive a one-for-one exchange on your investments of time, effort, and resources. You will experience setback, setups, and upsets. The outcomes from your actions will not always match your inputs. You will often give more and get less. You will be faced continually with the options to execute an action or offer an excuse. It is easier to offer an excuse than it is to accept responsibility for something that did not go the way you planned.

Sometimes when I play golf, I joke with the members of my flight about the excuses I have available in the event my game does not show up or goes awry. Although I work on improving my game, having an appreciation for the complexity of golfing consistently on different days, on dissimilar courses, and in varying weather conditions, I know the challenge and difficulty of getting the desired results. Therefore, I know a joke about excuses for one's golf game is relatable, common among golfers, and relevant. I tell the joke about my available excuses knowing I have no real excuses available to offer. I fully trust that the work I put in on my game will pay off and know that even if my game is off, I will continue to take one shot at a time and try to improve.

The reality is, if I were serious about my excuses, my attitude toward the game, my actions during and after the game, and others in my flight will be affected. With the use of excuses at my fingertips, I have no need to be concerned about how I play the game, no motivation or drive to improve between shots or after playing, and no concerns about how I am influencing others. Excuses excuse my attitude and my actions.

If you are the type of person who has an excuse handy, you will never be the best you can be, do all you can do, or succeed at your goal. Your excuses exempt you from your response-ability, actions, and expectations. Excuses will destroy your drive, minimize your motivation, diminish your destination, and dash your dreams. If there is something that you can always leave home without, it is your excuses. You have no need for them, and they are of no benefit to you. So do yourself a favor and get rid of excuses and make no more of them.

All that you can do is the best that you can. Once you have done that, even if you fall short of the desired outcome, you did your best, no excuses required. Additionally, if you have done only a portion of what you were capable of doing or could do and you did so knowingly, it is done. The past is past, with no excuses required. There is no going back to change the past. However, there is the option to change the future, if you learn from the past. If you decide instead to make excuses, you take the option of changing the future off the table. Your excuses prevent you from seeing a need for change and provides an explanation for the way things are. There is no need to change anything. Excuses work counter to your desire when you want to be successful. So stop trying to find or give excuses for your successes or failures because they are too easy to come by.

We all know people who are gifted and talented but are not living up to their potential, those who have settled for less than the best of themselves, thrown in the towel without fighting their best fight, settled for good enough, allowed a mistake in their past to define who they are today, and make excuses instead of taking action. These individuals say they are in the condition they are in or are where they are because of their birth, birthplace, parents, neighborhood, school, church, community, family, friends, jobs, positions, opportunities, or lack thereof. They blame their current condition on the rain, sunshine, moonlight, good times, or the boogeyman. They find an excuse instead of an action, something to blame instead of something to do, a reason to explain or justify their condition instead of identifying a way forward. Excuses give them an out, a pass, an exemption, or a reason for being in the state they are in. However, it does not give the power, authority, motivation, desire, will, or way to change their current condition or situation. Quite the contrary, it gives them the okay to stay where they are because they have an excuse to be there.

If you have no plans for progress or success, identify and collect as many excuses as you deem necessary and use them liberally. If, however, you have plans for a better future, a brighter tomorrow, progress, or success, you must dispense with the excuses. Get rid of them. They will hold you back, keep you down, and prevent you from progressing. Accept and live with the outcomes resulting from your actions and the actions of others who affect you. You could say that so-and-so happened to you because you were not part of the in crowd, you had a certain skin color, you did not grow up with a silver spoon in your mouth, you were not raised on the other side of the track, you did not have the connections, you did not go to an Ivy League school, you were not a good student, or you do not play politics. You could say tou tried, but it did not work.

You could offer these and a thousand other excuses for why you are not doing something or not taking an action that you are equipped to take, but what do they accomplish? Maybe the excuses make you feel or look better in the eyes of your onlookers. Perhaps the excuses are a true justification for you being where you are. Again, what do they accomplish? They do not position you any closer to your goal, inspire you to action, or incite you to do your best. Instead your excuses excuse you.

Excuses are not entirely bad, as the fact that you are offering one suggests that you know that there is something that should be, or should have been, done differently. So instead of offering an excuse, focus your attention on the reason for the excuse. Are you offering an excuse because you feel you failed, you did not accomplish something, you were not equipped to do something, you believe the ball was dropped, you have to save face, or you must avoid being embarrassed?

Rather than making an excuse, you should plan and take an action, one that will reverse, revise, revert, redo, or replace the excuse. Your excuses make it clear that there is something else that you expected, a different outcome. Do not waste your time or energy crafting the reason or justification for why the outcome is the way it is, given that it is not what you desire. Focus on changing the outcome. Follow the Nike slogan, "Just do it." And if that does not work, add again to the Nike slogan and "Just do it again." Everyone comes up short, falls short, or misses the mark every now and then.

In addition to us being human who are prone to making mistakes, there are days and times when we just do not feel like giving our best. Sometimes we give our best, and it is just not enough. What separates individuals settling for good and those desiring to be great is how they view the input and handle the outcome. Those settling for good put in the time and the work and expect a corresponding return on their investment. Those settling for good are concerned about the outcome, so much so that they react to it, are affected by it, and will offer an excuse if it does not go the way they expect or plan. Those desiring to be great are concerned about their input and will accept whatever comes from it, no excuses allowed. If the outcome is not what they expect or anticipate, they will review and revise their plan if necessary and continue to work without excuses to affect the outcome, learning as they take actions.

Let's be honest. Most of us grew up making excuses to cover our childhood and childish behavior, teenage nonsense, and youthful indiscretions. We developed the habit of making excuses for our actions and inaction as a means of survival. Instead of owning up to our mistakes, taking the punishment for what we did wrong or confessing our faults, we determined that excuses were the better option. It was easier to talk our way out of something by offering an excuse than to work our way out or take the punishment. Unfortunately for us, this worked more times than not. So instead of dispensing with the behavior, we enhanced, improved, and in some ways perfected it. Now we are masters at the art of excuse making.

Do you remember a time when you made an excuse for something, for example, not doing homework, making a poor grade, getting caught doing something you should not be doing, lying, cheating, or stealing? If the excuse you provided worked, do you remember how motivated you were to change your behavior? I suspect you, like me, were not motivated at all, figuring the excuse worked. Why mess up a good thing? "If it ain't broke, don't fix it." If the excuse worked, why work on the thing that caused the excuse? If someone is called on the carpet for making a low grade in a subject that was difficult for them, if they offered a good-enough excuse, for instance, "I studied, but this subject is just not my strong suit," and the person calling them accepted the excuse, what do you think will happen next? Do you think the person's grade will improve? Given that the excuse is accepted and the person offering the excuse believed it was good enough to offer it, I would not expect the grade to improve. Instead I think the standards expected of the student would be lowered, and they will either meet it or come up with another excuse. That is, if the person were reprimanded for making a C when an A was expected, the excuse offered and accepted lowers the grade expected now and going forward to a C. The person does not have to change, work any harder, or do anything different. A C is understandable, justified, allowable, and acceptable. Is the person able to make an A through hard work, tutoring, and dedication? Was the C the best the person could do? Was it the skill or the will that caused the C? Was the subject, the difficulty, or the act of studying the real cause for the low grade? I suppose we will never know, as the excuse offered was accepted.

When you put in minimal, limited, or controlled effort, do something wrong, or do not get the expected outcome from your input, offering an excuse is not your best option, as it does not change anything, get the job done, motivate you to work to create a different outcome, and ensure that you leverage your skill sets, will sets, or potential. When you make an excuse for something, that something still must be addressed. An action still must be taken. The fact that you have an excuse for why it did not get done still does not contribute to the action of getting it done. Instead excuses give you the right to not take an action. Excuses give you a pass and say, "It's okay the way it is. You do not have to do anything. It is not your fault. You do not have to worry about it because you have a reason for not getting it done. Take it easy. Don't sweat the little stuff. You do not have to do what you are required to do. Just explain (offer an excuse) why you did not do it. You will be fine."

Excuses do not contribute to you being a better or the best you. They support you being the lesser you. This becomes problematic if you aspire to be successful, to lead or move up in an organization or in life, as you will have to compete with others and be the best that you can be. If you aspire to be successful, lesser of you is not a viable option. Your success demands that you strive to be the best you that you can be, that you work out and not rust out, that you put your best foot forward, or that you exhaust every option before raising the flag or throwing in the towel. Your success is as dependent on your response to negatives, for instance, controversy, challenges, struggles, and setbacks, as it is on your response to positives. Excuses are generally a response to a negative, unwanted, undesired, unexpected, unplanned outcome. When things did not go your way, the easiest way out is to offer an excuse. While you get out of a required action or a responsibility, you still do not get the desired outcome.

As life happens and things do not go your way, there are always excuses to shift the focus and the blame, to justify your actions or inaction, to explain or deny what happened, to make you feel better about not accomplishing something, or not doing what you were supposed to do and capable of doing. There are always excuses that will justify to others why you did not accomplish something, even things that you were clearly able to accomplish. A problem with excuses is that they are impartial to your knowledge, skills, and abilities. That you can do something does not preclude you from offering an excuse. In fact, more times than not, excuses are offered when the ability to secure the desired outcome is within your reach. For whatever reason, you did not reach your goal, but instead of looking at what you could learn or do differently to reach your goal, you chose to offer an excuse. Excuses create approval for inaction where ability exist. They make it okay to stop when you have a green light to go.

People make excuses when they can do what is required of them and when it is in their control to change what happened. Given that excuses do not change anything, make you better, or position you for a brighter outcome, you must make up your mind that you will not make any more excuses. You should make it your goal to live with the consequences of your actions or inactions, to not give up when you did not accomplish something but look for the lesson you can learn from the experience, to accept your faults and your flaws but never give in or give up to failure, or to commit to your success with no excuses.

Life is built to build us, not to break us. We grow with pain (growing pains). We progress through struggle. We get a testimony from our test, a message from our mess, and a story from our stumbles. Failure is not the mistake we make trying to do something. Failure is not trying at all. The mistakes you make are your building blocks for your future, your lessons for the day, and your memories to not repeat. They are not failures. If you are doing something productive, if you are trying to succeed, you will make some mistakes. Accept that and keep it moving. Mistakes indicate that you are doing something. People who are not making mistakes are not doing anything or doing exactly what they are told. Neither is good. Learn from your mistakes.

If you accept your mistakes and learn from them, you can take that lesson forward to your next effort or initiative and be better because of it. Wilber and Orville Wright did not invent, build, or fly the first successful airplane on their first try. Thomas Edison did not create the light bulb on his first attempt. The automobile was not invented on the first attempt. When something is done that is valuable, impactful, useful, or worthwhile, there is a great possibility that it will be accomplished after several attempts, tries, upgrades, modifications, mistakes, or changes. It will not be accomplished on the first try.

The significance of your accomplishment is highlighted by the fact that it was not abandoned after a mistake. It was important enough to continue after several tries, mistakes, and improvements. You can learn from your experiences. Life happens, and you learn. Good or bad, ugly or pretty, whatever happens in life teaches you something that you can use in the next phase of life. So instead of sitting down and making excuses for what you did not accomplish or what did not happen, you should keep it moving and look for the lessons your experiences are trying to teach you. There is always a takeaway when something goes wrong or the expected does not happen. At times, however, the takeaway is not so obvious.

No more excuses. Accept the truth for what it is, the truth. "And ye shall know the truth, and the truth shall make you free" (John 8:32 KJV). The truth, not excuses, will free you to be yourself, to make mistakes, to learn, and to be the best you that you can be. The truth allows you to not know some things and say, "I don't know," not be good at some things and say, "I will try, but I have a lot to learn."

The truth is that some things come very easy and we can succeed without much effort; other things require our undivided attention, focus, and dedication. Why cover up the ease or effort with an excuse that will only create more problems? It is not how you look or are perceived when you take on an initiative. It is about who you are, what you do, and how you do what you do. Are you a hard worker, dedicated, and determined, willing to make a mistake and learn from it, or do you give up at the first sight of conflict or challenge? Are you so satisfied with yourself that you see no need to improve, make changes, or grow? Are you content with where you are but always looking to get better?

When you offer excuses, it suggests that you are good with where you are. When you acknowledge that an excuse could be offered but you refuse to offer one, you acknowledge that you could, should, and will do better. You are not alone. We can all do better. No matter how good we are or how well we performed, there is room for improvement. There is a quote that I learned when I was very young by St. Jerome that said, "Good, better, best. Never let it rest. 'Till your good is better and your better is best."

No matter how good you are, you can be better. You must strive to be your best. Please understand that your best may not be the best, but it is your best. In a competitive environment, there will always be someone better or learning from the best to become the best. Some will say that Muhammad Ali and Mike Tyson were the best boxers, Jack Nicklaus and Tiger Woods were the best golfers, and Michael Jordan and Magic Johnson were the best basketball players. Please note that I said "were" because there are better boxers, golfers, and basketball players today or on the way that have studied and learned from the best. One important point to note is that the latest best did not just learn from their predecessor's successes. They also learned from their failures.

You cannot afford to settle for less than the best of yourself. There is a book titled *Good Is the Enemy of Great*. The title alone speaks truth to power and volumes. Your good can prevent you from being great. How many times have you accepted your good as good enough, your stopping place? You have the potential and possibilities to be and do so much more, but you settle because you are good. If you are not careful, your being good will drain you of your dream, hijack your hopes, destroy your desires, and excuse your action.

Good is not bad, but it is not great. When your good enough causes you to believe that being good is enough, it becomes your excuse. After all, nobody is complaining about what you do, right? Please know that the lack of complaints does not mean perfection. It could mean that you are not doing anything or enough or have settled for the lesser of yourself.

There is a line in the movie *A Few Good Men* where Tom Cruise (Lt. Daniel Keffe) says, "I want the truth!" Jack Nicholson (Col. Nathan R. Jessep) responds, "You can't handle the truth!" The truth with its benefits and power often comes with its own burdens. The burden of a reality you are not willing to face, an outcome you did not want, a secret that heretofore was well kept, an ideal that has been shattered, or others knowing that you are not as gifted as you want them to believe. It's the burden of you being and accepting who you are.

It takes courage to accept and face the truth. There are two reasons I want to encourage you to accept and face the truth: you cannot hide from it, and it will help you. First, William Cullen Brant was right, "Truth crushed to the earth shall rise again." There is no getting away from the truth; it will catch up with or find you. While you may offer excuses, they never leave. You may manage to cover it up for a while, but it is coming up again.

Scripture supports this. "No man, when he hath lighted a candle, covereth it with a vessel, or putteth it under a bed; but setteth it on a candlestick, that they which enter in may see the light. For nothing is secret, that shall not be made manifest; neither anything hid, that shall not be known and come abroad" (Luke 8:16–17 KJV).

So instead of trying to cover up or hide the truth, face the music, deal with what you are trying to avoid, and do not make excuses. Excuses serve you no good purpose. Second, the truth about yourself will help you be who you are. While I agree with Abraham Lincoln's quote, "You can fool all the people some of the time, and some of the people all the time, but you cannot fool all the people all the time," I would add that you should not fool yourself anytime. Trying to be someone else guarantees you second place, while being yourself guarantees you first. The truth about you, "warts and all," can help you grow, improve, get better, and become the best you that you can be.

You have all that you need right now to get to where you want to go. If you continue your journey without making excuses, you will gather up anything else you need as you travel to get to your destination. You do not need to pretend to be someone else, make excuses for yourself, or cover up the truth. Just keep moving. Each step takes you closer to your destination. No excuse required. You do not have to make excuses for where you are, what you are doing, or how things are going or turned out. Just proceed. Create a plan and work it. Instead of making excuses for your lot in life, plot a course for your future state. Instead of looking back and trying to find reasons, causes, justifications, and excuses for where you are, look ahead to a brighter tomorrow. Instead of complaining about being here, start walking and working on being there (somewhere other than here or where you want to be).

For every complaint you have, you overlook a gift you were given. There may be some truth to the fact that you were not given the same opportunities as everyone else, but have you stopped to think that maybe you do not need the same opportunities because you have been given a different task and separate talents?

Life is our training ground, and each of us has been given everything we need to succeed. If you make excuses, you justify your inaction or give in to your challenges. Instead of getting better, you get bitter because you know you are better than this. You are equipped and responsible for your input, but you are only responsible for your response to the outcome. At your best, you may not be better than the competition, but you do not need to be. That is not your calling. Know your skill, knowledge, and abilities as well as your strengths, weaknesses, and motivations. Put your best foot forward, live with the outcome, and make no excuses. Be true to yourself and know that there are many ways to get to where you want to be, but all require that you make no excuses, accept the truth, and continue to move from where you are to where you need or want to be. No excuses. That is the truth. Can you handle it?

Blame Is Not an Option (To Thine Own Self Be True)

Blame is assigning responsibility for a fault or a wrong. While we generally look at the product of blame—the fault or the wrong as the negative—I submit that the process of blame, the assignment, is equally negative and should not be done. Success demands ownership, not blame. It is in your best interest to accept responsibility for your actions and whatever outcome and avoid the desire, will, intent, or interest to blame anyone or anything.

While blame superficially appears to remove you from the responsibility, it does not solve the issues you are blaming someone or something else for. So you must question blame's utility or futility, benefit, or loss. Yes, you are correct. If something does not get done, someone or something is responsible, but what good does it do to place blame? I recall a story, a joke, or some advice I was given about blame.

> It was a little story about four people named Everybody, Somebody, Anybody, and Nobody. There was an important job to be done, and Everybody was sure that Somebody would do it. Anybody could have done it, but Nobody did it. Somebody got angry about that because it was Everybody's job. Everybody thought that Anybody could do it, but Nobody realized Everybody wouldn't do it. It ended up that Everybody blamed Somebody when Nobody did what Anybody could have done.

Everybody, Anybody, or Somebody could have done this important job, but Nobody did. Who was responsible? Who dropped the ball? Who did not do their job? Was it you? Are you being asked? Are you Somebody, Anybody, Everybody, or Nobody? Does it matter? Isn't it more important to know your next step than who to blame for your misstep, miscalculation, mistake, or slipup?

Even with someone to blame, the job still needs to get done. Blame does not do it. Even if you blame yourself, it does not change the outcome. The outcome has already come out. Your next move should be to focus on what has come out and determine your next steps to accept it, advance it, change it, or get rid of it. You are responsible for what you are responsible for, your input and your response to the outcome. You are responsible for your input while you are putting in work and your response after the work is done. You can change your input while you are putting in work and your outcome after it comes out. When the outcome comes out, you cannot change what has been put in, as that has been done. It is past, over, finished. If you do not like the outcome, change it, but don't waste your time making excuses or blaming yourself or others for what has already happened. Own what belongs to you.

You may manage, supervise, lead, or guide others, but you cannot control their behaviors or actions. You may want the best out of others, for them to perform at the highest level possible, but you cannot make this a reality, as you cannot control their behaviors or actions. You can influence and encourage them to give and do their best, but you do not control their behaviors or actions. Truth is, you would do well to control your own behaviors or actions. Some days you feel like it, and other days you do not. Your behaviors and actions reflect the same. Focus your energies on you, your input, and your response to the outcome. Own your outcomes, whether they result directly from your actions or indirectly from the actions of others. If you were negligent or lazy, procrastinated, made a mistake or an error, led someone wrong, or did something that had a negative impact on your outcomes, own it. Do not look for someone or something to blame. That will "b lame." Accept what has come out. Be responsible for your input, and take your next step.

It is easier not to place blame when or if you are totally responsible for the outcome. To place blame when you are to blame only exposes you, opens you to criticism, and makes you vulnerable to attacks. So why do it, right? I agree but recommend you go even further and not place blame even when someone else in the chain of actions is responsible. If your outcome is affected by other's input and they drop the ball, blame seems the correct and logical response or next step. I would agree with you if the goal you sought were to identify someone to blame for an action that was not taken. However, if your goal were to deliver an action that was missed and now you are looking for someone to blame, I disagree with the blaming option. Blame will not get the action done or even assist with your efforts. Now that the outcome has come out and you know it does not match what was desired, you do not need to look back to point fingers and place blame but identify a way forward.

I want to be clear when talking about my views on looking back, as I am not saying or suggesting it should not be done. I am saying that it should be done, but with the goal to live and learn, not to offer excuses or to place blame. Your past is a great teacher. It tells you what has been done, how it was done, or if it worked or not. If you accept its lessons and use them to pass future tests, you will do well. However, if your focus on the past is to complain about failures or blame someone for something not getting done, I recommend you forget it. When you focus on the past with the aim to analyze, criticize, or dramatize it, you lose sight of or miss out on the opportunities the present and the future affords you. I believe this was the mind of God when speaking through Isaiah. "Forget the former things; do not dwell on the past. See, I am doing a new thing! Now it springs up; do you not perceive it? I am making a way in the desert and streams in the wasteland" (Isaiah 43:18–19 NIV).

If you focus backward, you will miss forward opportunities, fresh and new things. If you are crying over spilled milk, making excuses, and blaming the past, you are missing out on new opportunities and next steps. Therefore, I posit the past actions, inputs, and experiences are lessons for a brighter future. The past can direct you away from trouble, guide you around the wall you keep bumping into, and teach you that water is wet and you can drown in it, that fire is hot and will burn you, and that friends are there through thick and thin but enemies will thin out when it gets thick. The past is a great teacher but a poor student.

Therefore, when you are learning from the past, you are in the best possible position and doing the right thing. However, if you are trying to make the past a student by attempting to change what has already been done with the additions of excuses or blaming others, you are wasting your time. The story of the past has already been told by the past. It is His-Story. You should use your energy taking lessons from His-Story to write your story.

To write your story, you cannot afford to blame others or yourself, for that matter. What has been done has already been done. If something that you are responsible for did not go the way you expected or planned, even if someone else were responsible, blaming them is not the best option. You should examine what happened and identify a way forward to ensure that it does not happen again. For example, if, after examination, you determine that the action that caused the unexpected outcome was the result of someone else's inaction in the sequence, instead of blaming them, you should determine what should have happened to ensure that it happens next time.

Instead of waiting until the deadline to determine something has gone wrong, you should include an additional step in the process that requires you to check the status of others' actions to ensure they have what they need and are on track with their delivery. While this will neither change the past nor the outcome, it will shape the future to ensure a better or desired outcome. Blaming someone will not change anything. Quite the contrary, it might make things worse and create tension, distrust, and disfavor with colleagues you depend on to deliver a product.

Blaming someone else for an action that you are responsible for is not new, and it continues to have no impact on desired outcomes. Blaming goes back to the beginning of time. You may recall the story of Adam and Eve and the serpent and how they blamed someone/something else for their actions. It all started when God commanded Adam not to eat of the tree of the knowledge of good and evil (Genesis 2:16 KJV). Seeing his loneliness, God added a woman, Eve, to Adam's team.

One day while going through the garden, the serpent persuaded Eve to eat of the tree God had commanded Adam not to eat of. Now exposed, when God called to them, they hid themselves.

(It is interesting that by hiding themselves, they exposed their misdoings.) When God asked them about how they knew they were naked, the blame game began.

> And they heard the voice of the LORD God walking in the garden in the cool of the day: and Adam and his wife hid themselves from the presence of the LORD God amongst the trees of the garden. And the LORD God called unto Adam, and said unto him, Where art thou? And he said, I heard thy voice in the garden, and I was afraid, because I was naked; and I hid myself. And he said, Who told thee that thou wast naked? Hast thou eaten of the tree, whereof I commanded thee that thou shouldest not eat? And the man said, The woman whom thou gavest to be with me, she gave me of the tree, and I did eat. And the LORD God said unto the woman, What is this that thou hast done? And the woman said, The serpent beguiled me, and I did eat. (Genesis 3:8–13 KJV)

Each person involved chose to blame someone or something else. Adam started the conversation blaming God; Eve blamed the serpent. One could argue that Adam was right, Eve was right, or each had a reason to blame someone or something else. It is important to know that the issue is not the ability to blame, but the response-ability not to blame. Scripture support that they were each told about God's command not to eat of the "tree of the knowledge of good and evil." God told Adam, Adam told Eve, and Eve told the serpent.

However, after falling short of God's command, instead of owning their fault, they chose to blame someone or something else. The blame, however justified, reasoned, right, or true, did not change the fact that God's command had been disobeyed. The "tree of the knowledge of good and evil" had been eaten of.

When you are given something to do—a task, an assignment, a project, or a command—it is incumbent on you to see it through. Even if you are distracted, misled, or given new directions inconsistent with the written directions given to you by someone in a position to do so either by influence or authority, you are still responsible. Blaming someone else for what did not get done or done correctly, like an excuse, does not get you any closer to your desired destination. Blame shifts the focus and the conversation from you or the issue or problem, but it falls short of getting the job done.

Think about it. If you were assigned to write a paper and something happens to prevent you from accomplishing this, for instance, you or a family member gets sick, an animal dies, or someone else demands and draws your attention, blaming someone or something does not change the desired outcome. The paper is still due. You would be correct when citing the reason why you did not accomplish the task you were assigned. You may even be right when blaming someone else, but it doesn't change the fact that the paper is not done.

In the garden, Adam and Eve ate of the forbidden tree. Each disobeyed God's command. Regardless of why they did, they did it. They disobeyed. Any explanation offered to soften, explain, justify, or detail what has happened will not change what has happened. When you have been given responsibility for something, if it does not get done, the reason does not matter because it does not change what has not happened. The reason is useful only if you use it to assist with future decisions or to inform your next steps and actions. If you are aspiring to be successful in life, stop pointing fingers, and drop the blame game. Blaming does not change anything.

When blame is an option, it can easily become your mode of operation. You can always find something or someone to blame for anything. For example, you could start with the fact that you are less talented than someone. We all have different gifts, talents, and abilities. No matter how gifted and talented you are, there is always someone more gifted and talented. You may be able to do the job and do it well, but there is always someone who can do it better.

If blame is an option, your inaction could be attributed to their action. You would have done it, but you know they would do it because they are more talented and could do a much better job. This is b-lame (blatantly lame), but if you make blame an option, it could get worse.

You must be true to yourself. If there is something that you have been assigned to do, a project that you want to accomplish, and there are reasons for you not accomplishing it, there is no need to blame someone else, yourself, or something. Blame, like excuses, does not get you any closer to your destination and provides you justification for just getting by. Blame points the finger at the problem and may explain the issue but does not aid in solving it. It gives you a way out of the outcomes but does not change or impact the outcome. If you are seeking a way out, perhaps blame is an option. However, if you are seeking a way in and up in the organization and in life, blaming does you no good. Even when you have a reason and blame is just speaking the truth about what happened, it does not change the outcome or history.

For example, you may be correct in noting and highlighting the fact that you were not given the same opportunities as your colleagues, that the manager or supervisor preferred your colleagues over you, or that you were disadvantaged because of favoritism, skin color, the texture of your hair, or the way you walk or talk, but blaming will not change this reality. Blame is not about the solution. It is about shifting the responsibility, reassigning your response-ability. Instead of shifting the focus, assigning fault, or reassigning response-ability, it would be better to identify what needs to be done and "just do it." Calling out others' mistakes may make you look and feel better, but it will not change what has happened, and it will not exempt you from your responsibility. Paul wrote a caution to this type of thinking. "And thinkest thou this, O man, that judgest them which do such things, and doest the same, that thou shalt escape the judgment of God?" (Romans 2:3 KJV).

In this passage, Paul makes it clear that highlighting someone else's faults does not exempt you from your fault. If you blame someone for your inaction, it does not change the fact that you are inactive. You may shift the focus from you to the other person or from the task at hand to an error made and who made it, but this will not change the outcome. Placing blame may have an emotional impact on individuals involved, but it will not change what has happened. Please note that the emotional impact may be twofold: positive if you are placing the blame and negative if you are being blamed. The negative impact resulting from placing blame may cost more than the benefits derived from you feeling better.

Blaming someone or something else is not a viable option. Take it off the table. Put it out of your mind. Remove it from the mix. Just do not do it. If the outcome has come out and it is out of line, get blame out of the way and get to work on your future. If you missed it, you missed it. The reason can inform you going forward but should not be used to identify and blame the culprit. Stuff happens, and it happens often. There is no need to place blame. So acknowledge that these things happen and move on. Don't blame yourself or someone else. Don't blame the situation or your circumstances. Don't blame your background or skin color. This does not get you any closer to where you want to be.

Maybe you have seen or experienced the blame game played in an organization, as this is a real problem when you have talented people competing for positions, promotions, recognitions, or relationships. No one is willing to expose their weaknesses or to let down their guard for fear that they will lose something. Many of them suffer from a victim mentality and believe that others are out to get them or want to keep them down or from where they want to go. Therefore, they are less inclined to expose their weaknesses, as this would give the enemy, the opponent, the opposing force, or the competition an edge, if not an unfair advantage. They feel that they are left with only one course of action, to blame their shortcomings on someone or something else. They lash out or point their fingers in the direction opposite of themselves.

If this is how you feel and operate, you must be aware of the risk involved. First, you will not improve. You cannot get better if you will not acknowledge and accept your weaknesses. Second, your team membership will be suspect, and you could have a difficult time recruiting talent and resources. This could become a major problem if you want to move up in the organization. Blaming others will be viewed as a shortcoming, and it will not take long for the story to get out. Teams will question whether you can be trusted and relied upon to carry your load without blaming.

Please note that when you blame someone for your shortcomings, in addition to exposing your weakness for the task, it exposes an issue with your integrity and a character flaw. Most teams, especially the strong ones, can handle a weakness in your skill set. However, very few teams, even the strong ones, will want to have a member on their team with integrity issues or a character flaw. Teams, like relationships, are built on trust. Blaming shows your inability to accept responsibility. Can a team depend on you, or more specifically trust you, to get something done when your first response if you miss the mark is to blame someone or something? You should also note when you place blame, your leadership abilities and influences are negatively affected. Who wants to follow someone who blames them when something goes wrong? When you blame others, you alienate yourself from them. No one wants to be blamed for something that they are not responsible for. Honestly, very few people like to be blamed for something that they are responsible for.

If I am a part of your team and you blame me for not getting something done, even if I am your subordinate, my ability to trust you wanes, especially if I am not to blame. Alternatively, if you accept responsibility, you demonstrate that you are a team player, you take ownership for your outcomes, or you are mature but willing to learn. When you do this, it builds trust and creates loyalty. This type of loyalty will push others to step up for you, speak on your behalf, and fight for you and your initiatives, to give more than 80 percent of themselves to the task. Blame makes people feel guilty, inadequate, incompetent, and unqualified. Blame does not get you any closer to your goal or destination. So why do it? Rather, just do not do it.

CHAPTER 7

INCREASE YOUR VALUE

WHEN YOU KNOW WHO YOU ARE, WHAT YOU BRING TO the table, and what your motivations are and you can own your outcome without looking for an excuse or someone to blame, you can be of real value to the organization and to yourself. Given that people are an organization's most important resources, not its rules, regulations, policies, and procedures, if you know and can increase your value, you can plot yourself a successful course. The organization is an organism and depends on its people to accomplish its vision, mission, and goals. If you know how you can have an impact on the organization and its people, policies, procedures, and processes, you can influence, impact, and increase your importance, worth, usefulness, and value to the organization. Yes, people, like love, make the world go around and make the organization alive, live, and thrive. Being a part of the organism that makes the organization turn, do you know your value? How important are you to the organization's survival? What do you contribute, add, or bring to the table? What difference are you making? If you left the organization today, will your absence be felt? You should know the answer to these questions and inquiries like these, as the answers to them speak to your value.

I realize I have suggested and supported the assumption that all people in the organization are valuable, as they are its most important resource. While this is a true reflection of my thinking, I want to be clear that all people are not of the same value. Yes, everyone is valuable, but not of equal value. I know this is an obvious statement given the diversity in pay, positions, promotions, and paths. However, it is something you must grasp and appreciate if you plan to increase your value. The questions that you need to know and understand the answer to are the following: Of what value are you? Are you of high, low, or no value? How do you increase your value?

When thinking about the organization as an organism, I am reminded of Paul's analogy of the body and the church. He sees the church like the body, one body but many members. In Paul's letter to the Corinthians, he makes it clear that the church is one body but has many diverse members. He emphasizes the importance of each member's role and responsibility. He lets the Corinthians know that each member's role is significant and of value, that it should not be replaced by another member with a different role, and that it should not be devalued by the member or another member. He writes,

> For as the body is one, and hath many members, and all the members of that one body, being many, are one body: so also is Christ. For by one Spirit are we all baptized into one body, whether we be Jews or Gentiles, whether we be bond or free; and have been all made to drink into one Spirit. For the body is not one member, but many. If the foot shall say, Because I am not the hand, I am not of the body; is it therefore not of the body? And if the ear shall say, Because I am not the eye, I am not of the body; is it therefore not of the body? If the whole body were an eye, where were the hearing? If the whole were hearing, where were the smelling? But now hath God set the members every one of them in the body, as it hath pleased him. And if they were all one member, where were the body? But now are they many members, yet but one body. And the eye cannot say unto the hand, I have no

need of thee: nor again the head to the feet, I have
no need of you. (1 Corinthians 12:12–22 KJV)

This analogy works for the organization, as it is one organization
but many organisms. Each individual or organism has a unique set
of skills, is of value to the organization, and has a role to play. If
each organism plays its role well, the organization can be high
performing, efficient, and effective. However, if the organism
does not play its role well, the organization will perform, but its
performance will not be optimum. An organization that seeks to
be high performing must address the issue it faces when one of
its organisms is not performing optimally. The choices to address
this concern are many, including replacing or strengthening the
organism, having other organisms carry the excess load, or settling
for being less than the best. Another look at Paul's guidance to
the church could help with this, as he recognizes the importance
of each member and their impact to the functioning of the body.

Paul makes it very clear that in the church, Christ has placed
individuals in the body for a significant reason, and there are no big
Is or little Yous. There are those who would say that this is where
Paul's theology of the church breaks with organizational theory,
as he views each member has an equally important role. They see
an even greater break as Paul goes even further and emphasizes
that the feebler members of the body are more honorable, that God
constructed the church to honor the part of the body that lacks. He
notes that the reason God did this was to prevent schisms in the
body. Members would care the same one for another. He writes,

Nay, much more those members of the body,
which seem to be more feeble, are necessary: And
those members of the body, which we think to
be less honourable, upon these we bestow more
abundant honour; and our uncomely parts have
more abundant comeliness. For our comely parts
have no need: but God hath tempered the body

together, having given more abundant honour to that part which lacked: That there should be no schism in the body; but that the members should have the same care one for another. And whether one member suffer, all the members suffer with it; or one member be honoured, all the members rejoice with it. (1 Corinthians 12:22–26 KJV)

I would submit that Paul does not part with organizational theory in his reasoning and that he makes the case for preventing schisms that organizations should pay attention to. Like Paul's description of the church's focus on the feeble, organizations spend a great deal of time, energy, resources, and focus on their underperforming organisms and the high performers' weaknesses. Organizations spend significant resources bringing more honor to those viewed as less honorable, making the uncomely comely, and ensuring the weak are made strong, as all organisms are necessary. More specifically, organizations invest a significant portion of their budget developing the bottom 25 percent of its personnel and an even greater amount of its time and focus identifying, highlighting, and developing the weaknesses of its employees.

Evidence of this can be seen in the annual or periodic employee evaluations. While nearly 100 percent of the employees' performance documentation is focused on detailing their strength, the predominance of the feedback is focused on their weaknesses. In the feedback, there appears to be an underlying assumption that there is no need to dwell on the employee's strengths. On the contrary, the employee's weaknesses need to be addressed in full detail, including how to develop and strengthen them.

This handling of feedback is also evident in other competitive selection processes, for instance, assignments and quota courses/training. Feedback given to employees is generally based on their weaknesses: what they do not have, not on what they do have as well as what they lack, not their strong suits. For example, if you apply for a competitive position and are not selected, the feedback you are given is generally focused on why you did not win the assignment. Your feedback may be more about how much more qualified the selected candidate was for the position, even though what you are told will not be in these terms. You may get the dutiful commentary on how you had a great interview but your years of experience were recognized. "But you answered all the questions extremely well, and we believe you would do a great job. But you lack what we are looking for." What they are looking for is what they found in your competition. Again, your feedback is focused on why you did not secure the position, what you lack.

Other examples of this type of feedback are seen when bonuses and promotions are given. The conversations during bonus or promotion season is not frequently on the individual's strengths. Yes, the one who receives the bonus and awards may receive a few kind words for their contributions, but those who do not (most of the employees) are told what they lacked and should do to improve their chances next time. They are told what they need to do to get promoted and increase the bonus payouts. They are told what they lacked. The goal is to provide them information so they can improve, get better, and become stronger. After all, "feedback is a gift," right? So in some respects, Paul's theology of the church and organizational behavior are in line, as each values the individual and are concerned about the weak, the feeble, and the uncomely.

Organizations want to be high-performing, to be the best they can be. To that end, they learn. They share and transfer knowledge. They are constantly changing and improving. They invest in their people. They find and recruit the best and brightest people with the requisite skills, knowledge, and abilities. They establish onboarding, mentoring, training, and development programs to assist with and accelerate their employees' introduction, acclimation, and growth and to maximize their potential. They want the best for their employees so they can get the best from their employees. Given this reality, much time is spent developing the employee's weaknesses. It is not uncommon for an organization to spend more on developing weaker employees than on the growth and potential of their stronger employees. Typically, this type of spending is on a valued employee that is not living up to their potential.

If you plan to move up in the organization or progress in your career, you must be aware of the value you bring to the table. Do you have the requisite skills to do what you are assigned to do? Do you have the potential to do more? Are you a part of the 10 percent at the bottom or 10 percent at the top? Do you know where you stand, sit, or lean? Your answers to these questions will directly affect your behavior, actions, networks, motivation, and energy.

Think about it. If you are a part of the in crowd, the top 10 percent, your attitude, action, and altitude as well as your sense of belonging is quite different from someone who is in the bottom 10 percent. That said, you should know that your value largely depends on you. Yes, the organization will ascribe value to you, but you determine what value it ascribes.

So the question burning inside of you is, "How do I determine my value?" The short answer to that question is that your impact on the organization determines it. What are you doing for the organization daily? Is what you do making a difference for the organization or the organisms? Is your presence in the organization being felt or known? Are you singing the song of the Carter Family question, "Will You Miss Me When I'm Gone?" or making the statement of Araya, "You're Gonna Miss Me When I'm Gone"? Is what you do for the organization worthy of your pay? Do they need you? Do you go above and beyond? Do you do just what is required? Or do you do just enough to get by? Are you the feeble, uncommonly, lacking, or on the bottom 10 percent? You must know where you rest or reside in the organization. You must know your value or, more clearly, how valuable you are to the organization. Please note, when I say you need to know your value, I am talking about your present value, not your past or future value.

Your contributions to the organizations should be viewed as having time value—past, present, and future. As for the past, it is past. You may be where you are today because of what you did yesterday or last week, month, or year, but that is done. What now? Your present value cannot be about your past accomplishments alone. You have already been reviewed, rewarded, and recognized for past actions and results. If you were not, you must question if your views of your actions and their associated values are aligned with the organization's views and values. Maybe you were not promoted, rewarded, or recognized for something you did in the past because they did not believe what you did was deserving of such. Your past actions, efforts, and initiatives may have been good, but they will not be enough to carry you through your career. Very few people have a one-time success that will have such an impact or lasting effect that it extends throughout their career. It may propel them to a position of prominence or a promotion, but generally it will not keep them there. Do not allow yourself to get caught up with yesterday's successes. Celebrate them and keep it moving. Focus on today and deliver. Your success depends on your present and future values and your ability to have an impact daily and go forward.

If you are not contributing to and affecting the organization daily, you will be viewed as not adding value, which will precipitate your downfall, destruction, or demise. If you are not affecting the organization, you have no value to the organization. If you have no value, any resources paid to you or for your development are an opportunity cost. Those resources could have been used on something or someone else who would have had a positive impact.

Instead of being a cost to or a liability of the organization, be a valuable or valued asset. When you are valuable enough to the organization, you're having to create opportunities for yourself decreases, as opportunities will come your way. That is, instead of having to seek out and find opportunities, you will have to choose the one you believe is best for you. Given the importance and affect your value to the organization will have on you and your career, you should make it your priority to not only know your value but to increase it.

As noted earlier, the organization only assigns a value to you. You determine how significant that assignment will be. If you are unsatisfied with your current assigned value, if you are finding it difficult to secure assignments or positions or get selected for opportunities you know are reserved for individuals the organization sees as future leaders, this may be a great time to change your value equation, to increase your value.

To accomplish this, you must first know and understand what the organization values and commit yourself to delivering it. If you are not willing to do what is required to increase your value, to do what you need to do to get what you want from the organization, get comfortable where you are. You have nothing to complain about if you know what you need to do to get what you want, but you do not do it and, consequently, do not get what you want. That said, when you know what the organization values, you can increase your value by delivering.

For example, if the organization values timely customer service and you always deliver on time or ahead of schedule, you will increase your value. If your organization values difficult/stretch assignments, you will increase your value by securing a difficult assignment and performing at a high level. If your organization values change, you will increase your value by being a change agent (one who initiates change) or an agent for change (one who responds positively to change).

You should not be the same person tomorrow that you are today. We grow and change. Change is not an option. It is a must. Your current or present value to the organization should not represent your future value. You, like the organization you seek to affect, must constantly and consistently look for opportunities to grow, get better, change, and increase your value.

The organization changes constantly because its organism constantly changes. In order to be relevant and productive, to survive and thrive, the organization must change. To accomplish this, it depends on the change of its organisms. That is, the organisms must change the organization, but to do this, they must change themselves. Doing yesterday's business today will not get it done. Doing it the way it was done yesterday because you know and are comfortable with the way it was done will not do.

You must change, and you must alter the organization and bring it into the new century. Educate it on the new ways of interacting with its employees. Teach it the new ways of valuing its customers. Show it the new ways of measuring its success and accounting for its funds. If you can be the catalyst for change or chart the new direction for the organization going forward, you will be of significant value.

Change is indispensable. Human growth is the result of change. The human body is structured in such a way that change is automatic and constant. From birth to death, there is constant change—cells dividing and dying and new cells growing. As the body grows, it changes, develops, matures, and thrives. If change does not happen in the body, rigor mortis sets in, and the individual will die. The only place where change is not occurring is in death. Where there is life, there is change. If you are living, you must change. So instead of settling for where you are, your current/present value, which is derived from your past actions, you should choose to change. Increase your value.

To increase your value, your first step is to accept and agree that you must change. What got you here will not get you there. What you did yesterday that made you successful will not make you successful tomorrow. You must know and understand that as the organization changes, you move positions, people around you evolve, and the mission, vision, and goals of the organization are modified, you too must change, that is, make adjustments, generate new strategies and skills, grow in knowledge and understanding, develop new relationships, and make new moments. You increase your value by changing, improving, and getting better. If you do not change with the organization or change the organization, you will be left behind. However, when you change and increase your value, there is a corresponding increase in your net worth, income, opportunities, impact and influence, and roles and responsibilities.

With these increases, you will likely experience an increase in your own individual happiness, as happiness depends on something happening. When this happens, given "a happy employee is a productive employee," your productivity will also increase. Your decisions and actions, the changes you make to increase your value, creates a positive cycle of occurrences that affects you and the organization.

In order to increase your value, you must change and grow. Your growth results from you changing positions, accepting new challenges/initiatives, stepping outside your box, taking stretch assignments, developing your expertise on the job and in the classroom, collaborating with colleagues, interacting with interesting individuals, mentoring, and leading. And the list goes on.

As you change and grow, your roles and responsibilities will increase. As your roles and responsibilities increase, you must grow to meet and exceed them. You cannot keep doing the same things the same way when everything around you is changing. Your actions should reflect your responsibilities. As an employee, you may have been expected to do the work, but as a manager, you are expected to lead and supervise the employees doing the work. If you continue doing the work as a manager, who is minding the store? Who is leading the team?

It should be noted that with change comes discomfort, as dormant dysfunctions appear and weaknesses are exposed. That is, real and positive change will often pull you out of your comfort zone, into a place where you are required to do things you have never done, activities that do not match with your strengths, and functions you have not been doing for the past several years. This is one of the reasons why it is important that you know and understand your weaknesses, as you may have to use them one day. By knowing them, you can develop a plan to strengthen them and are not surprised when they show up.

Weaknesses are not the problem, as it is not uncommon for you to experience them several times during your career. As you move up in the organization and take on assignments of greater responsibility, you will recycle your discomfort. You may even become the weakest link. The exposure of your weaknesses, your discomfort, or you being the weakest link indicates that something you are involved in has change and a notification that it is now time for you to make some changes. If you continue doing things the way you have been doing them, the discomfort will continue, and your weaknesses will cause you to fail. However, if you choose to change, you could turn things around and grow in the process.

If you continue to grow and thereby increase your value, change will be constant, and your comfort will be interrupted continually. You should get comfortable being uncomfortable. Get comfortable walking in the gray. Your ability to be flexible and adaptable, to be willing to be placed or put yourself in a learning environment, will prove critical to your success. I must caution you not to be a know-it-all, not to "believe your own hype," or not to "drink your own Kool-Aid."

It is not uncommon for people who ascend to a higher level in the organization to assume or behave as if they know everything. They do this to protect themselves from being exposed for what they do not know or because their ego is large enough to convince them they are smarter than everyone else. Whatever the reason, knowing everything is not a viable option. It is an impossibility. The higher you go up in the organization, the more you need to know or the more information you must have access to. You may have been able to do and know everything in your previous assignment. However, in your new senior assignment, you may have to rely on the knowledge and expertise of your subordinates or colleagues.

If you get confused and assume that with the authority of your new position comes the knowledge, you will set yourself up to fail/fall. You may have positional authority but lack the knowledge required for the position. If you assume the authority and knowledge come with the position and act accordingly when you lack the knowledge, you will not command the respect of your team and will be viewed as arrogant. The higher up you go, the more you rely on your experts, subordinates, and team to keep you informed and get things done. If you are going to be effective, you must realize your limits, the impossibility of you knowing it all, and the incredible possibilities afforded you and your team.

Your humility is an asset; your arrogance is a liability. If you are going to profit by your growth and opportunities, you must always know that there is room for improvement, that you need to continue to grow. Do not get in your own way thinking or acting like you know everything. Paul offers this caution to the church at Rome.

> For I say, through the grace given unto me, to every man that is among you, not to think of himself more highly than he ought to think; but to think soberly, according as God hath dealt to every man the measure of faith. For as we have many members in one body, and all members have not the same office: So, we, being many, are one body in Christ, and everyone members one of another. Having then gifts differing according to the grace that is given to us ... (Romans 12:3–6a KJV)

Paul again displays his wisdom of relationships and how individuals should work together to be most effective. He cautions against arrogance, warning individuals not to see themselves as more than they are. When you see yourself as more than you are, you see no reason to improve or grow. The opposite is true if you are humble. Humility recognizes the need for and the importance of improvement and growth. Greatness is the product of hard work, improvements, and growth. Even those gifted will only realize their greatness after hard work, improvements, and growth. LeBron James is not considered one of the greatest basketball players of all times because he plays the same game year after year. He holds this badge of honor because each year during the offseason, he works on and improves aspects of his game and gets better and better. Even though the years have increased, his game has not decreased, as he continues to make changes and improvements and gets better.

If you are going to have a real and lasting impact on the organization, you must make it your personal business to become better every day. While "there will be days like this mama said," moments when despite your best efforts, things will not go your way or Murphy's Law ("anything that can go wrong will go wrong") rules, this is understandable and expected. After all, it is not the stuff that happens that is important. What is important is how you respond to the stuff that happens.

If you are not improving and developing your skills, the organization and its organisms will rightfully pass you by. Without improvements, you will easily fall prey to the Peter principle, which suggest that employees will rise and get promoted to the level of incompetence. That is, eventually you will be put in jobs or positions that you will not be able to fulfill the requirements. If you understand the importance of increasing your value, you will agree that there is no excuse for Peter's principle being active in your life. I understand the impact Murphy's Law could have because this is outside of your control. However, you can declare the Peter principle null and void by taking actions to improve with each advancement. Try this alliteration to remind you, "Purposed and purposeful preparation prevents Peter principle possibilities, period."

Being prepared and constantly improving will position you to always see Peter's principle possibilities but not experience them. As you advance and take on assignments with greater responsibilities, you will continue to move the envelope/"the cheese." As this happens, the potential for you to meet Peter and his principle becomes increasingly more possible. It is up to you to decide if you want to have the meeting or if you want to prepare so you do not waste your time with Peter. Preparation is the key, and it must happen before and after your next move. If preparing for your next move is your only action, prepare to meet Peter and his principle after the move. Continuous improvement should not be just a catch phrase. It should be your way of life.

If you are not prepared for your next opportunity, you could make excuses, blame others, find cause for pause and give up, identify a reason why this is not your season, or do nothing to change your situation. Alternatively, you can begin to prepare yourself to better your chances for success or to create additional opportunities. Please know that if you are going to be successful, you are going to be given opportunities to serve and work in positions where you are not yet qualified or equipped to handle. Stretch assignments and out-of-the-box challenges afford you this opportunity. These types of opportunities should be welcomed as they contribute to increasing your value through development and growth.

To increase your value, you cannot sit back and wait or take positions that have little impact on the organization. You must step up and seek opportunities that demand more of you than you were demanding of yourself in your previous or current comfortable assignment. Yes, your stepping up will create some discomfort. However, you must know that success and struggle are bedmates. You may not be prepared, equipped, or have what it takes to do the job, but if you are willing to learn, struggle, stretch yourself, and push yourself past your sticking point, not only will your stock go up and you become more valuable, your sense of net worth will also increase.

Your value to the organization opens doors, creates opportunities, and affects your rewards and recognitions and could be what keeps you employed. As we have noted, organizations go through changes. Sometimes these alterations have employee-employment ramifications. This happens when the organization makes decisions to downsize, right size, or even size to increase agility, reduce overhead, increase profit margin, or position themselves to better meet their mission requirement.

For example, when an organization decides to right size, the organisms are directly affected, as they are looking to retain the right people. The "right people" are determined by the value they bring to the mission of the organization. If you are part of the bottom 10 percent of the organization, it may be difficult to determine what you do. Your impact on the organization may be invisible, or you may not have made yourself valuable. When this happens, you are likely to be released, fired, let go, terminated, or realigned.

If you are valuable to the mission, part of the top 10 percent of the organization, and known by your impact, you are likely to be a part of the group deciding the fate and future of the organization. Your value to the organization will create a place for you during times of change. You may not know what the future holds, but you know change is a constant part of the present, future, and daily business of the organization. Being a part of this change will only increase your value. To further increase your value and secure your position, you must know and understand the direction the organization is headed and leverage this information to affect its mission, vision, and goal. You should also leverage this information to affect your continuous improvement program to ensure you are prepared or getting ready for what's next.

It is important to know who you are and what you bring to the table, but it is equally significant to know and understand your impact. That is, you need to know who you are, what you bring, and what you are doing and can do for the organization. It should be noted that you should never become comfortable. You should always be growing, developing, and improving. You should be actively increasing your value. As you increase your value, you enhance your opportunities and your impact on the organization.

PART
3

WHAT TO DO
WHEN YOU
DON'T KNOW
WHAT TO DO

CHAPTER 8

IDENTIFY
AND MODIFY
YOUR SUCCESS
STRATEGY

THERE ARE TIMES IN EACH OF OUR LIVES AND CAREERS when we find ourselves not knowing what to do, moments when we could not determine our next move. We tried everything we could thing of: talking through things, applying previous productive plans, struggling with several strategies, thinking through the troubles and details, working with written and unwritten words and rules, examining exits and entrances to figure out how we got here and where to go from here, and looking at ourselves and assessing our strengths and weaknesses to determine what we did right and could do better.

How did we get here? Despite our best efforts to do everything right and required, we still found ourselves in a position where nothing seemed to work and we did not know how to get it to work. We were committed to the cause, dedicated to the destination, mindful of the mission, focused on the fight, purposed with a plan, and believed we were doing our best, and yet somehow we ended up in a place where we questioned, "What do you do when you don't know what to do?"

It may help you to know that this experience of not knowing what to do has been had by everyone aspiring to do something of worth. No matter who you are and where you happen to be in life—your status, background, nationality, geographic location, pay grade, or rank—you will experience not knowing what to do. This could happen when your back is against the wall or you are floating on cloud nine, your head is down or is in the clouds, or all doors are being closed or you have too many opportunities to choose from. It happens when you are looking for the right answer and cannot find it, you want to move but are not sure in what direction, you can hear the call to do something greater but feel paralyzed, you want to jump but fear keeps you grounded, or you know you should do something but don't know what something you should do.

As common as the experience of not knowing what to do and the question of "What do you do when you don't know what to do?" are, one would think the answer would be equally common. As many people who have had this experience and question, you would think there would be a frequently asked question (FAQ) manual on the topic. Suppose this is much like the cure for a common cold. There are many remedies, but the cure is on the way. That said, much like the common cold, while there is no cure and one remedy does not fit all, your next step or action to aid in your answer is critical. Yes, the experience is common, but what happens next seems to be uncommon.

When you are at a crossroad and you have a choice to make, the choice you make could mean the difference in daylight or darkness, failure or success, winning or losing, changing or remaining stagnant, or going up or staying down. A decision this important "is not to be entered into lightly or unadvisedly, but reverently, discreetly, soberly and in the fear of God." Even when you know how important it is that you decide, you may still find yourself not knowing what to do because the decision is critical and difficult and the results are evasive. You want to do the right things to ensure the appropriate outcomes, but you don't know which choice will produce what you desire. If this is where you find yourself, keep reading. This chapter is for you. The first thing I recommend you do is identify and modify your success strategy.

Crossroads in life are a constant. You will often find yourself at a crossroad where you are uncertain about what choice to make, but you must choose. You may feel that you have exhausted your options, taken every sensible action, made every reasonable decision, and thought through every possible consequence, and still you are uncertain about what to do to create or produce a desired outcome. When you are in this place or situation, you should review your strategy to see if you have the right approach to determine your next steps. If after your review, you determine that you have gotten off track, that you need to get back to the basics of your strategy to get to the desired outcomes, you should make the adjustments and proceed.

However, if you determine that you have done everything as planned, that you have done everything right and you are still not getting the desired outcome, this may be a good time to change courses or course correct. If you continue the current course and keep doing what you have been doing, you will likely continue to get what you have been getting.

Einstein said, "The definition of insanity is doing the same thing over and over again and expecting different results." By this definition, if we are honest, maybe we are all a little insane. When you are doing what you believe is right, it is not uncommon to repeat that action over and over again, as you trust that it will yield you the desired outcomes. When you are doing the right thing, it is difficult to change course because you assume and expect that you will eventually get the desired outcome. This is not necessarily a bad thing, as it shows your commitment to a course of action. How many NBA star players or three-point shooters have you seen take and miss the next shot over and over again, as they believe the next one will go in? The question is, "When is enough *enough*?" Too often when you get caught in this cycle, you lose sight of the goal and are committed to the process. You just keep doing what you know and are comfortable with. You must remember that the outcome is the goal, not the process.

One big challenge facing you when you don't know what to do is yourself. You can be your own worst enemy. You would change courses sooner, but it goes against how you were raised, what you were taught and believe, your ideologies, and how you do and have been doing things. In addition to the outcome telling you, you know it is time to make a change, but it's uncomfortable and hard. It goes against the grain. This is the point when you should accept the challenge afforded you by this situation and do something different. Stop beating your head against the wall and make a change.

As difficult as change is, it is constant and required when you want to make any progress in life. When you find yourself at a crossroad and you do not know what to do after you have done everything you know to do and it has not worked, you must change. It is imperative that you consider, examine, adopt, and implement other alternatives. If you were taught growing up that hard work alone was the key to your success, but after working hard and putting in the extra hours and success evades you, what do you do? You may be inclined to work harder and put in more hours, only to discover that success is even more elusive. Now you are disgruntled, unhappy, upset, and ready to throw in the towel and surrender.

Maybe your concept of success by hard work alone is fallacious. Perhaps hard work is good for the position you are in, but not all that is required to get a supervisory or management position. Maybe you need to review your strategy for success and question its tenets. Maybe the question you are asking yourself about what's preventing or inhibiting you for being successful should not be "What else do I need to do?" but "What else am I not doing?" It could be that hard work, leadership, and collaboration are the necessary elements for your next move.

You should know that progress comes with a price and the price changes. Marshall Goldsmith was right. "What got you here will not get you there." If you believe everything you were taught growing up as a child holds true throughout life, you are in for a very rude awakening. Even if everything you were taught was true, things change. In corporations, industry, and in life, you will find that things change as you progress up the ladder of success. That is, as you move up, your requirements for success change with each progression and advancement. As a result, the things that you did and were required to do when you first joined the organization may yield you immediate and short-term success. However, as you get experience, mature in your position, and advance, you will find the things that you did when you first joined the organization have gotten you the requisite rewards and recognitions. They will not continue to pay you dividends or yield the same outcomes as you move up.

There is nothing new or novel about this concept, and it is applicable physically, mentally, and spiritually. For example, if you go to the gym to work out and build muscles with the goal to bench 250 pounds, you do not start working out with this weight on the first day. You gradually but progressively build up to this weight over time. You may start out lifting a hundred pounds for ten repetitions. After you are stronger and these weights appear lighter, you will increase your weights and repetitions. You will continue this process until you reach your goal. When your norm becomes ten repetitions at 250 pounds, it is highly unlikely that your use of the lighter weights that you began with will have any effect on building new muscles. To go beyond your achievement, you will have to push yourself and add additional weights and repetitions. What you did before will not have the same effect on building your muscles.

The growth, strengthening, or building concept is true of building your mental strength as well. When you began learning your alphabets or more specifically how to read, you start with the alphabets and a small set of words. As you advanced and became more fluent and your vocabulary grew, to increase your knowledge you had to read more or learn new words. You will not increase your vocabulary by studying and using words you already know. If you already know a word and it is in your vocabulary, how can you add it? This is not to say or to suggest that a review would not prove productive, as it could refine, enhance, or solidify what you already know. However, it is not an addition or increase of your vocabulary. To increase your vocabulary, you must add new words.

The same is true of your spiritual growth. When you start out on your Christian journey, you do not start out as grown men or women in Christ. According to Peter, you start out as babes in Christ. "Wherefore laying aside all malice, and all guile, and hypocrisies, and envies, and all evil speakings, As newborn babes, desire the sincere milk of the word, that ye may grow thereby: If so be ye have tasted that the Lord is gracious" (1 Peter 2:1–3 KJV).

While Christians begin their faith walk as newborn babes, they are to grow and mature. To remain a baby would be an indication that something is wrong. As cute as babies are, they are only to remain babies for so long. They must grow. Christians are called to be disciples, students, and learners who grow by studying, talking, and walking God's Word. Christians are even called to review, restudy, and remember what they have read, heard, seen, and learned so they do not forget or repeat past mistake. Paul said, "Therefore we ought to give the more earnest heed to the things which we have heard, lest at any time we should let them slip" (Hebrews 2:1 KJV). He also said, "When I was a child, I spoke as a child, I understood as a child, I thought as a child: but when I became a man, I put away childish things" (1 Corinthians 13:11 KJV).

Your growth as a Christian is reflected here as a change in your understanding and thought. Your understanding as an adult is not the same as when you were a child. Even your thoughts as an adult are not the same as when you were a child. When you grow and mature as a Christian, the things that used to tempt, try, and trouble you no longer have the same effect. Your experiences mature you and cause you to see and say things differently. Your growth will have you saying like Paul to the Philippians,

> I have learned, in whatsoever state I am, therewith to be content. I know both how to be abased, and I know how to abound: every where and in all things I am instructed both to be full and to be hungry, both to abound and to suffer need. I can

do all things through Christ which strengtheneth me. (Philippians 4:11b–13 KJV)

The need to change or to grow are mandatory to your success. You must know when it is time to change course and have the courage to do so. The advice Kenny Rogers gives in his song "The Gambler"[5] should be heeded. "You got to know when to hold 'em know when to fold 'em know when to walk away know when to run." There are no gains to be had by staying in a comfortable place too long. Your production may be the standard. You may be outdistancing your competition, and you may be the talk of the town. However, if you are not growing, learning, or developing, how is what you are doing benefiting you? When there is no return on your investment, it is time to get your investment returned, to no longer invest. This is true of finances, relationships, and life.

How many people do you know who have invested too much time in a relationship that was going nowhere? How many times have you stayed in a job, location, or relationship because it was comfortable? You felt that there was something else for you. The thrill of what you were doing was gone. You were no longer excited about what you were doing. You wanted to leave, to get out, but you were comfortable. You wanted to leave but were afraid to. You know it is time to go, to do something different, but you are afraid of the unknown. You don't know what to do.

The answers to "Where do you go from here?" and "What to do when you don't know what to do?" are stated in the questions. Where do you go from here? Answer: "From here." What to do

---

[5] "The Gambler" was written by Don Schlitz in 1976 and recorded by several artists, including Johnny Cash, but the tune was made a hit by country music icon Kenny Rogers.
Kenny Rogers' rendition was a No. 1 country hit and even crossed over to the pop charts— a rare feat at that time. The song was released in November 1978 as the title track from his album *The Gambler,* which scored him the Grammy Award for 'Best Male Country Vocal Performance' in 1980.

when you don't know what to do? Answer: "Do." When you find yourself wondering where to go, start going. Or if you're in a place where you don't know what to do, start doing. The reason you are asking the questions is because you know it is time to move, jump, or change courses. Something inside or outside of you has signaled to you that where you are and what you are doing is not optimal, beneficial, or acceptable. It is time to move.

Staying where you are, remaining static, or doing nothing, while choices and options, are not viable as they leave the questions unanswered. You are dissatisfied, disoriented, dismayed, disillusioned, distraught, or disappointed with where you are, and it is time for a change. Your first step is to step away from where you are. Begin to move in a new direction; modify your success strategy. What you are doing may have worked before and got you to where you are, but it is not working now. A step away, a change of course, would be good.

If you are going to get to a place where you know what to do, you must do something. You should start by leaving the place where you don't know what to do. As simple as this may sound, the first step to change is the most difficult, but it is the most significant and mandatory. Most people do not like the idea of moving from where they are. Comfort is a positive and a very negative thing. When you are comfortable, you are inclined to stay where you are and keep doing what you are doing, even when it is not your best option. As good is the enemy of great, comfort is the enemy of creativity. You may have the greatest opportunities afforded anyone in the world, or you may have greatness inside of you waiting to come out, but you will be unable to tap into it because you are comfortable. When you are comfortable, you do not have to do anything else.

We are where we are because we choose to be. We can also choose to be somewhere. So instead of staying where you don't know what to do, as comfortable or familiar as it may be, choose to be somewhere else. When you don't know what to do, do. Modify your success strategy, change courses, or take a step. It will be your difference maker.

CHAPTER 9

TAKE A STEP AND GET MOVING

WHEN UNCERTAINTY HITS YOU, LIFE HAS COME AT YOU so fast that you find yourself in a place where you don't know what to do and all that is in you has you feeling afraid, stuck, trapped, locked down, or immobile. Take a step. Get moving. When you do not know what to do next, it seems only right that the next course of action is to do nothing. You have learned that in the process of solving problems, by whatever method, doing nothing is doing something. Just as not deciding is a decision, doing nothing is an action. It may be inaction, but it is a choice of actions. Since you do not know what you should do, the easiest thing to do is nothing. Therefore, doing nothing becomes your default. Default means failure to act, inaction, or neglect, which is what happens when you do nothing. While it seems logical, safe, comfortable, and perhaps right to do nothing when you don't know what to do, it creates a vicious cycle of inaction and repeated questions. To break this cycle, do something. Take a step and get moving.

When you don't know what to do, do something. The only reason the issue or question of what to do has come up is because something needs to be done. Something or anything is better than nothing, as it represents a break from the norm, the usual, what is happening that needs to change. You may be afraid, but if you face your fears, you will free yourself. Try doing something. Even if you get it wrong, you win because you learn what not to do. There is no failure in trying. The failure is in not trying. You have heard the sayings or quotes that suggest that the best cure for falling off a bike or a horse is to get back on and ride. The best cure for falling is getting up. Donnie McClurkin said it best in his song We Fall Down[6], "We fall down but we get up … For a saint is just a sinner who fell down and got up." Scripture in Proverbs support these words. "For though the righteous fall seven times, they rise again, but the wicked stumble when calamity strikes" (Proverbs 24:16 NIV).

It is not in the falling; it is in the calling. When you have something that you are called to do, an action that is bigger than you but requires your input, or an activity that you are committed to getting done, you cannot afford to waste time bemoaning, lamenting, or crying over spilled milk. Clean it up, keep it moving, and try not to make the same mistake next time. Instead of dwelling on mistakes, use the experience you gain from attempting to and recovering from them to build your resilience and flexibility. You should get to a point where you see and welcome setbacks, mistakes, or challenging decisions as parts of the process of getting the job done and growing and developing your maximum potential. When you do this, your perception of challenges change, as does your belief in yourself to handle them. Carrie Law Morgan Figgs was right. "'It's hard to keep a good man down.' The storm may rage, the wind may blow and beat him to the ground, but one of the hardest things on earth to do is to keep a good man down."

When you find yourself in that old familiar place, where the question of what to do lingers and you don't know what to do, do something. If you do something and you make a mistake, get it wrong, or fall, do not spend any more time on the ground than you must. Get up and get moving. The worst thing that you could possibly do is to stay on the ground and waddle over your

---

[6] Published on Jan 5, 2015
Description
Song – "We Fall Down"
Artist - Donnie McClurkin
Licensed to YouTube by - SME (on behalf of Verity Records); LatinAutor, Capitol CMG Publishing, Adorando Brazil, UMPI, LatinAutor - UMPG, CMRRA, ASCAP, and 6 Music Rights Societies

weaknesses or stew over your struggles. Get up and get back on the bike or the horse. Get back in the fight. When you do this, you accept the lessons, the experiences of doing something taught you, and you can incorporate it with your next or new actions. Even a bad experience from doing something can be a good lesson. So get accustomed to doing something when you don't know what to do. Free yourself by moving into the unknown, the gray. Take a step.

Lao Tzu was correct. "The journey of a thousand miles begins with the first step." The first step you take will always be the first step. It represents your new beginning. Your first step is the beginning of a new set of steps. So whatever steps you took before, they only got you here. You will have to take another step to leave. Whether you are beginning a thousand-mile journey or you are several miles on the thousand-mile journey, your next step is a new beginning, a fresh step in the direction you are going. This was the thought of Charles E. Dederich Sr., who said, "Today is the first day of the rest of your life."

Today or your next step represents a fresh start. This is important to note because on this journey, you will get off course, confused, and disoriented; deviate from your plan; or get stuck and not know what to do. This could happen because of something you did or something someone else did to you or that just happened. When you understand that each step in your journey is unique, new, and just a piece of the whole, you can see how no matter what step brought you here, another step can get you out.

You should also know, understand, and recognize that every step you take is different. This is not just because the step itself is different, but things around and affecting the steps are also different. Even when your steps are the same, because you take them at different points and times on your journey, they feel different. For example, if you're running a marathon, the first step you take to begin the race may be easier than the last step you take to finish the race, even though they may be the same. Besides your physical status, so many other factors affect your steps to make them different, even when there may be similarities in your steps.

Even the two factors of your steps—distance and pace—that are more likely to be the same are different because of other things affecting them, for instance, terrain, turf, and texture.

What is common and consistent about your steps is each one represents a change in position; each one is new and comes with its own challenges. Unique physical, social, spiritual, mental, external, and internal experiences will affect every one of your steps. Whether your step is energized and exciting or slow and deliberate will be largely determined by how you feel physically, spiritually, mentally, emotionally, socially, and economically.

Even when you feel in control of your steps, there is a very likely possibility that someone or something that has no direct bearing on you will affect or interrupt them. For example, if the landscape changes and you must go uphill instead of downhill or you must work out on stairs instead of a level field, the distance and pace of your steps will change. You generally walk downhill faster than you walk uphill or on a level field. Things and people who have nothing to do with your journey can affect your steps. While you may be able to control some of your steps, you have no control over other things that could directly affect them. However, you do control the taking of your next step.

Steps represent your actions, your movement. They do not guarantee safe arrival to your destination, the correct choice from among your options, or ease of travel. You take each step as they come and live with whatever they come with and you adapt. There may be similarities in some of your steps, but generally each one is unique, different. What is common is that each step is next and new. Even if you could develop consistency in the pace and distance of your steps, they will feel different during separate times on your journey. Sometimes taking a step will be easy. Taking that same step on a different day may be very difficult. There is no sequencing of step difficulty. It does not get harder as you go along; nor does it get any easier. It depends, which is one of the things that makes taking a step when you don't know what to do so challenging. The fluctuation in the difficulty of your steps may be the result of you learning as you go, growing, and getting used to the steps.

If you run long enough, you will get a second wind where your breathing becomes easier and you are reenergized. This could happen because you see the end in sight or your body movement and breathing syncs up. Prior to your second wind, you struggle, but afterward, you level off and are ready to go longer. You experienced your most difficult steps in the beginning before your second wind. If you would have given up during the early part of your run, your struggle, you would have never experienced a second wind. Thus, you are ready to log more miles and understand that if you keep pressing through your difficulties, things may level off. You learn from this experience that the difficulties of your steps are not predicated on where you are on your journey, that you must keep moving.

You should not allow your experience with struggle determine the outcome of your actions, as things change. Taking the required steps could be easy today, hard tomorrow, and easier the next day. If you choose to give up because you are struggling because you don't know what to do, you may give up to soon, as your next step could be your breakthrough, your second wind. Midnight (12:00 a.m.) occurs in the dark, but it represents the end of a day and the beginning of a new one. If you give up because you are in the dark, you may be giving up on your morning. Keep moving. Take your next step despite where you are currently located, despite what you may not understand or what you do not know. Your action, your step, is necessary.

It is important that you take your next step because it represents movement. Your step says that you are going somewhere. Your movement is critical to your continued success. If you get stuck where you are, in a place where you don't know what to do, you will begin to rationalize and justify your being there. You cannot afford, after experiencing some difficulty or challenge trying to go forward, to follow the path of least resistance and get comfortable where you are. While staying is easier or familiar in known territory and much more comfortable, you must move. You know from experience, gained from being in a place where you don't know what to do, that change will be difficult. You also understand a change in your position will require an action that will be uncomfortable. Finally you know that in order to do something when you don't know what to do, you must walk out on faith into the unknown, that you move from a position of comfort to a position of discomfort. The changes you make may require you become a student when you were accustomed to teaching or an amateur when you were accustomed to being an expert. It requires that you accept the fact that the unknown is your operating space.

A key to getting to the next level in your organization and life is to move and keep moving. Newton identified three laws of motion. The first law of motion states that "an object either remains at rest or continues to move at a constant velocity unless acted upon by force." The reason many of us are where we are is because we are at rest or an external force that stopped us has us halted. Let me first suggest to you that there is nothing wrong with rests, if you choose it. However, if you are in the state of rest because an opposing force arrested you, you need to get moving. You cannot afford to allow your foes, friends, haters, negative influencers, or difficulties outside stop you and your attention or take you off task. You cannot allow the external forces to determine your fate. When you have been pushed, you need to push back and push harder.

Newton's second law states that "the rate of change in momentum of a body is directly proportional to the force applied, and this change in momentum takes place in the direction of the applied force." In other words, your momentum or movement forward can and will be affected by a force that is seeking to stop you. So if you are moving forward and heading to your destination of success, if failure is coming toward you and your force of movement forward to success is less than the force of failure coming toward you, you will be forced backward.

The opposite remains true. If your force of success is greater than the force of failure, then failure will be pushed back. In the former example where the force of failure is greater, it is important to note that Newton's laws does not say or suggest that you will remain in your affected state, just that the force of failure will affect you. You should know that your current state, even if the force of failure affects it, does not have to be your permanent state. It is only a temporary state of things, which will change once you regain your momentum and start moving.

Newton's third law states that "when one body exerts a force on a second body, the second body simultaneously exerts a force equal in magnitude and opposite in direction on the first body." In other words, as I learned in school, "for every action there is an equal and opposite reaction." So while you may be inclined to sit on the sideline because a force against you has placed you there, you should consider what you bring to the table before you give up. You bring an equal force to the force against you. You simply must use what you have. If you determine or discover that you don't know what to do, you should consider that it is not as bad as you think, as you are in a neutral place where matching forces have collided. To change your position, you need to apply force in the direction you want to go. You can be an object that remains at rest or choose to be an object in continuous motion, applying your onset of force to your journey. If you stay where you are in a place of rest, you will not go forward. And in time, due to movement of those around you, you will be going backward.

In the details of Newton's laws of motion, it is not my intent to take you back to school. Rather I want you to see that motion of any sort has two primary forces as it relates to you: the force that you apply and the force that is applied to you. Given this reality, you should know when you don't know what to do because the force on you has halted, stopped, paused, impeded, or interrupted your progress that you have a choice. You can remain at rest or apply force to change your position. If you are going to be successful, you cannot allow the force applied to you to equal or exceed the force you apply. If you do, you will remain in place, static, at rest, or being pushed or going backward. You must choose to not stand still, to take the next step and keep moving whether you feel like it or not. If you push when you do not feel like it, you can become a force to be reckoned with, one that does not depend on external support, a force multiplier where your presence enhances the force of others.

When you are in a place where you don't know which choice or options to take, you must choose, move, or take a step. Sometimes the movement is more important than the choice of movement, especially when you cannot decide where to go. We know there are forces at work to stop or impede your movement and progress. There is nothing new here. Given this knowledge and reality, you should push harder, run faster, and keep stepping. If you stop, not only is it harder to get going again, you run the risk of staying where you are.

If you stay where you are, you will remain who you are and not become who you are destined to be. If you move, you grow. If you remain still or at rest, you become stale, familiar, tasteless, and ineffective. To remain who you are today may sound good today, but is it? Imagine you remaining in high school and at home with your parents while your friends and classmates go off to college and experience life afterward. What do you think the conversation would be like with them in five or ten years? Not having moments when we don't know what to do may sound optimal, but think about the experiences you miss out on, the knowledge you gain, and the lessons you learn.

Far too many people are unhappy and frustrated where they are because they did not take the next step. They froze and settled, and as a result or reward, they are now where they were then. While then was good then, it is not good now. More specifically, because they decided by not deciding (remember, to do nothing is a choice and a decision), they are where they were. Now instead of being happy and healthy, they are tired of the monotony and wish they had made a different decision. They feel trapped and possess the need to explain themselves and justify them being where they are. This does not have to be you. You can make a choice and decide when you don't know what to do and live with the results or learn from the consequences. Either way, you are living and learning.

When you do not take the next step, you will remain in place and become a part of the place you are in. There is a story in the book of John about a certain man at the pool of Bethesda who had been there for thirty-eight years. I believe this story teaches us something about the risk of getting comfortable in an uncomfortable situation.

> Now there is in Jerusalem near the Sheep Gate a pool, which in Aramaic is called Bethesda and which is surrounded by five covered colonnades. Here a great number of disabled people used to lie—the blind, the lame, the paralyzed. One who was there had been an invalid for thirty-eight years. When Jesus saw him lying there and learned that he had been in this condition for a long time, he asked him, "Do you want to get well?" "Sir," the invalid replied, "I have no one to help me into the pool when the water is stirred. While I am trying to get in, someone else goes down ahead of me." Then Jesus said to him, "Get up! Pick up your mat and walk." At once the man was cured; he picked up his mat and walked. (John 5:2–9a NIV)

You notice that in this passage that the "invalid" or the "man with the infirmity" was in a place where the sick assembled to be healed by stepping into a pool that an angel troubled at a certain season. This sounds like a good place to find oneself if one is sick. However, because this was a place where healing was possible, a multitude of sick folk lay around the pool. What made it even more challenging was that when the water was troubled, according to verse 4, only one was healed, the first one who stepped in. This challenge placed this certain man in an awkward position, not knowing what to do. So for thirty-eight years, he tried to be the first, but he got cut off.

I do not mean to criticize this man, but thirty-eight years is a long time to be at the pool and not get in first. I wonder if his condition and challenge caused him to be more comfortable than creative. For thirty-eight years, I wonder if he could have used his creativity and ingenuity, his influence and negotiating skill, and his seniority and situation to better position himself to be the first. Did his condition and challenge cause him to throw in the towel and just go through the motion? Had he become comfortable with his environment in his new place? What causes me to wonder about this is that when Jesus asked him, "Do you want to get well?" He did not give a resounding, unequivocal yes.

After thirty-eight years of seriously trying, I would have expected an exciting and affirmative response. Instead he gave an explanation or excuse for why he was not healed. Jesus asked him if he wanted to be healed. Did he want what he came for thirty-eight years ago? Did he want to finally take the step he had been missing for thirty-eight years? Instead of answering the question, he offers an excuse for why he was not healed. This is the response of many who have given up on their dream, their desires after a force hits them that impedes or stops their progress. After some time of failed attempts, they give up. Now the only thing left is to make repeated veiled attempts at success and add them to your list of explanations and justifications for why you are where you are.

"I have no one to help me into the pool when the water is stirred. While I am trying to get in, someone else goes down ahead of me." This is your response, if you become comfortable in your place after giving up because you did not know what to do. You set up residence. You have accepted things as they are. You are committed to the idea that everything is outside of your control. There is nothing that you can do. You believe you are where you are and that is where you are going to be because "no one will help me" and "someone is blocking me."

You have lost your motivation to be different and to do more. You believe you will not get the position, so you do not apply. You believe you will not be promoted, so you do not put in the work. You do not believe you will be selected for the training, so you do not put your name forward. Instead of acting, you react. Instead of taking ownership for your behavior, you blame others. Instead of taking a step, you make excuses.

To make matters worse, when nothing happens because you did nothing to make it happen, you have the gall and audacity to say, "See, I told you." This is not a good place to be and not a good place to stay. The good news is that you can change things. Instead of accepting where you are, pointing fingers, or blaming others, you can take a step and get in the pool anyway. It may be more difficult now than it was then, but it can be done. "Nobody told you that the road would be easy ..." Your experiences, however good or bad, that result from you taking actions will make and mold you into the person you are destined to be. You must keep moving.

To stay where you are and blame others is not a productive or viable option. When you are not getting what you want from your life experiences, the natural, although childish, tendency is to look for someone or something to blame. Maybe someone stepped in front of you or someone else's idea got selected instead of yours. Perhaps that person got the job you wanted or has a degree that you do not have from a school that you did not attend. Or someone else is just better at this work than you.

Now what? It happened. It happens, and it might occur again. The questions you must answer are, "What am I going to do to ensure it doesn't happen again, to be ready the next time it comes up, or to move past it now that it has?"

You will always be able to make excuses, blame someone, explain, or justify being where you are. However, you must ask yourself, "What good will it do? What will it change?" Unfortunately, when you are successful at identifying a justifiable reason for being where you are, you have no reason to act. There's no reason to change.

Could this man have done something different in his thirty-eight years that could have changed his life? If he did not have an excuse or someone to blame, could he have gotten there first? Honestly, I think the man was where he was because this was his time. That said, his-story does not have to be your story.

Let me also caution that you not judge your steps or journey by someone else's. You should not gauge your growth and development by them. You should not assume that just because someone else got their second wind at the half-mile mark that this is where you will get yours. It is not. We are all different and have many distinct things affecting us. We may be on the same track, running the same race, competing against the same people, and having the same destination, and yet we have different experiences and separate outcomes. If the steps from your two feet are having different experiences in the race that you are running, you can rest assured that everyone in the race is running it uniquely and having different experiences at various times. You must control what you can, including your response to what you cannot control.

If you are in a place and you don't know what to do, it does not matter how you got there, how you arrived. The question is: what are you going to do? History does not have to be your story; your future does not have to be your past. One of Job's friends reminded him of this in Job 8:4. "Your beginnings will seem humble, so prosperous will your future be."

While his view of God's judgment may have been misplaced or misguided, the friend's desire for Job's welfare was not. So he tells Job to take one step and seek God, and he, Job, would be restored to a place of blessing, a site different from where he was.

Unlike Job's friend, I am less concerned about how you arrived and more concerned about your departure. However, I agree that a step is required if you are going to change things. You can point your fingers, identify, and provide legitimate justification and reasons for why you are where you are, but they will not change anything. After you have explained, justified, rationalized, and memorialized your situation, even if the tables were turned against you to create your lack of certainty, you are still responsible for if you stay where you are or move out. You may not determine the stimuli, but you govern your response. If you stay, it's on you; if you leave, it's on you. The difficulty or the impact of your response does not determine your ability to respond. While there are no guarantees that your response will secure your desired outcomes, you are still response-able. If you make a responsible decision, you will better position yourself to secure your desired outcome. Your response to what happens determines what happens next. Take a step and change your position. Change your life for good.

Finally, like the journey of a thousand miles beginning with that first step, the step you take when you do not know what to do will not be easy. That said, if you want something bad enough, you are willing to put in the work. The question you should ask yourself is, "Do my actions align with my desire?" People want a lot, but they are not always willing to pay the cost and put in the time, energy, and resources. You want the car and the house, but do you want to work for it? You want the mashed potatoes, but do you want to peel and slice the potatoes? "Everybody wants to go to heaven, but nobody wants to die." Everything comes with a cost. Are you willing to pay? How bad do you want it? Saying you want something is not the same as acting like you want something. Your effort must match your desire. You cannot expect to put in minimal effort and get maximum return. "Garbage in, garbage out."

"A man reaps what he sows" (Galatians 6:7 NIV). When you are at a crossroad and you do not know what to do, your next step is not only critical. It is difficult because you do not know if it is the right step. Will it lead you to your destination? Will it take you further off track? Will it be a waste of your time? Will you be better off staying where you are? A step into this space is uncomfortable, uncertain, and frightening. For these reasons, many people stop, throw in the towel, throw up their hands, and give up. They lack the commitment and fortitude to decide to move forward and live with the consequences. If your next step would change your life, would you take it? Would you be willing to commit to a course of action, to take a step if you knew your life depended on it? Well, it does!

This man at the pool talked a good game. He spoke of his seasonal commitment and dependence on others. He spoke of his frustration from being prevented to step in when the water was troubled. However, when asked if he wanted what he came to the pool for over thirty-eight years ago, his answer showed more disappointment than desire, more doubt than deliverance, and more deterrence than dreams. After thirty-eight years, he could have been tired from trying, comfortable in his common area, passive-aggressive, or aggressively passive, waiting for someone to put him in the pool.

Regardless of his history or past action, he now has another chance to decide what to do. This is your life; this is your chance. Do not waste time wondering or waiting; do not squander your second (third, fourth, fifth ...) chance being comfortable and contrite. Rather, align your efforts with your ambition, your deeds with your desires, and your dedication with your dreams. Take a step and keep it moving. This is the beginning of the rest of your life.

CHAPTER **'10'**

Stop Tripping: It Is a Journey, Not a Trip

Trust the Outcome

ONE OF THE RISKS OF BEING IN A PLACE WHEN YOU don't know what to do is getting caught up or stuck there. As noted in the previous chapter, to prevent this you need to move, do something, or take a step. If you are moving and taking the requisite step, you should not be overconfident or disillusioned, thinking that movement alone is enough to get you to your destination. Yes, movement is essential, critical, and indispensable, but it is not the end all, be all. Movement alone does not reduce the forces that work against you to make you stop. It does not take you directly to your destination; it does not continue without you continuing it. Yes, a step will solve some of your problems. However, you will need a new set of solutions for the problems you face after you start and while you are moving.

Knowing that you are on a journey and not a trip will prove helpful. I know these words are interchangeable, synonymous, and have each other as meaning. However, to clarify how they differ for this book and our conversation, let us define journey as the travel from your starting point to your destination and trip as a single round or tour on your journey. A journey is to the finish line; a trip is to the next stop. A journey is long term; a trip is intermittent. This distinction is being made so you can separate your travel to your destination in two parts, short and long term.

WALKING IN THE GRAY

While this may seem insignificant, it is not, as you need to separate the challenges you face and the opportunities you are given as you travel to ensure that you do not get off track. Your commitment and dedication are to your destination, your journey. With your destination, your end game, your journey set, you know where you are going. You may even have a plan in place to get there. While you can and will anticipate challenges, there is no way for you to accurately predict what they will be, when they will happen, what impact they will have on you, and what adjustment you will have to make. All you really know for certain is that you will be challenged time and again. Knowing the certainty of you being challenged, you can now accept that this is part of your journey. As part of your journey, your challenges only represent a trip. That is, your challenges are intermittent. They occur in intervals, not continuous. Your challenges are there to cause you to stumble, fail, and trip.

If you are going to make it to your destination, you must know and remember that it is a journey that you are on and not a trip. So whatever happens as you travel, don't trip. It's a journey. When you hit a wall and are not sure what to do as you travel, don't trip. It's a journey. Your travel will be so much easier if you understand that you are on a journey and not a trip. Knowing this, you are less likely to spend time tripping.

The Merriam-Webster Dictionary defines tripping as catching your foot against something and stumbling. The Urban Dictionary defines tripping as freaking out, acting crazy. Either of the definitions accurately describe what is often the desired outcome of your challenges. When things are going your way, things are flowing. It is smooth sailing. There is nothing to impede or negatively affect your travel.

Life's journey needs no assistance. Your future is bright, and the way is clear. This type of living does not last forever and often not very long. Most people can handle the good days. It is when the good days must be counted to remind you not to complain that you are likely to trip. These are days when the lyrics of Rev. Paul

Jones's song "I Won't Complain,"[7] speak to you on a very personal and deep level.

> I've had some weary days
> I've had some sleepless nights
> But when I look around
> And I think things over
> All of my good days
> Outweigh my bad days
> So I won't complain

I want to focus your attention on these other days:

- when you feel like tripping because you have been tripped by someone or something
- when you fall and think you cannot get back up
- when the force against you seems to get the best of you and you must take two steps backward instead of going forward
- when life deals you a lemon and you cannot find your recipe for lemonade and, if you do, you realize you have no sweetener

Let me start by encouraging you to stop tripping. You are on a journey.

For the sake of clarity, when tripping is used in this book, it means that you are over the top, exaggerating the issue. You are focusing on things that do not matter and can be changed. You are getting caught up in the minutia or the small details that, if missed, will not be missed. You are sweating the little stuff that could be accomplished without sweat. You are getting off track when the track is still in tack. When you do not know what you should do next, lashing out, complaining, blaming others, and

---

[7] **I Won't Complain: Platinum Edition** Rev. Paul Jones Christian & Gospel Released: Dec 31, 1992

pointing your fingers are common and, in most cases, expected behavior. After all, there is nothing you can do, right?

So you do what you can do. You trip. The problem is that tripping gives you something to do, but it is not something that is productive or gets you any closer to your destination. You take significant energy, dedicated resources, and your unredeemable time and counter your situation, doing something that makes you feel better for a moment but does not get you any closer to your destination. You are tripping.

You and your organization would be better served if you focus on the things that matter, those that will help you get to where you are going. If you can begin to see that you are on a journey headed to your destination and that to get there you will have to take several trips, trips that contribute to but do not conclude, cancel, or determine your destination, you are ready to begin.

When you focus on the journey, you can see that this is not just about where you are but about where you're headed. You have not arrived your destination; your destination is not here. Here is a temporary location, a layover, a stopping point on your journey to your destination. Where you are is just a transition spot. It is not your destination. The sooner you understand the journey you are on, the quicker you will value and appreciate the trips you have to take or experience in order to complete your journey, and the sooner you will stop tripping.

Trip denotes to stumble or fall. When you fall, you have options: stay down or get up. What you decide will determine your future. If you stay down, you stay, where you are and in whatever condition you are in. If you get up, you have options. The same is true of you journeying to your destination.

If you stumble or fall on the way, you have options: stay where you are or keep it moving. What you need to know here is that you have options. If you choose and do not like your choice, choose again. Take another step. After all, "We fall down, but we get up." When you find yourself in a position where you are not making any progress or not at the pace you believe you are capable of, you have options.

Choose one. I recommend you choose to take a step forward in the direction of, or what you believe is the direction of, your destination. Do not waste time engaging excuses or bellowing blames. Don't trip. Own your situation regardless of how you arrived. You are here. If knowing how you got here helps you get there (there being where you are going), do your homework. Research. If it does not, use this time discovering your next move because you must take a step.

Taking a step when you are in a position where you do not know what step to take is critically important. If you do not move in this position, the possibility of you tripping becomes more likely with the passing of each moment. It is very common when you are in a position where you do not know what to do that you do something to make matters worse. This generally happens because you lose sight of the goal, the destination, or the big picture and get caught up in the moment, which becomes momentous and more important than the mission.

To make matters worse, the momentous moment that resulted from you having stumbled or fallen creates a perception where your view of impending possibilities is limited at best. You cannot see your way out, so you begin to complain and gripe about how you got in. Instead of going forward to fulfill your dream, you end up making poor decisions and going backward. Backward would not be bad if you were using it to gain momentum to make a forward push, but this is not the case. Your backward movement solidifies your surrender, you raising the white flag, retreating, or throwing in the towel. This is unfortunate given the reality that, in the scheme of things, this is just a trip on your journey. This is a trip that you can chalk up to experience. Take as a learning opportunity. It may not be easy, but the best lessons or teachers are not. When you understand and accept your travel as a journey and not a trip, you will be able to take your next step knowing that whatever happens is only a part of the process, a trip. Knowing this, you will not trip over things on your journey.

What makes our journey a success is how we respond to difficulties, the trips we must take to complete our journey. Difficulties are a part of the journey; they are as certain as the journey. Their certainty almost makes them insignificant. What makes them valuable is our response to them and the lessons they teach us. Are you going to trip and act as if this is the end of the world? Or are you going to take the lessons these distractions/forces offer and use them to learn something valuable?

I am endorsing and encouraging the lessons. Stop tripping and look for the lessons to learn from these experiences. I know this sounds like the old proverbial saying, "What does not kill us will make us better." However, the challenges of life are real. The question is: will you turn these challenges into opportunities to learn, that is, lessons? If you can accept your challenges as stepping stones or opportunities to get you to the next level on your journey, you will not succumb to them. Instead you will learn from and leverage them to ensure your success. How you view your challenges will determine how you approach them and how you allow them to affect you and your journey. When you view your challenges as opportunities, when you do not know what to do, you know you are not at the end of your road. You know you will figure something out, if not immediately, surely after you learn the lesson this challenge is teaching you. After all, this is a point in time on your journey to your destination. It is a comma and not a period, as it represents a pause and not a permanent stop. If you change your view about your situation, if you alter your perspective on what you are going through, you will change your experience and outcome.

If you go into a challenge or are facing a challenge or a setback with the understanding that you will come out of it and it will lead you to something greater, you will engage and experience your struggle differently. This is analogous to you going to the gym to suffer physical stress in order to build muscles and get stronger. You enter the gym with a plan in mind and a workout goal to help you accomplish it. You know that each drop of sweat represents calories and/or fat burned and each weight lifted gets you closer to your goal. While you are struggling, breathing heavily, feeling tired, and questioning yourself, you continue to push because you know this will get you to the next level physically. You understand that in order to accomplish your physical goal, you must be spiritually and mentally focused and physically committed. You must accept the fact that the outcome outweighs the input. The benefit outweighs the cost. You must commit to the cause and the course of action.

You cannot afford to trip, as tripping creates an attitude of ingratitude, a cause for justifiable permanent pause, an excuse to exit, a front to fail. When you trip, you acknowledge that you cannot see your way out, that you believe or feel that you are stuck and lack the freedom of movement to change your situation. You lash out at others or something to blame. You do not see the opportunities your challenges are affording you or are trying to teach you. You see your current situation only, and you lack the view of your future that shows that you are not in this position or place permanently. Here and now is your focus and your future. You have managed to get caught up in the moment in whatever you are experiencing that is causing you to feel like you have no options.

This approach to dealing with problems is very common. When you are in this place, you can easily find a support group, people who are where you are and completely understand what you are dealing with. Unfortunately, the answers or solutions they have for you are the same ones they had for themselves, the same ones you currently have for yourself: do nothing, blame others/ something, or make excuses. Their solutions, their answers, are what caused them to flock or migrate to you. Maybe it's true that "misery loves company" and "birds of a feather flock together." You must be careful when you are at a low point that you do not accept or seek advice from someone in the same predicament you are in. If they have not figured out what to do, what can they tell you to do? They can console you, understand your situation, or provide you support and comfort. This is exactly what you do not need, if you are going to get out from among them, change your circumstances, and take the next step.

A change in your perspective on challenges, your surroundings, and your circumstances are warranted if you are going to get to your destination. You must not get stuck, caught, or mired down under the load of your challenges. Your current experiences, however difficult, are just moments or points in time on your journey.

If you take a closer look at the workout analogy, you may be able to see the importance of mind-set, focus, and commitment to your journey. People who work out and have a habit of doing it understand the value of having the right perspective. They have a habit of working out and can focus on their goals and push themselves to get the desired results. They get up in the morning with the goal of going to the gym to build muscles. While they may be driven, determined, and dedicated, they do not feel the same every day. They may not even enjoy the habit of getting out of bed early to go to the gym and push themselves to their very limit. However, they know and understand that if they are going to reach their goal, these are critical parts of the process. So they do it. Rain, snow, sleet, hail, or sunshine, they do it. Whether they feel like it or not, they do it. They do it because they have a goal in mind and see the value of the process, the growing pains, the interim struggles, and successes.

Individuals with this perspective see their worst days as their best days. While they do not feel like getting out of bed, going to the gym, and working out, they do it. When they do, the sense of accomplishment they feel from having pushed through their struggle, having taken the next step, and having gotten the workout in despite how they felt outweighs the end of their feel-good days.

You have undoubtedly had this experience of finally doing something that you needed to do but did not feel like it. While the task itself may have been menial, the sense of accomplishment you felt was superior and exciting. When you put in work, when you do not feel like it, you feel accomplished. The same is true of your struggles, your challenges.

If you are going through something that makes you feel like you have no alternatives, think you have no way out, and believe you are at the end of the road, if you can do something, anything, your sense of accomplishment and confidence will grow. When you do something when you feel like nothing is your option, make a decision when you cannot seem to decide, or take a step when you cannot see the ground, your sense of accomplishment grows, as do your accomplishments.

When you experience the feeling of moving when the forces pushing against you are greater than the energy you feel like exerting or the energy you have available to exert, your sense of accomplishment skyrockets. You almost feel like you have done the impossible. You now have a story to tell. Everybody likes a Cinderella story. We all want to see the underdog win. When you are Cinderella or the underdog, do not waste the opportunity to be the main character in the comeback story of the century. Don't trip. Do something.

If life were easy, it would be boring. Who wants this to be their story? You are on path to your destination. It is not going to be easy. It will be eventful, but you can make it. When we travel from the Washington, DC, area to Arkansas by way of Tennessee, we start knowing we are going to take a certain route. The road we travel is at times straight, narrow, wide, bumpy, hilly, curvy, slippery, wet, or smooth. On our way to Arkansas, we may encounter detours, accidents, speed traps, speed bumps, traffic jams, weather changes, police, speed changes, or other challenges. Whatever we encounter, we will view as temporary, as our destination is Arkansas. That is where we are going, and that is where we will be. Since we have taken this trip several times, we have had a sundry of experiences. We have yet to make the trip and not have a story to tell about something that happened that impeded our progress. We started out one trip in a new car but arrived in a rental.

Please note, when you are journeying to your destination, you will have a sundry of struggles, a plethora of problems, a myriad of mishaps. When these things happen—and they will—you can trip or start tripping and call it quits. Alternatively, you could take these as opportunities to build your repertoire of recollections. Nothing is better than a good story of triumph over trouble to remember, recall, recollect, or tell. You will not only have the experience of feeling like a winner. You get to share that feeling of accomplishment with someone else.

When you don't know what to do, you do something, and it turns out right, you feel great. When you share your story, someone else will feel great too. Maybe you got it wrong. You made the wrong decision. Now you have the benefit of your experience and something to tell someone else to avoid. This is another win. On your way to your destination, maybe you saw an accident or a police officer when you were speeding but did not get stopped. Or perhaps you almost had an accident. You ran off the road but managed to get control of your car.

In either of these situations, when you are clear of the trouble, you have a story to tell. When you make it to your destination, you are not only excited about seeing the people you journeyed to see, you are excited that you made it and have something to talk about, something to tell about how you made it over. There is very little to tell about a journey that is uneventful, that goes perfect and as planned. What can you say? *We had a good trip?* Not so when you have a trip with experiences.

Overcoming your difficulties has given you something to share, some advice to offer someone who may benefit or learn from your experiences. If during your travel you encountered construction, you can tell someone to avoid the area if they want to save time. Whatever your experiences, if you see them as a part of the process, a step on your journey to your destination, you are less inclined to get caught up, bound down, wound up, twisted, stuck, or stopped. You know this is a journey, not a trip.

People typically trip, fall, or fail because they get stuck, get caught in a place that they believe they cannot get out of, or get comfortable and view change as too much of a challenge. They may have been in a good position and moving forward with good momentum, but something happened. Maybe their foot got stuck on something; perhaps they looked behind and something caught their attention long enough to capture their focus and cause them to miss something important to their next step. They never saw the hole, the gap, the bump in the road, or the trap. They may have been doing great, moving at a good pace and on the right trajectory, but they tripped when someone else on the journey distracted them. They may have been doing great until they started comparing themselves to others and began to feel that they deserved more, should be further along, or should have the position the other person has.

The number of reasons people trip equal or exceed the number of people who trip. There are many. The reasons to trip, much like excuses, do not require validation, proof, or justification, and they vary by individual. If you do not have the proper perspective on your challenges, you will trip and start tripping. The key to alleviate the possibility of this happening to you is to have the proper perspective on your challenges and a keen focus on your destination. You must be focused enough to know where you are going but keenly aware of where you are. You must know that where you are is not your destination, just a point in time along your journey. So regardless of what happens to you now, given that it is only for a time, you should accept the lesson that it is teaching and not get caught up tripping. It is only temporary.

While the solution to tripping seems easy, the sundry of reasons prevents this from happening. Because the reasons for tripping are personal and unique, they are individually attached and sometimes emotionally felt. For example, you may trip because of past experiences. You cannot get over what happened to you yesterday. You blame your past for being where you are. So instead of letting go of your past or accepting it as a teacher, you hold on to it with all the associated emotions as you try to go forward and then stumble. The additional weight you carry holding onto the past often prevents you from being able to move freely and successfully. This adds to your frustrations and provides more fuel for your internal fire, which burns brighter with each unsuccessful step. The more weight you carry, the more frustrated you get; the more frustrated you get, the more your personality and performance suffers. The more your personality and performance suffers, the more you are overlooked for awards, recognitions, and benefits. The more you are overlooked, the more frustrated you become. The more frustrated you become, the more you trip. And the cycle continues until tripping becomes your norm and you do not know what to do.

The cycle causes you to believe that you are justified tripping; it causes you to lose sight of the real reason you tripped in the first place. You are on a journey to your destination, and you hit what should have been a bump in the road. However, instead of continuing your journey, you tripped and kept on tripping until you lost sight of where you were going. Now you are trying to justify where you are and are not looking at where you are going. You are on a trip and tripping instead of being on a journey and taking one step at a time. Your past has consumed your future; the small things have become huge. Molehills have become mountains. Your journey has been reduced to a trip, and you are tripping.

If you are going to be successful, you must see life as a journey and not a trip. It is not a one-time event; it is a process. It is not a battle; it is a war. Like strategically winning a war, you may lose a few battles, but you must keep fighting. Life is filled with many ups and downs, opportunities to learn how to succeed and how to bounce back. If you have the proper perspective and see life as a journey and not a trip, you will welcome its pluses and minuses, positives and negatives. With the proper perspective, you will know that life's downs are not there to take you under but to elevate you higher, to grow and develop you, and to prepare and purpose you. If you see life in the long haul, as a journey, not a trip, you can face each challenge as a building block, not a stumbling block. You will understand that struggles are there to make you strong, not to weaken or destroy you. Frederick Douglass may have said it correctly,

> If there is no struggle, there is no progress. Those who profess to favor freedom, and yet deprecate agitation, are men who want crops without plowing up the ground. They want rain without thunder and lightning. They want the ocean without the awful roar of its many waters. This struggle may be a moral one; or it may be a physical one; or it may be both moral and physical; but it must be a struggle …

Struggles, trials, tribulations, suffering, and challenges afford us the opportunity to become stronger. If you do not experience struggles, you are not likely to know your strength. Like darkness brings out the best in light, your challenges will bring out the best in you. Losing a game during the regular season may better prepare you for the postseason. The loss could teach you something about the areas you need to work on, develop, and strengthen. The proper perspective will inform you that when you are faced with a challenge on the job or in an assignment or life, it is not to destroy but to build you; it is there to afford you an opportunity to become better in your lot in life or at your craft. So when challenged, don't trip. Remember, it is a journey, not a trip.

CHAPTER **11**

ENCOURAGE YOURSELF AND KNOW YOUR WHY

THERE WILL COME A TIME IN YOUR LIFE, IN YOUR professional journey, when you will feel alone, abandoned, or ostracized. You will struggle with being by yourself, being left alone because no one seems to understand or appreciate the challenges you are facing, or being excluded. You will find yourself with your back against the wall and your opportunities limited. There will be times during your journey when

- You will find yourself by yourself and others at odds with you.
- Your decisions to move and how you move will be inconsistent with the advice and guidance provided by your mentors, colleagues, friends, and family.
- The decisions you make will not produce the desired outcomes and you will find yourself wondering what to do.
- Others will intentionally and unintentionally contribute to putting you in positions where you are not sure about your next course of action.
- You are in a difficult place without knowing or understanding why.
- Your decisions to do, when you don't know what to do, will put you in a worse position, create more challenges, and cause more disappointment.

- Your actions will not only negatively affect you but those around you.
- You have done all the right things, put your best foot forward, and put in the necessary work and you cannot see any fruit from your labor.
- You end up in what seems to be the worst possible position despite your best intentions and the best advice and guidance from others.
- You wake up in the morning and not want to get out of bed because you feel you have given all you have to give and have gotten nothing in return.

These are the times when you must encourage yourself, when you must know why you do what you do and how to motivate you. During these times, the external factors, forces, sources, or causes will not be enough to keep you on track or moving forward. The pats on the back, the attaboys, the monetary rewards, or the written or spoken words of inspiration from others will not only not be enough, but they are likely not to be present. You will have to find the strength, courage, and motivation within yourself to keep moving. You will have to recall your reason for doing what you are doing and remember why you are doing it. You will have to encourage yourself.

In Scripture, there is this wonderful story of David having to encourage himself during his most difficult struggle. In 1 Samuel 29, David managed to get himself into a real jam. After being delivered many times from the hands of Saul, David got tired of being on the run and living like a fugitive. So he came up with a plan to escape from Saul, which involved him colluding with the enemy, the Philistines. He took 600 of his men and their families into the land of the Philistines, thinking if Saul discovered where he was, he would give up his pursuit. He was right.

After building a relationship with the Philistine king, Achish, establishing his cover, David and his men settled in Ziklag. Interestingly, they used this location as a base of operations to attack the enemies of Israel. Things were going well until the Philistine king asked David to participate in a war against the Israelites.

While David agreed in order to retain his cover, the princes of Philistine angrily protested, and David and his men were sent home. When they got home, they found their city burned to the ground, their homes destroyed, and their wives and children gone. The Amalekites had invaded and taken captive all that was precious to David and his men. David and his men yelled and cried until they had no more tears left to shed. David was distressed, and his men were talking about stoning him. He had come to the end of his rope, and he was discouraged. Feeling like a complete failure, abandoned by God, and rejected by those who once cared, David is all alone, with no close friends and no family. However, instead of despairing like others, being angry like others, or blaming someone else like others, David distinguishes himself. He encouraged himself in the Lord.

> And it came to pass, when David and his men were come to Ziklag on the third day, that the Amalekites had invaded the south, and Ziklag, and smitten Ziklag, and burned it with fire; And had taken the women captives, that were therein: they slew not any, either great or small, but carried them away, and went on their way. So David and his men came to the city, and, behold, it was burned with fire; and their wives, and their sons, and their daughters, were taken captives. Then David and the people that were with him lifted up their voice and wept, until they had no more power to weep. And David's two wives were taken captives, Ahinoam the Jezreelitess, and Abigail the wife of Nabal the Carmelite. And David was greatly distressed; for the people spake of stoning him, because the soul of all the people

was grieved, every man for his sons and for his daughters: but David encouraged himself in the Lord his God. And David said to Abiathar the priest, Ahimelech's son, I pray thee, bring me hither the ephod. And Abiathar brought thither the ephod to David. And David inquired at the Lord, saying, Shall I pursue after this troop? shall I overtake them? And he answered him, Pursue: for thou shalt surely overtake them, and without fail recover all. (1 Samuel 30:1–8 KJV)

As bad as it may have seemed, appeared, or been for David, he encouraged himself in the Lord and sought guidance on his next course of action. There is much that we can learn from David's struggle, reaction, and response. While David had already been anointed to be king of Israel, he had to go through and suffer a lot before he was crowned. I am of the belief that each of his trials, struggles, and challenges prepared him for the assignment he was destined to. If David were to become the man God wanted him to be, he had to be stripped of everything, including his reputation and self-will. He cried his last tears of self-pity so he could understand the place for tears ("Weeping may endure for a night" [Psalms 30:5b KJV]); faced the full fury of loneliness and overcome it ("Yea thou I walk through ..." [Psalms 23:4a KJV]); and put away all memory of applause and praise for what he had accomplished and draw his strength from God ("I will lift up mine eyes unto the hills, from whence cometh my help ..." [Psalms 121:1 KJV]).

If David were to be king of Israel, he had to learn to trust and depend on God. With each struggle he faced and challenge he overcame, he became more of the man he needed to be the king of Israel. While this was true of David, it is also true of us. To become who you are destined to be, you must go through something in order to get to something. You must suffer to reign (2 Timothy 2:12 KJV).

Experiencing stress or being distressed is common to most of us. The differences in our outcomes results from how we handle ourselves when we are stressed. The story of David is a compelling one because instead of despairing or distressing, David did something that we all should take note of. He encouraged himself. He did not have his family, friends, or foes to tell him what to do. He had to deal with this by himself. At first, he was distressed and discouraged.

You are no different at your lowest point. Your most difficult times will occur when you are alone, when you do not have family, friends, or foes to tell you what you should or should not do next. As a result, you are very likely to become discouraged. You may be discouraged because you know why you are in the position you are in and you feel you are responsible or in a hopeless situation. You may be discouraged because you are not sure what actions to take. The last ones you took brought you to this position of uncertainty. Regardless of why, you are now discouraged, and you feel lost or like you have lost everything. You question your tomorrow, and you do not have a solution for today. To make matters worse, instead of seeking or crying out for help, you fake the funk, forge the façade, choose to save face, or decide to guard and protect yourself by looking and acting in control. Alternatively, you may feel responsible and therefore feel that you do not deserve an opportunity or another chance; you feel that you deserve what you are getting.

David clearly was at this point. He was discouraged. However, he realized that his future did not end with his present. Truth is, your future does not end with your present. It begins with your present. Yes, you should accept this moment for what it is, a moment in time, not the end of time. You should use this moment to gather momentum for your future. You may be discouraged, but brighter days are ahead. You may be confused and uncertain of your next steps, but you can take a step and see what happens. You may have a lot of questions, for instance, "Where do I go from here? How do I get up from being down? How do I move forward when standing still seems to be a safer, if not a better option?" You may even feel that anything you do will be a waste of time, that you have "been there done that." You may be at your lowest point and feel like doing nothing.

When you find yourself in this position—and you will—you should make it your business to not look out at your situation but look in for your solution. During your distressful and discouraging times, you would do yourself a service to remember your why, your reason for doing what you do. You may have to look deep within yourself, when you are at your lowest point, to remind yourself why what you are doing is so important, how it is required for you to get to your destination.

During your low points when you feel beaten and beaten down, you will have to look inside to identify your motivation and the courage to keep moving despite what is going on around you or is happening to you. You will have to look in yourself to identify the courage, that is, you will have to get courage from inside yourself, "in-courage." When you identify the "in-courage," you will be able to encourage yourself. Yes, you can sit where you are and blame yourself. You can stand where you are and point your finger at someone else. You can stay where you are and feel justified because you made poor decisions. Alternatively, you can find within yourself your reason to move forward. You can recall the reason you set out on this journey to your destination and use this as a call to action. You can look in to see the future your dreamed of and use this as your motivation to keep moving. You can look in to find the courage to face your challenges. Your feeling of fear and doubt about your decision should not be allowed to paralyze you and keep you in a place where you know in your heart of hearts is not where you are supposed or are destined to be.

Your uncertainty about where you are and doubts about your next steps serve as a reminder that there is something else that you must do. Your doubt is not a decision. It is a sign that tells you that there is something else for you, that there is something else that you should do. Your doubt creates a level of stress that forces you to take note of your situation. The stress may be so powerful that it causes distress or discouragement. Like pain, this stress reminds you that you are alive and that you have a choice. How you handle the pain, or the stress, will determine your future. You can ignore it and hope for the best, or you can take an action and continue to chart your course. Instead of staying in a place for you are doubtful, distressed, or discouraged, why not identify your why and keep it moving? Why not use your doubt, your distress, or your discouragement to make a difference?

There is some truth to the fact that life comes at you fast. When it does, sometimes it knocks you off your feet, pushes you up against the wall, knocks you flat on your back, and provides you with more challenges than opportunities. When this happens, you must decide whether to stay where you are or proceed forward. To get back on your feet, off the wall, or up may not be easy and will certainly not be the easiest option. It would be easier to wait for help, wait for something to change or happen.

As a result, you may be inclined to wait for someone to tell you what you already know. Get moving. Because the decision to move is difficult and the outcome unknown, you may be waiting for someone you respect, admire, look up to, believe in, or trust to lift you and get you to move forward. You may even be waiting for time, which many believe heals all wounds, to fix what you are afraid to face. Waiting gives you time to ignore the immediate, delay your decision, postpone your problem, defer your doubt, remit your requirements, or do nothing when doing something is required. You may continue to wait, but delaying an action that needs to happen does not change the requirement. It is up to you to decide your next course of action.

When you are alone and must make the decision to act, you must look within and identify your motivation to act. You may need to go back in order to go forward. You may need to go back and discover the original idea, thought, or motivation that put you on this journey. You can see that you are in a difficult spot and you do not know what to do, but if you can discover what inspired you to take on this task, perhaps then you will have what it takes to move. If you can remember what motivated you to move and take that first step, maybe it will be what the doctor orders to get you going. Sometimes all you need to get you out of a tough spot is the memory of what got you in it.

Your motivation for this journey was enough to get you started, which is often the most difficult part of the journey. If it were enough to get you started, maybe it will be enough to keep you going or enough to get you started again. Perhaps you are in a place where you feel like you cannot get to where you were going. You have gone or been forced off track, and you did not expect it to be this difficult. You are at a crossroad, and a decision must be made. More correctly, a decision will be made. You need to ensure that you make the decision.

Remember when a decision is required, if you do nothing, that is a decision. Rather than do nothing, rediscover your motivation. Revisit what was inside of you that drove you to want to be on the track that led you to this point. David realized that his family and the family of his men had been taken and he had to do something. If he did nothing but sat around and mourned and yelled with his men, he would not have gotten his family back, and he would likely have been stoned. He recalled the memory of his family and decided he had to do something other than just cry over them being taken.

You will have to do that same thing when you are at your crossroad. Instead of crying over the position or promotion you did not get, the opportunity you missed or were overlooked for, the dream that appears to be deferred, or the difficulty of the decision you must make, you should look in to yourself, identify your courage and "in-courage" yourself, and get moving.

Looking inside yourself to remember or recall why you are here, your motivation, will be key to your survival and success. Remember, you are here because you decided you wanted to be the CEO of your company. Now that seems impossible because you are stuck in a position. Has your reason for being here changed?

Do you still want to be CEO? If you still desire to be the CEO, you know you cannot let the fact that you seem to be stuck in a position stop you. You must proceed forward. You may have to change your original plans because you did not expect or anticipate this bump in the road, hiccup, derailment, roadblock, delay, or stop. However, here you are, but you do not have to. Nor can you afford to stay here. So instead of giving in to where you are presently, you encourage yourself and keep it or get moving. While you are at a standstill, you tell yourself that you still have the time, talent, and tenacity to be CEO. You just must take your next step and get back on track.

Please note, a conversation with yourself about yourself is not a bad thing, as it represents the fact that you have looked inside for the answers to your questions. Sometimes all you have is you. Do not allow things external to you define you or determine your course of action. Yes, they may influence and affect your course of action, but they should not be allowed to determine it. Do not stay distressed and discouraged because things are not going your way. Accept the fact that this is the way things are, but it does not mean that they must stay that way. You have options. Choose one and exercise it. Act. "In-courage" yourself. Tell yourself to get up and get moving. Tell yourself who you are, where you are going, and why you are doing what you do. Encourage yourself.

You must know what motivates, inspires, and encourages you. You cannot rely on others to motivate or keep you going. This is not to say or suggest that you should not seek or accept the advice, guidance, directions, encouragement, inspiration, or motivations from others. Quite the contrary, you should welcome it. However, you must be prepared to handle it alone, as there will come a time when others will not be an option, will be the cause of your concerns, and, while present, should be allowed to watch as you figure things out on your own. You must know the key that unlocks your inner strength, the key that opens yourself up to be "in-couraged," the key that motivates and drives you. You must know what gets you up in the morning and keeps you up at night, what inspired and motivated you to begin this journey. Your motivation may be family, friends, foes, funds, fun, or future. Or it may be popularity, prosperity, posterity, or people.

Whatever your motivation, you should know what it is. You should also know that your motivation is uniquely yours. It is what makes you do what you do. What drives you may not be what drives someone else. Be true to yourself. If you are in it for the money, the prestige, the press, the popularity, the friendships, or the fun or to impress others or help your family, it is what it is. No one else's opinion or judgment matters.

While we are each marvelously and wonderfully made with many similarities, what drives each of us is unique. What people think, feel, or know about your motivation is not important. What motivates you may not motivate, inspire, or work for them, but it works for you. We each have our reasons for doing what we do. When you know what your motivation is, you can recall or remind yourself when things get tough and you are not sure what to do next or now. Your motivation will provide you the courage and encouragement you need when you are distressed or discouraged. To that end, do what you need to do to ensure that you have access to your motivation and it is available to you when you need it. Write it down. Repeat to yourself. Get it ingrained in your system. So that when times get hard, difficult, or doubtful and you find yourself distressed or discouraged, you can pull it from your internal file, your internal storage, and your gray matter and encourage yourself.

CHAPTER 12

BELIEVE IN YOURSELF

WHEN EXAMINING THE POSSIBILITY OF SUCCESS, EVEN when the tools are available, most of you wonder if success is for you. You wonder if you can get there from here. While success means to succeed at something, to achieve a desired outcome, its true meaning is uniquely defined by the individual. It is generally a distant goal or objective that requires effort, initiative, good luck, faith, favor, planning, training, strategy, and a willingness to extend, stretch, and commit yourself to achieve. Whatever you define as success, if you are going to achieve it, you must put yourself in a position to do so. You cannot allow yourself to fail out of the gate because you do not know how to get to your destination from where you are. Lack of knowledge on how to achieve your goal can have a crippling effect and prevent you from taking that most critical first step. You need to get moving. Take that first step. Your desire to be successful is a sign, an indication that you have what it takes. Start by believing in yourself. You do not have to make your dream a reality today. You do not have to achieve success today. You just need to get started today. Dreams delayed become deferred and eventually die. You do not need to know how to make your dream a reality. You do not need to have all the tools in your toolbox. You have the most critical key to your success, your desire and your dream. You just need to take that first step.

Your dream will become a reality when you put in the time. Your dream will not fail because of the dream, as you can never dream to big. If your dream is not realized, it will be because you did not believe enough in yourself to make it a reality. When you do not believe in yourself, you begin to question yourself as well as your abilities, resources, connections, upbringing, training/ education, aspiration, and commitment. You start asking yourself, "Is it worth the effort? Can I do this? Was I wrong?"

As a result of your disbelief, you fail before you even start, get out of the gate, or even give it a try. When you do not believe in yourself, you do not even give yourself a chance. You cannot see yourself being where you want to be. You cannot see yourself able to fulfil your desires. You cannot see yourself being successful. You limit your dreams to when you are sleeping, when your eyes are closed. You refuse to open your eyes to the possibility that what you are seeing in your dream is what you are destined to be. You never take the steps or actions that you take or execute so easily when your eyes are closed. You never wake up to the reality of your dream. Alternatively, you open your eyes and take timid, measured, and controlled steps so you can say, "I tried." You passively pursue your dream knowing it will not happen. Let me stop here and pause you here as well. You will never achieve your desire and realize your dream if you do not believe in yourself. Without believing in yourself, you cannot get there from here.

The assurance you need to realize your dream is a belief in yourself. You must first see yourself achieving your dream. If you cannot see it, you cannot be it. If you can see it, you can be it. You can rest assured that there will be those who do not believe in you. That should be anticipated and expected. However, you must believe in yourself. You must believe that you have, or will have when necessary, what you need to turn your ideas, thoughts, dreams, and visions into reality. This is labeled as the first step toward your destination because it all begins with a belief in yourself. Before you can take your first step to realizing your success, you must believe in yourself. A burning desire without a belief in yourself to make it happen will burn you up. A dream or vision without a belief in yourself to make it a reality becomes an illusion. Ideas and thoughts of success without a belief in yourself will flee and eventually pass. The realization of your ambitions, aspirations, dreams, desires, goals, and objectives begin with you believing in yourself. If you are going to achieve, you must believe in you. You can have everything at your disposal that you need to accomplish a task, but until you believe in your ability to accomplish that task, what you have is disposable. You may be the most talented or gifted individual for what needs to be done, but if you do not believe that you have what it takes, all will be wasted. How many times have you seen people with less but achieve the most? How many times have you watched the ugliest guy get the prettiest girl? If you were wondering what separated them, it was their belief in themselves. When you believe in yourself, you create an aura of success, and you attract the same. When you believe in yourself, it emanates confidence and changes your environment. When you believe in yourself, your abilities, tool kit, training/education, knowledge, or familiarity with the task do not limit you.

Like it or not, you are responsible for turning your dreams into reality. You have not been given the luxury of sitting on the sidelines while someone else duly details and develops your dreams. Your dreams and the tools to make them a reality may have been given to you or inspired by God, but it is up to you to believe enough to make them real. Hebrews 11:6 says, "Without faith it is impossible to please God." You have been given everything you need to succeed, but you must believe. Paul describes faith in Hebrews 11:1 as "the substance of things hoped for, the evidence of things not seen."

Faith, your belief, is the substance and the evidence of your dreams, ideas, visions, and what you hope for. More clearly, your belief gives you the proof you need to know that what you believe will happen. Substance and evidence provide proof of what you hope for and do not see. Faith allows you to believe in the then, the future, and the now. Your belief allows you to see the possible amid the impossible. It allows you to see the sunshine despite the rain, to know that tomorrow will be brighter than today. Your belief makes you feel and taste the reality of something that is not here right now. Your belief in yourself will keep you standing, walking, running, and fighting when all around you suggest otherwise. It will push you beyond your naysayers, your haters, and those whose intent it is to keep you down. It will drive you to accomplish things that others say could not be done and keep you on the path when you have taken days off or when life deals you a bad hand. You must believe in yourself to push yourself past your points of procrastination, to drive out your disbelief, to not take no for an answer when yes is required, and to continue your journey when others have given up on you and your loved ones lose heart and wonder why you keep trying.

There will be times on your journey to success that all you have is you pushing you to achieve your goal, vision, passion, purpose, and future. You must remember that "it's yours." Since it is yours, it is up to you to secure and to realize it. When you must go in alone, you must believe in yourself. You must know in your heart of hearts that you have what it takes to accomplish what you have set out to do. There is nothing wrong with you looking outside of yourself for advice, direction, and guidance.

However, you must be careful and balance what you hear with what you internally know. Not everyone shares your dreams, has your best interests in mind, or will be able to advise you on something that you have been given to do. Others may mean well, have good intentions, mean you no harm, or want what is, in their view, best for you. The problem with getting information for others on your journey is that it is yours. You are the captain of your ship, the driver of your car, the pilot of your plane, and conductor of your train.

Even when people have the best of intentions, they just may not be able to see what you dream about. Sometimes you will just have to rely on you. People come and go in and out of your life for seasons and reasons, and some stay for a lifetime. Some people are in your life for advice, a few make you think twice, and others help you play nice. You must be astute enough to determine in which category people belong and not try to force-fit them where they do not. Additionally you must know that you are a part of the equation that does not change. You are the common denominator.

You will always be involved in delivering on your dreams. You may seek advice from others, but you have the final say. You get to decide what actions you take. Given how important you are to realize your dreams, you must constantly evaluate and build yourself up as well as strengthen your belief in you. You are your most important resource, and if you squander your resources, you will assuredly squander your chances for success. When Paul spoke of his ability to do all things through Christ, he started with expressing belief in himself. "I can." "I can do all things through Christ which strengtheneth me" (Philippians 4:13 KJV).

Paul recognizes himself as a critical part of the equation. While he saw his ability to do all things through Christ, he did not put the work on Christ. He knew that the work of doing was his responsibility and believed he could do it. You would do yourself good to begin like Paul with yourself, believing in yourself. While God has great things and greatness in store for you, if you do not believe in yourself, you will not realize them. Your belief in yourself and God precedes your call to greatness.

Start your journey by believing in yourself. Your belief will inspire you to take the first steps, ignite the flames on your path to success, and sustain you during difficulties. Do not risk your future depending on advice and guidance from someone who may not know what is best for you. The person who has your best interests at heart is the one you see when you are looking in the mirror.

Instead of going to someone to validate your vision, to delight in your dream, and to ascertain your aspirations, start with the person in the mirror. Start with you. Start by believing in yourself. If you cannot believe in you, how do you expect anyone else to believe? I know how difficult it can be to believe in yourself when you are starting something new, stepping out on faith, or doing something others doubt or question. However, you have what you need. You just need to continue to believe and to identify ways to strengthen and develop your belief.

There are two key things that you can do to develop and strengthen your belief: talk to yourself and think on the right things. While you may know what you must do and believe you have what it takes to do it, life happens. When life happens, it sometimes throws you off your game, surprises you with things that you never thought would or could happen, or causes you to question yourself and doubt whether you have what it takes.

Knowing this will happen, when you start your journey and know it is yours, you should immediately identify ways to build your belief to weather the coming storm. A key to building your belief is to talk to yourself. You must develop a communications connection with the person most important to your success, the individual with your best interest in mind, the one who has been given the vision, dream, desire, thought, purpose, and passion, you.

As strange as it may sound, talking to yourself will prove to be your most important ally and action during the most critical times. When there is an important decision to be made, a crossroad to choose, a challenge to conquer, or a person to put in their place, your first reaction is to talk to someone to ensure you are doing the right thing, to get their thoughts, ideas, and input.

What if you have no one to talk to? What if the person you choose to talk to does not understand your passion, your dream? You know everything about the dream you are pursuing. At one point, you believed in you; you knew you were called, commission, charged, and equipped to do this, but now you are questioning yourself. Why? You hit a bump in the road. Something did not go as expected. You tried a few things, and none of them seemed to work. You feel you are at a standstill, stuck or frozen in place. You don't know what to do.

When this happens, you need to go back to the basic, the beginning, and remind yourself of who you are and why you are here. You know better than anyone what drove you to do this, the fire that once burned within, or the passion of purpose that called you to step out when staying in would have been easier. You just need to get back on track. This would be a great time to talk to yourself, encourage yourself, pump yourself up, get yourself excited, or give yourself some instructions. Before you go to someone else, spend some time alone going over your options, doing your own review and analysis, remembering your why, and talking to yourself.

Talking to yourself to rebuild and strengthen your belief is not new and not reserved for those who are socially inept or mentally ill. If this is not something that you practice, it is very likely that you are doing it automatically or you have seen it done with positive results. You may have seen this done in the gym when someone was getting ready to lift heavy weights. Before they put a hand on the bar, they pump themselves up. You may have heard them verbally talking to themselves, saying encouraging words, like "I got this. Let's do it. Light weight."

You may have heard them making grunting noises or doing something physical to themselves, for instance, pound their chest, hit themselves, and make faces. Whether verbal or nonverbal, what you observed was individuals talking to themselves to motivate themselves to get the job done. Maybe you have a similar ritual when you are getting ready to do something difficult. Whatever the ritual, you are doing it to tell yourself something, to build up your belief in your ability to do what may seem impossible or at least challenging. You use words, verbal and nonverbal, to encourage yourself. You talk to yourself to get yourself going. The kicker is that no one ever really told you to do this. It is almost automatic, human nature, like breathing. Why? I believe the answer resides in the power of words.

Words are power, or more correctly, "there is power in words." If you are going to build or strengthen your belief in yourself, your words are key. You need to hear them to remind yourself to tell all your faculties—your mind, body, and soul—your why. Paul recognized in scripture the power words have on your belief. In fact, he went so far as to say your belief comes from words.

"Faith cometh by hearing, and hearing the word of God" (Romans 10:17 KJV).

What you hear has a direct impact on what you believe and therefore do. Your words provide you the ability to influence how you act or react to something. What you tell yourself indirectly and directly influences your attitude, behavior, altitude, and outcome. If you were wondering just how powerful your words are or can be, Solomon provides some details in Proverbs 18:21 (KJV) when he says, "Death and life are in the power of the tongue." You have at your disposal the ability to speak life or death to your situation, and you exercise it often. Anytime you tell yourself you cannot do something, you kill the option, death. Anytime you tell yourself you can do something, you give yourself a chance, life. With this kind of power at your disposal, you must be very careful how you use it.

On another occasion, Solomon said, "Watch your tongue and keep your mouth shut, and you will stay out of trouble" (Proverbs 21:23 NLT). If you are not careful, you will be your own undoing. To start your journey, you must believe. To develop, build, or simply sustain your belief, you need to talk to yourself. Knowing the power of the tongue, think about the effect you could have if you knew how to harness it, how to use its power to affect your desired outcomes.

Your little member, your tongue that boasts great things (James 3:5 KJV), can get you in a lot of trouble. I remember my mother telling me, "If you don't have anything good to say, don't say anything at all." She was wiser than her years. Negative words are poison to the soul; they kill dreams, thoughts, and ideas. Not everyone was taught this invaluable and respectful principle, or maybe they were, but their intentions are not good. Regardless, you must know that as you travel on your journey to success, you will encounter much negativity. Not everyone wants the best for you. You will hear negative words, feedback, comments, commentary, reviews, and analysis from people who have their own agendas or do not understand or care about your purpose, desires, mission, or vision.

If you hear and accept what they are saying, your belief will be shaken, and you will sit or stand by and watch your dream die. You must be prepared when this happens, and it will. So spend some time doing what seems unnatural, perhaps a little insane, talking to yourself. You cannot wait for others' validation, approval, okay, acceptance, or consent to move out. You must believe in you, and you must continually strengthen your belief. The more success you experience, the closer you get to your goal, the greater your challenge. The higher the height, the deeper the debt. "For unto whomsoever much is given, of him shall be much required" (Luke 12:48b KJV).

The closer you come to your outcome, the more negativity will come out. You should expect negativity to come from without, but you must ensure that it does not exist within. Your preparation, the strength of your belief in yourself when you face these challenges, will get you through. If you have practiced the art of talking to yourself, having developed your communication connectivity, you will be equipped when you face your challenges.

You have the power to affect your future, to determine or affect your journey. What you tell yourself about yourself will influence your beliefs, which provide you the drive and motivation to keep going. You should be methodical and strategic about your selection of words. Oliver Wendell Holmes Sr. said it best, "Speak clearly, if you speak at all; carve every word before you let it fall."

Most people take Holmes's advice when it comes to interacting with others, but do not consider it when communicating with themselves. You may be thinking the rarity and frequency of you talking with yourself does not warrant such consideration. I recommend you reconsider. While you may not speak words to yourself consciously, vocally or verbally, you are constantly speaking to yourself on a subconscious level, quietly and nonverbally. The thoughts you have about your abilities, strengths and weaknesses, the conversation you hold in your mind and heart about whether you can or cannot do something, or if you have what it takes to succeed represent your conversations with yourself. What are you thinking? Are your thoughts, the private conversations you are having with yourself, building you up or tearing you down? Are they positive or negative? Are they producing life or death?

Paul also recognized the importance of our thinking and advised us to think on positive things. He said, "Finally, brethren, whatsoever things are true, whatsoever things are honest, whatsoever things are just, whatsoever things are pure, whatsoever things are lovely, whatsoever things are of good report; if there be any virtue, and if there be any praise, think on these things?" (Philippians 4:8 KJV). When you talk to and think positive things about yourself, you strengthen and grow your belief, which will prove critical as you face greater challenges and are afforded more opportunities.

Your belief in yourself is so important because it provides the foundation from which you spring into step, face different challenges, and take on new opportunities. Two sets of skills—skill set and will set—will determine your success. Your skill set are your abilities, what you bring to the table to accomplish the task, for instance, education, experience, and expertise. Everyone has a set of skills; everyone brings something to the table. However, not everyone uses the skills they have to the best of their abilities. I have seen very skilled people fail in places where less skilled people succeed. I have seen individuals who have the academic underpinning, the intellectual capacity, the physical athleticism, and the requisite experience and expertise to face challenges they were more than equipped to handle fail. You can probably attest to knowing smarter people who were not as successful as people who were not as accomplished. You probably know someone in your organization who was promoted before someone more skilled. I am sure you know some very skilled and talented people who are living on the margin of life. If skills were the only thing required to be successful, everyone would be successful, as everyone has some skills. Skills are not the only requirement. You can be the most skilled person in the world, but if you lack a will set, you will not "be all that you can be."

The second set of skills required to be successful and maybe the most important is your will set. While I am not sure who my mom was quoting, I remember her telling us often, "Where there is a will, there is a way." I am not even sure if we really knew what my mom intended for the phrase to mean. However, I do remember adopting into my life and using it when I am faced with a difficult task or up against a formidable foe. When I used it, it was my way of saying, "If you want something bad enough, you will figure out a way to get it."

Your will set is you wanting something so bad that you figure out how to get it. It is a belief in your ability to get what you want or desire despite the requirement or resistance. You may not have what it takes to get the job done, but your will set makes you a viable candidate. You may not be equipped to win the fight, but your will set makes you a worthy opponent. You may not possess the requisite skills, academic underpinning, intellectual capacity, or physical prowess necessary to accomplish the task, but your will set makes you competitive and competent. Your will set is by your availability and your desirability, not your abilities. Your will set causes you to look at the job description and realize that you have very few, if any, of the desired qualifications and ask for a chance to show what you can do. If you have the will set, you can accomplish the task most of the people fail at because you want to do it.

In the biblical story of David and Goliath, David did not possess the requisite military skills of his brother or other members of the armies of Israel. He did, however, possess a will set that was unmatched. He wanted to fight Goliath and believed he would win. He did not have the experience, expertise, or résumé, but he believed that with God on his side, Goliath did not have a chance. Your will set does not look at what you do not have, but it uses what you have. Your will set will set you up to succeed.

PART
4

HOW WILL
THEY KNOW?

CHAPTER 13

BE THE BEST YOU THAT YOU CAN BE

AFTER HAVING DETERMINED YOU WANT TO SUCCEED at what you are doing, it is critical that you know and understand how to ensure that those in positions to support and advance your career know your aspirations and qualifications. It is equally critical that you know what those in these positions are looking to promote, support, and advance, for instance, qualifications, character, work ethics, and experience. While you may know the organization and the organisms, the people, procedures, and protocols and be the best qualified for advancement, assignment, or position, if no one knows you, you will be overlooked or underutilized. If no one knows who you are or what you bring to the table, how can they support your efforts to ascend to the next level, be promoted, or take on a special assignment? It is not enough for you to know everything about the organization or the people in it. If you expect to advance, in addition to leveraging your skill sets and experience against the organization's needs, you must ensure that those making promotion, assignment, and advancement decisions for the organization know who you are and how you are affecting and can affect the organization's success or way forward. It is a mistake for you to think or assume that your actions, work ethics, and production will be enough. This is akin to the error of assuming that your hard work will yield the best results and that there is equity in actions and results.

I am not against the concept of equity; however, I am not naïve, and I recommend you not be as well. There may have been a day when your hard work yielded you the desired outcome. That day may not be today. If hard work alone merited promotions, how many people do you know who have been overlooked or passed over? I believe in hard work, but your success depends on much more.

If you are going to succeed in life and corporate America, you must be savvy and strategic. You must have a destination and a plan on how you will get there. One thing that you should include in your plan is a strategy or an approach to ensure that those in the leadership positions know your aspirations. This is not to say that if they have this information everything will work out the way you plan or expect. However, it is to inform you of the value and importance of communicating and demonstrating in a way that those in position of power know your desire to succeed. You should begin by asking and answering several questions:

- How will those making these decisions know of your desire?
- How will they know of your desire to manage or lead?
- How will they know of your productivity or the impact you are having on the organization?
- How will they know of your ambitions, goals, or aspirations?

Maybe you are thinking they will know because you told them ... by your words. Then my question to you would be, "Is this enough?" You may say that they will know by your performance and impact on the organization ... by your actions. Then I will repeat my question and ask, "Is this enough?" Words or actions alone, like faith without works (James 2:17 KJV), will not suffice, will not be enough. You will need both your words and actions working together, complementing one another to ensure your success. Then you must not assume that those in position of influence and power know what you are doing and saying. You must not leave your success to chance. You must have a strategy to ensure that what you do and desire do not go unnoticed, unrecognized, or unrewarded.

In the following chapters, you will be given some tools to ensure that your journey to success is not left to chance. We are going to share three actions that if taken—and taken seriously—will ensure that they know you have a plan and you desire to succeed. The first thing you should do is "be the best you that you can be." The second thing you should do is "expand your territory." Finally you should "help somebody share your story."

While this list is not exhaustive, if you do these three things, you will not only be known by those in positions of power, but you will affect those around you and leave a legacy for those you touch long after you have moved on.

When you have a burning desire to be successful, you have all that you need to succeed. You must recognize and accept this as your reality. Most people fail before they begin their journey to success because they fail to see that they have what they need to succeed. They have the desire, dream, and drive, but they do not believe in themselves. When you have a vision, a dream, or an aspiration, you have the seed within you that is required to grow your dream into a reality. When you can see it, you can be it.

Because you have been given a desire or a dream, you have received the most important element to make your dream a reality. Your dream, burning desire, and vision is a look into your future. Your dream is a foretelling of things to come. Your desires are predictions of your destiny. Your aspirations are passions for your purpose. When you have something within you that gives you insights into your future—desires, drive, dreams, visions, aspirations, and motivations—you have the seed necessary to achieve. However, the seed will not grow if it is not tended to, watered, cultivated, worked, or fertilized. If you do not act on the seed within you, it will die. Alternatively, if you choose to cultivate your seed, you can grow your new reality. It will not be easy. It will be work, but it will be well worth it.

The first action you should take to make your dream a reality is to start with what you have, you, and be the best you that you can be. Yes, you have within you the seed of greatness, which is necessary to turn your dreams into reality and your desires into destiny. You start your journey to success by seeing and accepting this truth. Do not get caught up in a comparative reality, thinking you must have what your neighbors have in order to be successful. Do not get confused thinking your success depends on the pace of the Joneses and therefore you must keep up with them. Your talents do not need to match the talents of others for you to achieve your dream or to reach your destiny. You can see the risk of this type of thinking in the parable of the talents told by Jesus in Matthew 25:14–30.

While each servant was given talents equivalent to their task and according to their several abilities (one was given five talents, another was given two, and one more was given one), the recipient of the one talent buried his talent. The ones with the five and two talents doubled the return on the man's investment who was travelling into a far country. The one who received the least failed to see the value of his talent by comparison and did not use his talent or put it in the bank to collect interest. Instead when he went in to give account of his actions, he made excuses and offered incredible explanations for his lack of action. He was called wicked and slothful, and his one talent was taken away and given to the one who now had ten talents.

It is important to note that the requirement of each of those given talents were different and based on their several abilities. They each were expected to use what they had to the best of their abilities. The ones with the five and two talents were equally praised ("Well done, good and faithful servant; thou hast been faithful over a few things, I will make you ruler over many things: ..." [Matthew 25:23 NIV]), although their returns were different. They each used what they had to the best of their abilities.

You have been given visions, dreams, desires, gifts, and talents based on your several abilities. While it is worth noting that your gifts and abilities will not be the same as others, it is also worth highlighting that even if they were the same, they will be used differently. One man's strength is another man's weakness. "One man's trash is another man's treasure." You have been provided skills and abilities equivalent to your tasks to ensure your success. What you lack in skills present in others is not necessary for you to succeed.

People succeed in administrative and support services, agriculture, art and recreation services, construction, education and training, electricity, financial and insurance services, food services, health care and social assistance, hiring, information media and telecommunications, gas, mining, manufacturing, portal, ministry and ecclesiastical services, professional transport, public administration and safety, retail trade, retail, real estate services, scientific and technical services, water, waste services, wholesale trade, and warehousing. And the list goes on.

There are billionaires, millionaires, thousandaires, and hundredaires in all fields of endeavor. They each have discovered their destiny, developed their desires, pinpointed their passion, achieved their aspirations, and realized their dreams. Having done this, they separated themselves from the pack by being the best they could be.

Successful people have given in to their drives, desires, and dreams and developed the requisite skills and abilities required for them to succeed. Their dreams gave them the motivation to do what needed to be done for them to be successful. The motivation to make their dream a reality provided the extra energy they needed to push through difficult tasks and do things they did not particularly enjoy doing. Their motivation to make their dream a reality allowed them to see the value in doing each task they were assigned to the best of their abilities, even when it was something they did not enjoy but could benefit from.

Too many people are working in areas they despise and are unable to identify a passion or a purpose for doing it. I emphasize their inability to discover a purpose or passion because the enjoyment of what you are doing is not a requirement for you to be successful; however, motivation is a must. You can be successful doing a job or in an assignment or field outside of your purpose or passion and not enjoy it if you can identify your motivation to be the best you that you can be doing it. You may not be the best at it because it is not your purpose, your destiny, but you can be the best you that you can be.

Truth is, you may not be the best at what you are destined to do, what you are passionate about, what you dream of, or what you aspire to, but you can be the best you that you can be. You are the common denominator in any assignment you take, task you are assigned, or position you are in. Your attitude in how you approach to diversity of your assignments needs to be consistent. You must commit to be the best you that you can be regardless of where you are, what you are doing, or whether you like or enjoy the task you are assigned. This is important, in part, because you never know why you are where you are or what it will provide you that will prove useful or critical to your future endeavors.

Success in life is like building with blocks or walking up a set of stairs. Each block adds something to the construction, and each step gets you closer to your destination. You may think that it would be much easier if you knew what the end was going to be before you started your journey. If you knew how the story of your life ended, you could plan your journey block by block, step by step. You could commit to doing the things necessary to ensure that your story ended the way it was supposed to.

What if you did not like how your story ended? What if you liked how your story ended but figured you did have to work for it? There is as much risk in you knowing how your story ends as it is in not knowing. However, not knowing demands that you put in the work. Not knowing causes you to choose a destination, make informed decisions, and adjust when mistakes are made. When you do not know, you may have a vision, set goals, commit to a purpose, be passionate and motivated to accomplish a desired outcome, and still not hit the target you were aiming for. You will go through in order to get to. Each challenge will offer you a new opportunity and provide you some fresh growth. Your experiences will become your story. Your story will include challenges and opportunities that will prepare you for your future. Your story will include accounts of things that happened to you that you will be unable to explain in real time, but in hindsight, you will see that nothing happened to you by happenstance. You will see that the hardships that you endured provided you the tools you needed for your greatest accomplishments. You will see that your most difficult tasks, your most difficult assignments, prepared you for your greatest success and provide you your greatest success story.

If you look back over your life, you will see that greatness is a product of difficulty, your test was necessary for you to have a testimony, and the mess you were in and came out of gave you a message. Your most difficult and challenging assignments in school, college, and life developed and prepared you to be the best you that you can be. Someone said it correctly that lapdogs do not get strong, but the dog that must run fast and work hard to get a meal gets very strong. This is true of humans also. Your greatest challenge, difficulties, and trials will yield your greatest success. "If we suffer, we shall also reign with him" (2 Timothy 2:12a KJV).

If you are going to get to where you aspire in life, you must be the best that you can be regardless of the situation. Please note, I am not saying that you must be the best, but I am stating that you must be your best. I recall asking my children when they came home with their report cards, "Did you do your best?" I asked this question not only when they made less than an A. I inquired of every grade, including and especially when they made an A. I wanted them to understand that life is not about making the grade. It is about being the best you that you can be. When you are talented in an area or subject, what you do may come easy. For example, if you are talented and strong in mathematics, the test results from a math test may not be an indication of your effort or what you have learned. You may be able to score high on a test without studying or putting forth any effort. An indication of your success would be whether you learn something. To do this, you will have to put in the work, put your best foot forward, and do your best.

You should note that your best may be less than an A. There are times when you can give it your all and do your best, but because this is not your area of strength, your best may not be good enough for the task. The question you must answer is not whether you made the grade, but "Did you do your best?" When you take on a task, accept an assignment, or sign up for a new initiative, if you do your best, you can live with the outcome. You may not be the best in sports, academics, organization, team, or group, but you can be the best you that you can be. All that you can do is what you can do, and when you have done the best that you can do, you have done all that you can do.

I recall reading a poem when I was growing up that speaks to this by Douglass Mallock, "Be the Best of Whatever You Are."[8]

> If you can't be a highway then just be a trail,
> If you can't be the sun be a star;
> It isn't by size that you win or you fail—
> Be the best of whatever you are!

If you are a poet or a preacher, a doctor or a ditch digger, a teacher or a student, a manager or an employee, a CEO or a servant, a ruler or a master, a bourgeoisie or a proletariat, black or white, or whatever you are, be the best. You do not have to be better than. You just need to be your best. You have been given all that you need to be the best you that you can be. You will be settling if you choose to be someone other than who you are. Your life should not be about copying, emulating, or duplicating. It should not be about relocating your lot in life. You should make it your passion and purpose to be the best you at whatever you do.

---

[8] **Citation MLA Format**
Douglas Malloch. "Be The Best Of Whatever You Are." Family Friend Poems, 2006.
https://www.familyfriendpoems.com/poem/be-the-best-of-whatever-you-are-by-douglas-malloch

Do not try to change places with someone else or imitate someone else. Be yourself.

Please note, if you choose to duplicate or emulate someone else, aside from being a fabrication, the best that you can hope or ever be is second. When you copy someone, the number-one slot, the best, is already taken. However, if you choose to be yourself, to be the best you that you can be, you are the original, the number one. Anyone who chooses to follow, copy, duplicate, or emulate you can only be number two. You have taken the number-one slot.

It is critically important that you take the life that you are given with all its benefits and use it and them to the best of your abilities. You do not have to be someone else, to be like someone else, to be better than someone else. You only need to ensure that you are not wasting your time, energy, expertise, knowledge, skills and abilities, and opportunities. To do that, you must work daily to be your best. A team, like the body, consists of many members from different walks of life, with varying experiences, talents, and levels of expertise.

As a member of the team, you are only responsible for your part. The more effective you are, the more effective the team is. A team cannot be effective when all its members are trying to do the same thing. An example of this is seen when all members of the team attempt to conform or create harmony or avoid conflict by thinking the same way. It creates a psychological phenomenon called "group think." When this happens, the group tries to avoid conflict even if it means silencing points of views critical to the success of the group. When all members of the team have the same function, the group is dysfunctional. An effective team seeks to leverage the talents and abilities of all its team members. Diversity within a group allows for critical evaluation of alternatives; promotes creativity, uniqueness, and independent thinking; generates the most thought out ideas; and evaluates outcomes.

When Paul was describing the church in Christ in 1 Corinthians, he used the analogy of the body to show the value of the individual parts and how they could work together to create harmony. He noted that while there are many members, there is only one body. He also noted that each part of the body was valuable and worked best when it was doing what it was supposed to do. No part could be discounted by another part or by itself, and no part was more important than the other part.

> For as the body is one, and hath many members, and all the members of that one body, being many, are one body: so also is Christ. For by one Spirit are we all baptized into one body, whether we be Jews or Gentiles, whether we be bond or free; and have been all made to drink into one Spirit. For the body is not one member, but many. If the foot shall say, Because I am not the hand, I am not of the body; is it therefore not of the body? And if the ear shall say, Because I am not the eye, I am not of the body; is it therefore not of the body? If the whole body were an eye, where were the hearing? If the whole were hearing, where were the smelling? But now hath God set the members every one of them in the body, as it hath pleased him. And if they were all one member, where were the body? But now are they many members, yet but one body. And the eye cannot say unto the hand, I have no need of thee: nor again the head to the feet, I have no need of you. Nay, much more those members of the body, which seem to be more feeble, are necessary: And those members of the body, which we think to be less honourable, upon these we bestow more abundant honour; and our uncomely parts have more abundant comeliness. For our comely parts have no need: but God hath tempered the body together, having given more abundant honour to that part which lacked: That there should be no schism in the body; but that

the members should have the same care one for another. And whether one member suffer, all the members suffer with it; or one member be honoured, all the members rejoice with it. Now ye are the body of Christ, and members in particular. (1 Corinthians 12:12–27 KJV)

Paul recognizes, as you should, the value of diversity. He even went so far as to say that God had placed the unique abilities of individuals in the church to serve specific purposes. It would be an unfortunate tragedy to have the hand trying to be an eye or an eye trying to be a foot. The body would not function properly; the church would be dysfunctional. The body works best when each of its parts does its part. There is no benefit in the body parts changing roles because they want to or because someone pressures them to do so. Each part has a purpose and serves best doing its part. The foot has a purpose, as does the hand and the eye. You have a purpose, and when you choose to copy someone else, it is a tragedy. In fact, each time you try to be someone you are not, it is a tragedy.

When you choose to be yourself and to be the best you that you can be, you give your team an opportunity to optimize its outcomes. You give yourself the opportunity to optimize your outcome and be the best you that you can be. This is not the case when you choose to imitate someone else. Whitney Houston said it best in the lyrics to her song "Greatest Love of All."[9]

> I decided long ago
> Never to walk in anyone's shadow
> If I fail, if I succeed
> At least I lived as I believe

I remember being all to the front office some years ago by my boss for an action that I had taken that he was not pleased with. He made it a point to let me know that he was the boss and that he was in charge. Specifically, he wanted me to know that he was the boss and I was nothing but, in a kinder way, a butt.

In my frustration with his approach, I shared with him a joke that I had heard that I felt was very fitting to this situation. The joke was about "Who's the Boss?" [10]

> When the Lord made man, all the parts of the body argued over who would be boss. The brain explained that since he controlled all the parts of the body, he should be boss. The legs argued that

---

[9] "The Greatest Love of All" is a song written by Michael Masser, who composed the music, and Linda Creed, who wrote the lyrics. It was originally recorded in 1977 by George Benson, who made the song a substantial hit, peaking at number two on the US Hot R&B/Hip-Hop Songs chart that year, the first R&B chart top-ten hit for Arista Records. The song was written and recorded to be the main theme of the 1977 film The Greatest, a biopic of the boxer Muhammad Ali. Eight years after Benson's original recording, the song became even more well known for a version by Whitney Houston, whose 1985 cover eventually topped the charts, peaking at number one in the United States, Australia, Canada and on the US Hot R&B/Hip-Hop Songs in early 1986.
https://en.wikipedia.org/wiki/The_Greatest_Love_of_All
[10] **All the parts of the body argued over who would be boss**
BY ADMIN · JANUARY 31, 2010
Who's the Boss?

since they took man wherever he wanted to go, they should be boss. The stomach countered with the explanation that since he digested all the food, he should be boss. The eyes said that without them man would be helpless, so they should be boss. Then the asshole applied for the job. The other parts of the body laughed so hard at this that the asshole became mad and closed up. After a few days ... The brain went foggy, the legs got wobbly, the stomach got ill, and the eyes got crossed and unable to see. They all conceded and made the asshole boss. This proved that you don't have to be a brain to be boss ...

My point here is that every member of the team is important to the success of the team. You should not allow words or labels ascribed to you determine your significance or cause you to function outside of your abilities. If you want to maximize your team, you must maximize yourself. You must be the best you that you can be. In the words of Kathryn Stockett, author of *The Help*, "You is kind. You is smart. You is important."

EXPAND YOUR TERRITORY (NETWORK)

HAVING COMMITTED TO BE THE BEST YOU CAN BE, YOU have taken the first step to let others know who you are. You have not left their awareness of your impact or aspiration to chance. You are actively involved in your future, including your legacy. Being the best you that you can be makes the next step of expanding your territory a way to leverage others to tell your story and to ensure that you have the right story to tell. Expanding your territory is not new to those wanting to do more and to have a greater impact. In fact, this concept is present in the Old Testament in a prayer we affectionately call the Jabez Prayer recorded in 1 Chronicles. "And Jabez called on the God of Israel saying, 'Oh, that You would bless me indeed, and enlarge my territory, that Your hand would be with me, and that You would keep me from evil, that I may not cause pain!' So God granted him what he requested" (1 Chronicles 4:10 NKJV).

While not much is known about Jabez, his prayer tells us that he desired something bigger for himself and he wanted God to ensure that he did the right things. He prayed for enlargement of his territory and God to ensure that He would not leave him but rather guide him from evil and causing pain. God granted him his request.

When you desire something bigger than you, growth, or success, you will need help. When you find yourself in a position where you don't know what to do but know you must take a step, you have no way of knowing if the step you take will be the right one. However, you can increase the chances of the step you take being the right one by doing your research and asking for support from the right source. Yes, you could take a step in the dark because you know a step must be taken, but the risks involved when you take the step in a vacuum is much higher than it needs to be if you can get help. Every step you take, even when it is a must, is risky, but when you take a step in the dark, you can alleviate the risk by soliciting support. Any step you take to get yourself out from being stuck in the mud could be viewed as a good step. This would be true if every step yielded a positive outcome. Taking a step to get out of the mud or the dark could put you in a worse position than you were in. This is true of any situation you find yourself in.

Having said that, this does not have to be, nor should it be your story. You should work to ensure the step you take has a modicum of success. To do this, you need to enlarge your territory. You need to add someone to your network who knows something about walking in the dark or getting out of the mud or simply has a better solution than you. Your territory is your network. Your territory is expanded each time you grow your network.

Do not think that you have all the answers, and do not act like you know everything. If you think or act like this, you are doing yourself a disservice and your "haters" a favor. As noted previously, you have your strengths and weaknesses. If you are at a crossroad and you do not know what to do, relying on yourself when the solution calls on your weaknesses will put you at a disadvantage. You being self-reliant or independent when the answer is outside of your area of expertise or strength will cause you more heartaches and pains than warranted. You may get lucky when doing it by yourself and working from your weakness, but why take the chance? You will serve yourself and your mission better if you engage someone who can offer advice from a position of strength. That said, during crisis is not the optimum time to develop relationships and expand your territory. This is done best when done strategically and in preparation for a crisis. In this chapter, we will briefly discuss the importance and benefits of expanding your territory (your network).

Most organizations realize the value, importance, and benefits of networks. To that end, they have formalized and systematized networking to ensure that officers or employees who join the organization can get connected and reap the benefits of an expanding territory. They realize that there is some real value in having your best friend or a friend at work. They know that when people are connected, they feel like they are part of something and are more productive and inclined to stay with the organization. They also see the impact networks have on assimilating, acclimating, inculcating, and accelerating the employee's organizational learning and development. Most organizations hire individuals who have the expertise, technical knowledge, or know-how to perform the task, job, or position for which they were hired. They are expected to figure out the rest.

High-performing organizations, however, do not leave this to chance. They know how impactful networking is to employee effectiveness. They know that for an employee to do what they are hired to do, they must interact effectively with other employees, people, and organisms. Employees and the organizations have failed them because they were not properly assimilated into the organization.

Organizations realized the value of its employees knowing and understanding things that are not formally documented, for instance, the unwritten and informal rules, cultures, values, and norms. They know that this information is not available to non-employees and can only be gotten when you are hired and on the payroll, which could be too late. They also know that people fail because of what they do not know. To curb the failure rate resulting from this, organizations have put systems in place to allow officers to network throughout the organization, including and especially with the senior executives. This allows them to provide new employees with insights and details on the organization that would not be available to them until they have served the organization for years.

The formal network that the organization has put in place and the informal one that it does not control are great tools available to aid you in learning about the organization at a deeper level. Kudos to any organization that takes this on as a project or an initiative to aid in the development of its employees. However, you must know that it is not up to the organization to build your network. If you are going to be successful, you must take ownership of constructing and building your own network. This must be done by you strategically, methodically, tactically, and practically. You must ensure that your network is effective enough to educate and enlighten you, intuitive enough to inform and incite you, and creative enough to care for and challenge you.

Additionally you must be constantly upgrading, changing, improving, and expanding your network. Your network will prove critical to your success, as it will be or should be there for you when you don't know what to do. Your network will prove invaluable during your most critical times. You will be able to talk to someone about what you are going through, discuss and debate ideas on your next course of action, and get thoughts on the impact of your actions, next planned steps, and future. If you construct, build, and expand your network properly, you will have people in your net who have experienced what you are going through and came out of it better than when they went in or are experienced enough to provide you advice and guidance on your best course of action. If you construct your network properly, while you may feel that you are the only one left to deal with what you are going through, you will know that you are not alone.

An effective network will be there for you when you don't know what to do or feel like you are the only one who has ever had to deal with the challenge you are facing. Your network provides you a team, a group, or someone other than you that can provide you an alternative view, a way out. Your network gives you someone else to lean on, to rely on, other than yourself. Your network gives you access to information beyond your limited knowledge. Your network knowledge is as broad and expansive as the people you have in it. Therefore, you want to ensure that it is inclusive and represents a wide range of diverse skills, knowledge, and abilities.

When you expand your network enough to include individuals who have already been down this path you are currently on, you have access to insights and information that can accelerate your learning and support your success. The benefits of an expanded network are many, including its diversity, experience and expertise, insights and intellect, and knowledge and know-how. With an expanded network when you encounter a problem, you are likely to have access to an available solution. What may be a challenge for you may be simple and effortless to someone else in your network.

What you are going through may not be unique; it may only be unique to you. One person's problem is another person's opportunity. One person's challenge is another person's cheese. What may be complicated to you may be easy for someone else. You will never experience the reality of this if you are totally reliant on yourself and do not expand your territory.

Take the low-risk, high-return approach and expand your territory. Expand your territory means to include more people in your inner circle, to grow your circle of influencers. It means to involve more people in your decision-making process, to include more people in the group of those who discuss your issues and concerns. Please remember that an organization is as much an organism as it is an organization. It is a group of people executing the regulations, policies, and procedures to accomplish the mission, vision, and goal of the organization. It is people getting things done. There is some truth to the fact that there is strength in numbers, especially when they are working together, dancing to the same music, and moving in the same direction. The more organisms/ people you have in your network working to support or assist with your success, the more likely you are to succeed. While more could and should be better, it must not be your goal. Your goal is to the number of people in your network; it is the people in the numbers.

You need to ensure that the people you include in your network have your best interests at heart and are committed to your success. You need people in your network willing and able to provide you advice and guidance, insights, and information. They are willing to tell you the truth, even when it hurts. You should include people in your network who have nothing to do with your work or area of expertise. You want to have access to people who can answer the question should the question come up. Having people who do not specialize in what you do gives you more access to information when something comes up that you are not familiar with. By expanding your network, they may not have the answer, but maybe someone in their network does.

When you are at a crossroad and don't know what to do but are trying to determine next steps because you know you must do something, it is easy to get tunnel vision, to see things one way, your way. When you are being challenged, relying on what you know, what you are comfortable with may not be your best option, your optimum solution. This is a great time to look to your network for support, options, alternatives, and solutions. Someone with a different perspective, optic, experience, knowledge, or insight into your challenge may see and understand where you are and know a way out. You may, because of your proximity to the problem, see your experience as a breaking point, but someone in your network may see it as a point to break through. The alternative views and options you receive from your network may be what you need to turn what could be a point of failure into a point of success. Your network could ensure that you do not become comfortable in a place that is uncomfortable. Your network could keep you from settling when settling is what you want to do because you cannot see your way out. When you do not know what to do, your best option may be knowing someone who does. I recommend you go one step further and ensure that those who know, know you. When you expand your network, it puts them and you in the know: you know them, and they know you. Franz Kafka said, "Better to have, and not need, than to need, and not have."

Expanding your network gives you access to a diverse group of people with varied backgrounds, opinions, and views. You may never need to call on them for advice or guidance, but when and if you do, they will be there.

You should also note that when you expand your territory, you are increasing your reach and positioning yourself to have a greater impact. An enlarged territory includes more people, which means a larger number of contacts, a greater base of support, and an increased number of people to influence. Your network interaction is not one way, flowing toward you only. Networking is a two-way street. You are influenced, informed, affected, assisted, and supported by your network, and you influence, inform, affect, assist, and support your network. Your relationship with your network expands your zone of influence, control, and power.

Therefore, as you expand your network, you enlarge your territory. You expand your base of power. If you have a limited network, you may have limited power and influence, and you may be limiting your impact on the organization. The opposite is true when you expand your network (territory). You increase your ability to have an impact on the organization. If you desire to move up in an organization, the size and strength of your network is critical. The larger your network, the more access and the more influence you have. The more people you influence, the greater the impact you can have on the organization without being in control of them. The more influence you have on an organization, the more likely you are to be a leader and one to be considered for organizational leadership.

An individual who does good to great work but lacks the ability to influence people may be effective as an employee, someone to be managed, led, and influenced—but would not be a good leader. Influence is a prerequisite for leadership. You may possess positional authority and be able to manage, but to lead effectively, you must be able to influence them. If you cannot influence people to follow you, get things done, step up, or stand down, you will not be able to lead them. When you have an expanded network and leverage it to affect the goals of the organization, you demonstrate your propensity to lead.

One reason for expanding your network is to expand you affect, your influence. With an expanded network, you get an enlarged territory, which means you can have a greater impact and accomplish more organizationally. The enlargement of your territory, or more accurately, the expansion of your network allows you access to more people in more places doing more things than you could have ever done by yourself. This allows you to do more and have more of an impact than you would alone. The worst thing that you can do for yourself is to assume you can get everything you need done by yourself. The poet John Donne said it correctly in "Meditation XVII," "No man is an Island, entire of itself; every man is a piece of the Continent, a part of the main ...")). This is as true in organizations as it is in life.

Your network, however large or small, reflects your understanding that you are not alone. It shows that you value community and understand that the organization is a group of organisms working together for the greater good. You will do your best work with someone else. The organization is connected. We are connected. We succeed or fail, rise or fall, or stand or sit together. When an organization has a vision, mission, and goal, the purpose and plan of the organism is to accomplish them. You are one of many organisms determined to accomplish the organization's mission. You cannot do it alone. Together with your network, you are closer than you have ever been.

Do not forget that one of the primary reasons for expanding your territory is to let those in positions of authority, those of power, know who you are and what you bring to the table. One key benefit of a network is bringing people together. Your specific network serves to introduce you to others in the organization. It provides you access to people in places doing things that are beneficial to the organization that you would not otherwise meet or know about.

While the same individuals in your network provide you advice and guidance on things that will affect your decisions and actions, they also provide you a venue to let the organization know who you are. They provide you a platform to communicate to and through them what you do and can do for the organization. If you select your network wisely, you will strategically identify individuals who will serve effectively in dual roles: assist you in decision making and provide an inlet and outlet for you to communicate your value.

In addition to those in your network knowing more about you, they will share this information with others. This is critical, as your network will always be more far-reaching and able to reach farther than you could ever do by yourself. It is worth noting that not everyone in your network will serve in a dual capacity, but each represents a greater reach than your own. If constructed properly, some people in your network will be so enamored, captivated, and impressed by you, your work ethic, and your experience or expertise that they will take it upon themselves to ensure that others know you. They will speak on your behalf when you are not in the room, and they will speak up for you when you are not at the table. These individuals will not only provide you advice, but they will guide you and introduce you to their network, further expanding your network and enlarging your territory. It is not uncommon for individuals in your network to serve in multiple capacities, for example, mentors, sponsors, advocates, guides, and advisors. They want the best for you and will work to help you secure your desired outcome and expand your territory.

In order to be successful, you cannot do it alone. You must include others in your plan. If you are relying solely on yourself, you will miss your mark. You need others to know of your plan for success and still others to communicate your plan. This does not work when you work in a vacuum. You need a network, and you need to be constantly expanding it to enlarge your territory. If you try to do this alone, you will limit yourself, your reach. If you include others, you will extend your reach. The more people you have in your network working with you, supporting you, and helping to keep you moving in the right direction, the better. The larger your territory, the better.

HELP SOMEBODY BY SHARING YOUR STORY

MOST OF WHAT YOU DO TO POSITION YOURSELF TO succeed will involve you doing something for you or someone else doing something for you. The final action required by you to ensure that people know you, however, involves you doing something for someone else. Help somebody; share your story.

When you help someone, you do not have to tell anyone what you did, as the person helped will make sure they know and the person you helped will not forget. Out of a simple act of kindness, you can become a legend with a legacy. You may ascend to the highest ranks in the organization and experience an incredible amount of success. You can become a legend, but if you do so without affecting the organism, the people, your departure will represent the end of your story, as it relates to the organization. Alternatively, you may remain on the ground floor and never make the C-suite, but if you have an impact on the organism, the people, when you leave, your legacy will live on. You can have both. In fact, you should make it your mission to succeed and to share, to be a legend with a legacy. Please note, an investment in others is an investment in yourself.

We have talked about the organization being an organism and how important people are to its success. If you plan to be successful, you should leverage the opportunity afforded each day of your life to help, influence, or share with the most important resource in your organization, the organism, its people. You have undoubtedly been taught or heard how important your investment is to your return. You have heard phrases, songs, and quotes all aimed at reminding you of the importance and value of your contributions or investments to your success. The following are just of few of the things you have heard:

- "No pain, no gain."
- "There ain't no such thing as a free lunch."
- "If you want something, you have got to give something."
- "Nothing from nothing leaves nothing."
- "You reap what you sow."
- "If you sow a bad seed, you will reap a bad harvest."
- "He which soweth sparingly shall reap also sparingly; and he which soweth bountifully shall reap also bountifully" (2 Corinthians 9:6 KJV).
- "If you put in garbage, you will get garbage out. Garbage in, garbage out."
- "You get what you pay for."
- "The more you give, the more you get in return."

The point of this is to remind you that your success depends on you making the right investments. People are your best investment. They may be considered high risk at times; but as the saying goes, "high risk, high return." Aside from the risk involved, there is a much higher reward. The feeling you get from investing in people and seeing them benefit from your contributions is difficult to measure, as it often exceeds your expectation and sometimes your imagination.

Words often fail to express how you feel when

- you tell someone something and it changes their lives,
- you do something for someone and they are more grateful than you feel the act deserves, and
- you see the fruit of your labor in people others gave up on.

When you help someone, it has its own reward.

The reality of helping people is that when everything else changes—the system, processes and procedures, technology, organization structure, pay and reward system, training and development models, and recruitment and retirement system—there will always be an opportunity to help somebody. When change happens, you may lose yourself, your position, your status, your office space, or your friend at work, but you will always have an opportunity to help somebody. You may get out of bed and head to the office with no clue on what your day is going to be like or what you are going to do because you have been displaced or your assignment is pending, but you will have an opportunity to help somebody.

What are you going to do when opportunity knocks? If there is truth to the fact that people are an organization's most important resources, what are you going to do when opportunity knocks? If an organization consists of two important parts and organism is one of them, what are you going to do when opportunity knocks and you can help? The most important resource in the organization, its people, needs help every day. When you have a story to tell, a thought to share, or an act of kindness to do, you have an opportunity to change somebody's life. Opportunity is knocking. What are you going to do? Do not take that knock for granted. Answer and get to work. Expand your territory by being of service to someone in need and sharing your story.

People tend to believe that in order to help someone, they must have arrived. Quite the contrary is true. In order to arrive, you must help someone. You cannot afford to wait until you have achieved your goal of being successful before you decide to help someone. Your ability to provide help is not dependent on your success. You do not have to wait until tomorrow to do something for someone else. You should not wait until you achieve a certain status or goal or are in a certain position before you help someone. If you are unable to find it in your heart to help someone today, in your current position, it is not likely you will do so when you arrive. If you are not practicing the art of giving back or being of service to someone else from where you are today, it is unlikely that you will be doing it later. Your lack of practice may cause it to be too difficult to do, or your success without it may cause you to question its importance. If serving others is not something you do as you move up in the organization, it is not something you will do when you arrive.

If you need to be able to benefit personally from supporting others in order to do it, please note that you will. Anything you do to help others will directly or indirectly help you. For example, when you help others, you will be expanding your territory. You can see the benefits of this in the last chapter on "Expand Your Territory." Each time you lend a hand, provide advice or guidance, or tell your story, you expand your territory from which you can draw information, let others know who you are, and have a greater impact on the organization. By supporting others, you expand your network, reduce your limits, grow your impact and communication link, and get to practice what it means to be a servant leader.

So even if you need a selfish motive to support someone, you have it. I recommend you help for help sake because it is the right thing to do, someone needs you, and you can. The organization is at its best when its employees are at their best. You can help facilitate this. Your assistance should not be dependent on what you will get, as much as what you can provide. Your goal should be to provide support to someone for the sake of support, not because it provides you anything in return. Yes, there are by-products of you helping others that will far exceed your contributions, your success being one of them, but you should not make this your motive or primary reason for doing it. You helping someone lets them and the organization know who you are. Whether you know it or not, you have a story to tell, and it is important that you tell it. It does not matter if your story is one of success or turmoil; it can be of help to someone.

Maybe someone is going through what you have gone through. Whether you just started in the organization or have been around for years, you have a story to tell. If you are new, while your story may be limited to how you entered on duty, this could help someone face their challenges like the ones you experienced because they now know that someone else went through the same thing and survived. If you are more seasoned, in addition to telling your story, maybe you can mentor or sponsor someone. Regardless of your years of service, experiences, and position, you can help somebody.

You work in an environment where the rules of engagement are, at best, gray. You are expected to deliver on your requirement and help the organization accomplish its mission. To do this, you work with a diverse group of people from different walks of life, skill sets, experiences, levels of expertise, races, cultures, ethnicities, creeds, skin colors, and nationalities. Everyone brings their own set of problems and opportunities, challenges and triumphs, and questions and answers to work with them. Everyone has good and bad days, ups and downs, and strengths and weaknesses. Most importantly, everybody needs somebody, for instance, to talk to, listen, share, understand, assist, and support.

You are no different, as you need others as much as they need you. To accomplish what you are assigned to do, you cannot do it alone, you need others, and you need them at their best. What can you do to assist with this? What can you do to help them be their best? These are some questions you should ask yourself. When you see someone in need—and there is always someone in need—you can assume that they will figure it out or work it out on their own, or you could offer to help. You helping them will help the organization and you.

You have a higher calling, one that goes beyond the things you do. If you think about it, as others have, it is not the things you have to do that you go to work for. It is not the projects, the processes, and the procedures. You go to work for the most important resource of the organization, the people. It is well documented that people leave organizations because of the people, for instance, managers and supervisors. It is also well documented that people stay with organizations because of the people. People who have a friend at work are much more productive and much more likely to stay with the organization. When people retire or resign from an organization, they generally do not miss the work, but they do miss the people. People connect with people. You may be doing great work, and you should continue to do so, but if work is your only connection to the organization, you are missing a very critical link.

You work in a gray space not knowing what tomorrow holds or who will affect your life or whose life you will affect. Given the human dynamic, while you may not know who you will have an impact on, it is certain that you will have the opportunity to affect someone. Your life and success are intertwined with the lives and success of others. Martin Luther King Jr. said it best: "Whatever affects one directly, affects all indirectly. I can never be what I ought to be until you are what you ought to be."

You have the gift and opportunity to be the best that you can be, but it is dependent on others being the best that they can be. You must make it your business to live the lyrics to Mahalia Jackson's "If I Can Help Somebody."[11]

---

[11] Song: IF I CAN HELP SOMEBODY
Alma Bazel Androzzo
as rec by Gracie Fields 1948
also rec by-
Michael Holliday
Mahalia Jackson
Josef Locke
Sir Harry Secombe
https://lyricsplayground.com/alpha/songs/i/ificanhelpsomebody.html
This song is by **Mahalia Jackson** and appears...
on the album _Let's Pray Together (1963)_
on the album _Gospels, Spirituals & Hymns (1991)_
on the album _The Essential Mahalia Jackson (2004)_
https://lyrics.fandom.com/wiki/Mahalia_Jackson:If_I_Can_Help_Somebody

If I can help somebody, As I travel along
If I can help somebody, With a word or song
If I can help somebody, From doing wrong
My living shall not be in vain.

Maybe you have been deterred from helping because you did not know how or felt the time investment was more than you could afford or wanted to spend. If this is your reality or reasoning, I have some good news for you. Helping others could be as simple and powerful as taking a few minutes to tell someone your story. When people are going through something or having a rough time or a difficult day, and are not sure what to do, sometimes all they need is a word—a word of encouragement, empathy, instruction, or inspiration. It's a word from someone who has walked in their shoes.

When people are in trouble, they do not always want someone to solve their problems. They just want to know that their problems can be solved. People will buy a picture that is broken in many pieces with many different shapes—a puzzle—and spend hours putting it back together because they know the pieces will fit. They know what the end looks like. They have seen it. Your experiences; optics; views on life, work, and people; and your story sometimes is all people need to hear to know that the pieces of the puzzle will fit. The fragmented pieces may not make any sense to them, but your story could be the piece of the equation that solves their problems, the answer to the question of "Am I the only one?", the inspiration to keep going when they feel like giving up. Imagine how easy it would be to help someone when all that is required is for you to tell them your story.

Your story is your story, your history. It is an account of what has already happened in your life: your experiences, challenges, opportunities, successes, failures, and so forth. It is an acknowledgment that you and your experiences are parts of something bigger than the moment. Your story provides you a retrospective and an introspective look at your life. It allows you to see where you have been and understand what effect and impact your experiences had on you.

Your story, your history, teaches you things about your past that you did not know or understand while you were experiencing them. It allows you to see connections that you did not see in the past. I am not sure where or when I heard this phrase, but I remember being told, "Hindsight is better than twenty-twenty vision." That is, when you look back at your life experiences, you have a clearer vision or understanding of what happened and why. While George Benson said it a little different in the lyrics of his song "20/20,"[12] his meaning seems to be the same.

> If I knew back then what I know now
> If I understood the what, when, why and how
> Now it's clear to me
> What I should have done.
> But hindsight is 20/20 vision

Regardless of which view you prefer, hindsight provides you a clearer view of your present situation and alternatives, as it looks back on your past with many of the outcomes realized. By looking at your history, you gain a better understanding of who you are, where you are, and why. Rev. Clay Evans, in his song "I've Got a Testimony,"[13] may have said it best:

> As I look back over my life
> And I think things over I can truly say that I've been blessed
> I've got a testimony.

---

[12] Writers & Publishers – George Benson from the album **Live at Montreux 1986** · Copyright: Writer(s): Randy Goodrum, Stephen Alan Kipner Lyrics Terms of Use
https://www.metrolyrics.com/2020-lyrics-george-benson.html
[13] "I've Got a Testimony" as written by and Anthony Tidwell. Recorded by Rev. Clay Evans & The AARC Mass Choir
General Comment Artist: Rev. Clay Evans & The AARC Mass Choir Project: I've Got A Testimony Release Date: 1995
https://songmeanings.com/songs/view/65800/

Your history is a teacher, an advisor, an instructor, a guidance counselor, an informant, and a study guide, as it provides you valuable information that you can use to understand your present and shape your future. It behooves you to follow the advice of Rev. Evans and look back over your life and think things over. You seldom, if ever, see the end before the beginning. However, when you have the ending as your beginning, you are in a good starting place. Your past represents the end of your actions to date, and all the results are in. With this as your starting place, you know the outcome of what you have done. You can determine if what you did accomplished what you desired or if you need to make some adjustments.

When you strategically plan for your future and establish the requisite goals and objectives to accomplish them, you are doing what is required, the necessary. However, you will only know if your decisions have secured the desired outcomes after the fact, in hindsight. You may be strategically focused and decisively correct, but circumstances beyond your control or that you were not aware of or did not anticipate may cause your outcome to go awry. You can do everything advised in this book and still will not know the outcomes of your decisions until they come out. You can do the right things for the right reason at the right time with the right motives with the right purpose in mind when the circumstances are right and still not know if you are going to secure the right outcome.

When you can look back on what you have done to get to where you are, you can assess the successes or results of your decisions or actions. In that assessment, you can see and determine if the steps that you took should be continued or modified. By looking back, you can begin to understand how your inputs affected your outcomes. Understanding your history, your story, is key to ensuring that you do not repeat mistakes. It also serves to help you secure your success.

When you are driving to your destination in a vehicle, you do so safely because you view things affecting your travel through several windows and mirrors. The windows allow you to take a panoramic view to see in all directions; the mirrors allow you to see things behind you. While the passengers in the vehicle have the luxury of spending most of their time looking out the side windows, the driver spends most of the time looking out the windshield, the side-view mirrors, and the rearview mirror. The size of the windshield versus the mirrors would suggest that the driver sees more through the windshield than the rearview and side-view mirrors. The windshield is much larger, you can see more, and what you are looking at is in front of you. The rearview and side-view mirrors are small and very limited in their scope. You can see things behind and to the side. The rearview mirror even gives a distorted view of what you see, and the side-view mirrors may be inscribed, "Objects in the mirror are closer than they appear."

With these diverse optics, it would be easy to conclude that the driver sees more through the windshield than through the rearview and side-view mirrors. On the surface this may be true, but if the driver has driven any amount of time, what has been seen is greater than what is being seen. Additionally, what has been seen is valuable to understanding what is being seen, including the location of the driver. Your journey to success is much like driving. What you see is not necessarily more than what you have seen; what you have seen can help you understand what you see.

When you are traveling, you must always be looking forward in order to know where you are going, but you must also continue to take a periodic look in the rearview mirror to see what is behind you. Your life is in front of you, but to appreciate and understand it, you must not forget what is behind you. What you see in front of you is limited by what your eyes can see. If you are fortunate enough to have twenty-twenty vision, you can stand twenty feet away from an eye chart and see nine-millimeter letters, what a normal person sees. Anything beyond your ability to see is up for discussion and debate, as your clarity or surety becomes less and less the farther away you look to see. When you must make decisions that affect outcomes in your life, things in your distant future, they will be much more informed and accurate if you can see farther than twenty feet or the distance you can see with confidence with your natural eyes.

What you can see is enhanced, extended, and expanded by your rearview optic, what you have seen and experienced. Most of what you see with your twenty-twenty vision is what you have seen. You draw conclusions about what you see from things you have observed in the past. For example, you are reading this book without looking at and reading every letter of every word and every punctuation mark on every page. Because of your past experiences with reading—learning letters, words, vocabulary, phrases, sentence structures, and punctuations—your eyes go across the pages smoothly, seeing what you already know.

Your study and reading history allow you to scan the pages, to read by making assumptions and drawing conclusions about what you see. Your ability to read without seeing every letter, to read quickly, or to speed-read is a direct result of your knowing what is in your rearview mirror. The contributions of your past to your present and therefore your future cannot be overstated. It is so interconnected that the preacher in Ecclesiastes 1:9 (NLT) said, "History merely repeats itself. It has all been done before. Nothing under the sun is truly new."

Think about the potential value of knowing your decisions, your actions, and their associated outcomes. You can decide today without having to rely on just what you see. You have your history, empirical evidence, to assist you to make that decision. With this information, you can avoid and learn from past mistakes and get better at what you are doing or attempting to do.

You have heard it said over and over and in a sundry of different ways that "experience is the best teacher." I like the way Benjamin Franklin said it: "Experience keeps a dear school, yet fools learn in no other." I prefer this way of saying it because I agree that experience is the best teacher. I just do not believe it has to be your experience. There is much to be said about you learning from others' experiences. Learning from others' experiences is the foundation of the education system, learning organizations, and religion, just to name a few. Why start over doing something when it has already been done? Why reinvent the wheel?

Instead of redoing what has been done, learn from it and do something better or different and better. Your story is your invented wheel, an account of things you have learned that others should do or avoid. Your experiences are the best teachers, but you are not the only student. At least you should not be. You must make it your business to tell your story and to share your history, your experiences, and your wheel.

I had the opportunity to tutor when I was attending university. I tutored subjects I was enrolled in. What I remembered most about my experience was that I learned more than I taught. In the process of tutoring or teaching others, I gained a better understanding of the subject matter. Maybe it was because I had to figure out different ways to teach the subject to different people, so in the process I gained a deeper understanding. Perhaps it was the sense of pride or feeling of satisfaction I got from helping someone who made me want to do better myself. Possibly it was both. There is something about helping others that causes you to see things more clearly and makes you want to do better. When you help others, you make your existence larger than yourself. You expand your territory. You affect the world.

If you share your story—information from your rearview, history, decisions and outcomes, or experiences—you may change the course of history for someone. If what you have learned has benefitted you, it will likely assist someone else. While your story is not for everyone, there is a group of people whom you see daily or will meet who are in dire need of a word from you. They would benefit greatly from hearing your story. Your story could keep them from entering into a pitfall, stumbling, derailing, making a grave mistake, or doing what you did that almost cost you your job, position, or career. Your story could be just what they need to keep them moving forward and on the path to success.

Why would you let someone step out the door and into a ditch when you could stop it? When you have walked out the same door and into the same ditch, why would you let this continue? You can break the cycle just by sharing your story. I know this analogy seems a bit crude, but you must see how something drastic can be stopped by you just speaking up and sharing your story. You may believe you do not have anything to share because what you have done or accomplished is no big deal. You could not be further from the truth. It is common practice to downplay or take for granted the things we know or experience. You may think that it is no big deal that you fell into and got out of an obvious ditch. So why share? You should share because the ditch is not so obvious to everyone and some people never made it out of the ditch. You did. How did you do it?

Your story on how you arrived where you are is filled with wisdom, knowledge, and understanding that will benefit others. It could keep someone from making the same mistake you made or from redoing what you have already done, from reinventing your wheel. As positive as inventing a wheel is, it becomes redundant, repetitive, unnecessary, and a waste of time if it has already been done. Your wheel has been invented.

If you share, instead of reinventing the wheel, the person can focus their energies and efforts on making improvements or modifications, for example, making it roll faster, improving the treads on its tires, or offering more options on sizes. By sharing your story, you provide your listeners with information and options, something they may have not been aware of or believed they had.

Your story positions those you share it with to climb higher, to do more, and to keep going. Your life and legacy are like climbing Jacob's ladder. If "every round is going to go higher and higher," you must do your part and pull those behind you up to your rung by at least telling them how you got there. You have taken steps to get where you are. If you tell no one about the steps you took or how you did it, your steps will fade, and no one will know. If you tell someone, you blaze a trail for those behind you to follow. You become a trailblazer.

Instead of requiring others to pull themselves up by their own bootstraps, to figure out what you already know, why not set them on the course to success? Position them for the next rung in the ladder. Show them the next part of the trail.

Something as simple as telling your story, something you already know, can provide critical assistance and create allegiance. If you have experienced any amount of success, someone shared their story with you. If you look back on your experiences in life, you will find that there was someone who blazed the trail for you. Maybe it was just a story that they told you that inspired you to go further. Their story may have been in words or actions, but you heard it, and it got you moving in the right direction. The reality is that the person sharing the story may not even know you heard it. Knowing how someone else's story influenced you, you should know your story will influence someone else. Just like your life may have been shaped by someone else's story without them knowing, your story may affect others without you knowing it. Paul described us as "epistles ... known and read of all men" (2 Corinthians 3:2 KJV).

Whether you want to or not, you are telling your story. Your life is an open book. Your actions are a part of your story. You cannot deny it, as your actions speak louder than words. That being the case, why not take control of the narrative and ensure you have an impact on the legacy you leave?

Everything you do becomes a part of your history, your story. While you may still question whether you have something to share, let me assure you that you do. If you have managed to stay on course while dealing with your challenges, you have a story to share. If you have managed a modicum of success and gotten even close to where you desire to be, you have a story to share. You may not be where you want to be, but you can be sure you are where someone else would love to be. You may not consider what you have done a success, but I can assure you that there is someone who does. If you want to know the distance of your travel, where you have come from, you can introspectively look at where you were and compare it to where you are.

If you want to know the significance of the distance of your travel, where you have come from, begin to share your story. When telling your story, you will not only influence the individuals you share it with, you will also gain insightful perspectives on how you got to where you are given your challenges and opportunities. You will find that true appreciation for your journey often comes only through the rearview mirror. When you are driving on a long trip, when looking forward, all you see is highway and distance. It can cause you to ask questions, such as, "How much farther? Are we there yet? How much longer? When is the next break/rest stop? How much longer will we be in traffic?"

With so much further to go, you can get discouraged and lose sight of your destiny. Distance combined with disturbances, distortions, and distractions will leave you doubtful, down, and distraught. If you are only looking at something that seems at times unattainable, you will likely lose heart many times and may not recover. However, when you can look in the rearview mirror and see where you have come from and how you made it despite the many struggles and challenges, you can put things into perspective.

In the rearview, your challenges and opportunities collectively made you who you are today and prepared you for what lies ahead. In the rearview, your challenges, struggles, trials, tribulations, setbacks, fights, failures, resistance, distractions, and losses all seem to work together for your good, making you stronger, better, and more equipped. In the rearview, you see that you are an overcomer, a fighter, a winner, a strategist, an achiever, a conqueror, or a trailblazer.

Paul spoke about this in scripture when he said, "We can rejoice, too, when we run into problems and trials, for we know that they help us develop endurance. And endurance develops strength of character, and character strengthens our confident hope of salvation. And this hope will not lead to disappointment" (Romans 5:3–5a NLT). Peter compares us to gold notes in that we experience trials to bring out the best in us. He writes,

> So be truly glad. There is wonderful joy ahead, even though you have to endure many trials for a little while. These trials will show that your faith is genuine. It is being tested as fire tests and purifies gold—though your faith is far more precious than mere gold. So, when your faith remains strong through many trials, it will bring you much praise and glory and honor on the day when Jesus Christ is revealed to the whole world. (1 Peter 1:6–7 NLT)

When you are going through something, traveling, or looking through the windshield, it is very difficult to see these experiences for more than what they are at the time. When you have gone through them and can look back, you can then see their values, lessons, and reasons for happening.

No one wants to experience hardships, but through your struggles, you gain strength and the proper perspective, including the ability to appreciate the beauty of a good day. When you gain a proper perspective on your difficulties, trials, tribulations, and setbacks, you will be able to approach new and similar challenges successfully and share your lessons learned with others. For example, when you experience hardships, you do not give up, toss in the towel, or become frustrated. You know this is just part of your growth process, as you have learned, as Paul said, "to be content whatever the circumstances" (Philippians 4:11KJV).

People struggle with life's challenges because they have not gained a proper perspective. They are battling with the here and now and the then and there because they fail to see and understand how and where they came from. They have not yet assimilated the knowledge of how life, through its ups and down, its smiles and frowns, prepares us for our next level. They have not yet gained the appreciation for their struggles. As a result, they give up before the struggle is over because they have not been trained to endure hardship as a good soldier (2 Timothy 2:3). They have not learned, as Friedrich Nietzsche said, "that which does not kill us makes us stronger."

When you understand the place of struggles, your perspective on struggles changes, and you can endure them without breaking. Once you have had these experiences, you can share your story with others who are going through and wondering if they will make it. It is up to you, as it is your task and responsibility to mentor, lead, and guide others. It is your duty, your responsibility, to help somebody else. How? Share your story.

There is a story in John 9 about a blind man who receives his sight at the hands of Jesus. After much questioning about who Jesus was, where he came from, and if the man was blind, the blind man said, "Whether he be a sinner or no, I know not: one thing I know, that, whereas I was blind, now I see" (John 9:25 KJV).

Embedded in the story is a very significant lesson I want you to take with you as you share your own story. The lesson is to stick to your story. You should not try to tell someone else's story or embellish your own. The blind man did not choose to have a conversation about what he did not know. He simply addressed those asking the question with what he knew. "I was blind but now I see." As insignificant or short as his story may sound, it was his story.

If you just share your story as it has happened with those who are coming behind you, you will discover the power of your experiences. Your story will affect others and help them with their challenges. Think about the impact of the blind man story. His story is our story. How many people do you know that have had that same experience as the blind man—people who do not know how they got to where they are? All they know is that they were in a bad place, and now they are in a better place, blind but now they see. These are people in need of your story. You do not have to make anything up. You do not have to wait for certain experiences. Just help somebody by sharing your story. It will change so many lives.

Printed in the United States
By Bookmasters